PASS Prepare, Assist, Survive, and Succeed

Barbara Bole Williams and Rosemary B. Mennuti are back with a thorough update to their essential guide to preparing for and achieving the best score possible on the Praxis Exam in School Psychology. Pulling from their years of experience and hands-on involvement in the continued revision of the exam, and using their PASS model (Prepare, Assist, Survive, Succeed), these two veteran school psychologists have revised this easy-to-use resource to reflect the most recent exam content, professional standards, and most current practical knowledge for school psychologists. Also included are student test reflections and information on how to obtain and maintain your NCSP credential.

Barbara Bole Williams, PhD, NCSP, is a professor and coordinator of the School Psychology Program at Rowan University, Glassboro, NJ. She currently chairs the National School Psychology Certification Board for the National Association of School Psychologists (NASP). She also serves as a member of the Praxis School Psychologist Test Development Committee for the Educational Testing Service (ETS).

Rosemary B. Mennuti, EdD, NCSP, is the former professor and director of the School Psychology Programs at the Philadelphia College of Osteopathic Medicine.

PASS
Prepare, Assist, Survive, and Succeed

A Guide to Passing the Praxis Exam in School Psychology

2nd Edition

Barbara Bole Williams
and Rosemary B. Mennuti

NEW YORK AND LONDON

Second edition published 2016
by Routledge
711 Third Avenue, New York, NY 10017

and by Routledge
2 Park Square, Milton Park, Abingdon, Oxon, OX14 4RN

Routledge is an imprint of the Taylor & Francis Group, an informa business

First edition published 2010 by Taylor & Francis

Library of Congress Cataloging-in-Publication Data
A catalog record for this book has been requested

ISBN: 978-1-138-91029-4 (pbk)
ISBN: 978-1-315-69349-1 (ebk)

Typeset in Times
by Apex CoVantage, LLC

Dedication

It is with heartfelt love and joy that we dedicate the second edition of this book to two very special people in our lives: Olivia Grace and Ethan Dakota.

Contents

Part II Content of the Exam

Part III Succeeding

List of Figures

List of Tables

Acknowledgments

This book has been a work in progress over the past 20 years. It grew out of the challenges we faced as graduate educators at Rowan University given the responsibility to prepare students in their final phase of coursework to obtain national certification in school psychology. The Praxis School Psychologist exam was still a rather new requirement when we began, and we wanted to help students achieve success. What evolved over the years developed into the PASS model: prepare, assist, survive, and succeed, an experience that helps graduate students in school psychology prepare for and succeed on the Praxis School Psychologist exam.

Our work is also the result of the efforts of many people—practitioners, colleagues, and graduate educators—who contributed to the ideas included in this book. Most of all, this book would not have been possible without the help of numerous graduate students we encountered over the years in our school psychology programs, classrooms, and workshops. We continue to be impressed by their dedication, energy, hard work, and competency, and we are indebted to them for their contributions. We also want to acknowledge the literary skills of Terry Molony, who contributed original writing expertise to the manuscript. Together with them, we were able to compile a guide to support students preparing for the Praxis exam. Thanks to all of you who dedicated your time and effort to this project.

Thank you to the graduate students who wrote reflections about their experiences preparing and taking the Praxis School Psychologist exam. These are school psychology graduate students from Rowan University, including Regina Lyons, Winnie Thompson, Abina Duncan, Gena Pacitto, Mary Beth Zenyuk, Alexandra Vartanian, Andrew Midgley, Sarah Larson, and Courtney Casey.

Finally, we are indebted to four terrific Rowan school psychology graduate students who assisted us in the revisions necessary for the second edition of this book. A big thank you to Danielle Genovese, Lindsay Hendricks, Jessica Mark, and Rebecca Mark who helped to update tables and references and review sample questions. These are four talented young women who will soon become accomplished school psychologists.

Barb and Roe
July 2015

Part I

Process of Preparing

Chapter 1

Introduction to the PASS Model

Prepare, Assist, Survive, and Succeed

Many professions have competency examinations that, once passed, designate readiness for professional practice. These examinations assess candidates' mastery of subject-area knowledge and are utilized as a requirement for certification/licensure. In school psychology, the Praxis Series serves in this capacity. The Educational Testing Service's (ETS) Praxis® Subject Assessment School Psychologist exam (5402) is a high-stakes test for graduate students entering the profession of school psychology. In addition, school psychology practitioners desiring to apply for the credential of Nationally Certified School Psychologist (NCSP) through the National Association of School Psychologists (NASP) are required to take the Praxis® Subject Assessment exam. In many arenas, attaining a successful score on the Praxis® Subject Assessment in School Psychology is a critical performance-based outcome measure of one's knowledge in the field of school psychology.

The importance of the exam as a "high-stakes test" in school psychology extends to the requirement that all candidates enrolled in a NASP-approved graduate program in school psychology are required to take the Praxis® Subject Assessment School Psychologist exam as a requirement for graduation. NASP-approved programs must then document a pass rate of 80% or more of their candidates in order to meet one of the content knowledge indicators required by the Council for the Accreditation of Educator Preparation (CAEP) (formerly National Council for Accreditation of Teacher Education) and NASP as part of the program approval process.

A Little History

Batsche and Curtis (2003) describe the history of the Praxis Exam in School Psychology, with origins in 1983 when the National Commission on Excellence in Education prompted a movement of school reform. States adopted legislation requiring professional competency examinations for educational personnel, in part to identify who was a "qualified professional." In 1986, NASP formally began working with ETS in the development of a competency examination in school psychology, including assisting with the identification of content domains and the development of test items for the exam. Through continued collaboration, in fall 1987 ETS and NASP formulated a national pilot testing program and completed the necessary field-testing. Then, in July 1988, 7,200 school psychologists nationwide took the exam for the first time in order to develop norms. By the end of that year a "staggering number" of 12,654 school psychologists had taken the test (including the two authors of this book). NASP joined with ETS in 1989 to conduct two national validation panels to establish validity of the examination. The joint endeavor between NASP and ETS has continued until the present time, providing for subsequent revisions of the test specifications and item content to assure the Praxis® Subject Assessment exam in school psychology remains up-to-date and reflects contemporary school psychology research and practice.

In the mid-1990s, the authors of this book were contributors to the first revision of the Praxis Exam in School Psychology. ETS approached the revision of the exam by first gathering together school psychologists from around the country in order to discuss and identify knowledge necessary for competent practice in school psychology. From the list of competencies, another group of school psychologist (we were in this group) was invited to the ETS site in Princeton, New Jersey, to participate in the development of a bank of questions, which would potentially be items used in the exam. These school psychologists were considered "content specialists" and, together with professional item writers, took on the task of developing first drafts of questions for the exam.

The process for developing initial questions was an interesting one. The content specialists were given the list of school psychology competencies and asked to write items covering any of the competency areas. The ETS leader who provided training to the content specialists suggested that the initial efforts in writing items should cover the most obvious content, which was considered the "low-hanging fruit," that is, the basic knowledge in school psychology that would lend itself to good multiple-choice questions (e.g., asking about the stages in Piaget's developmental theory). These were questions that were factual in nature and knowledge common to a typical school psychology graduate program. Next, the task was to develop questions that tapped the application of knowledge and the skills essential to becoming a competent school psychology practitioner. For example, a scenario was written to describe an academic or behavioral problem a child experienced in a classroom, and the possible responses included various strategies for intervention.

Once the draft bank of questions with correct responses and plausible distracters (incorrect answers) was completed, ETS conducted a validity study in order to select the most appropriate and accurate items to make up the final bank of questions to be used for various formats for the Praxis® Subject Assessment School Psychologist exam.

The Praxis® Subject Assessment School Psychologist exam underwent a second revision that became effective on September 1, 2008. The first author of this book once again played a role in this process by working with ETS as a member of the National Advisory Committee for the Praxis School Psychologist exam. With this revision, a new version of the test was developed and first administered on September 13, 2008. The changes in the new version better aligned the test content with the NASP (2000) Standards for Training and Field Placement Programs in School Psychology (NASP, 2000). During this process, some new items were gradually incorporated into the test, but the content was not changed extensively. ETS's objective in revising the test was not only to update the test but also to alter the scale upon which the scores are reported. Previously, scores for the Praxis School Psychologist exam ranged from 250 to 990. Now, the Praxis® Subject Assessment School Psychologist scores are on a scale ranging from 100 to 200. While this rescaling of the test scores resulted in a different score range, it did not change the major statistical properties of the test. Moreover, the statistical process did not change the individual states' passing standards but simply determined the equivalent passing scores on the new scale. At the time, the qualifying score for the National Certification in School Psychology (NCSP) awarded through NASP was 165, which was the statistical equivalent to the former qualifying score of 660 on the old scale.

In September 2014, the Educational Testing Service (ETS) released of a new version of the Praxis® Subject Assessment School Psychologist test (5402). The revised test has been designed to align more closely with the NASP (2010c) Standards and is offered exclusively as a computer-delivered exam unless accommodations for disabilities are necessary.

The revised Praxis® Subject Assessment School Psychologist test (5402) content is built on test specifications that are aligned with NASP's (2010a) *Model for Comprehensive and Integrated School Psychological Services' Ten Domains of Practice.* Figure 1.1 provides an overview of the four content categories and further breaks down each category into topical areas.

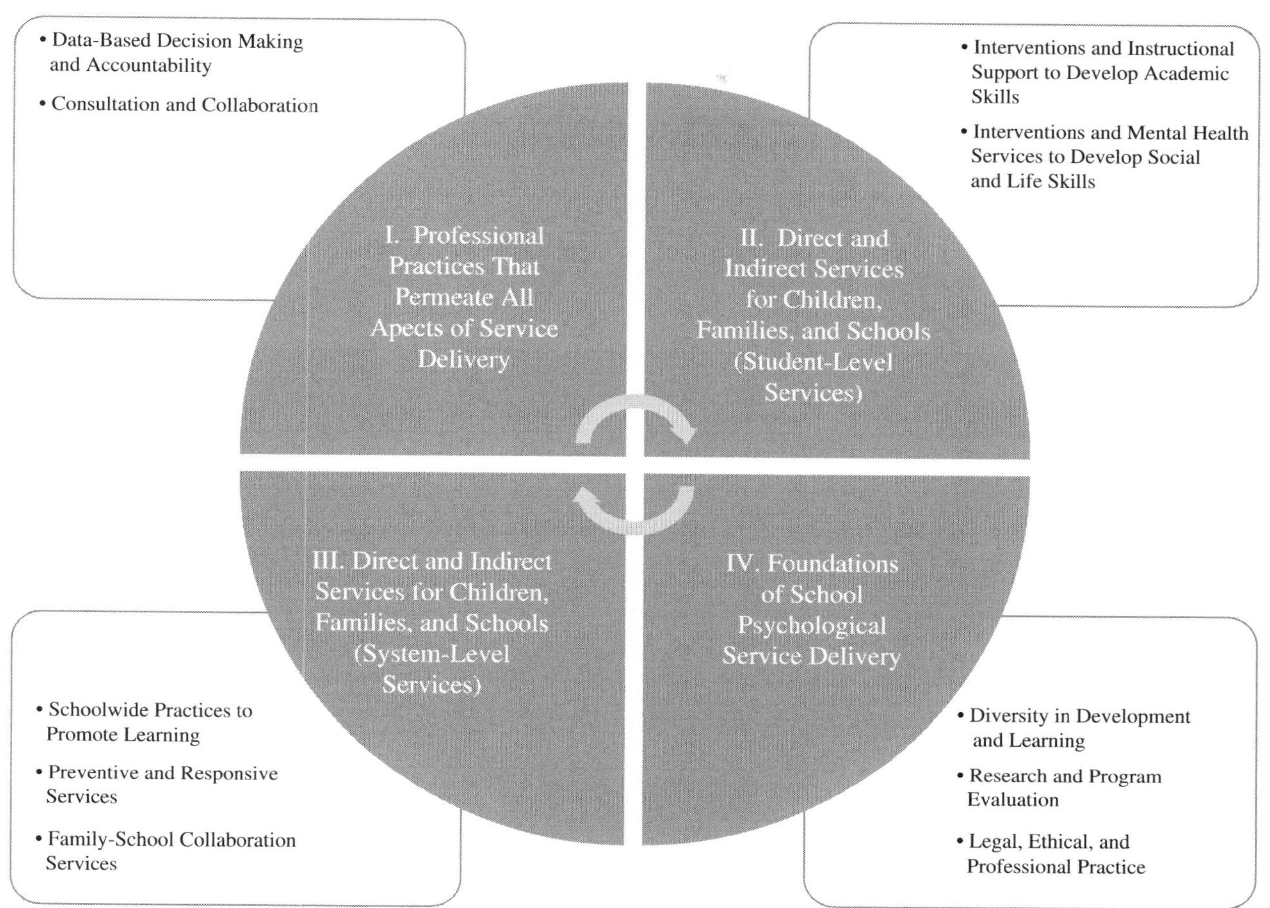

Figure 1.1
Praxis School Psychologist Test (5402)

The test consists of a total of 140 questions. Within the four content categories, the number of questions in each category varies as follows:

I. *Professional Practices That Permeate All Aspects of Service Delivery* is assigned approximately 42 questions or 30% of the exam;
II. *Direct and Indirect Services for Children, Families, and Schools (Student-Level Services)* accounts for approximately 32 questions or 23% of the exam;
III. *Systems-Level Services* has approximately 22 questions or 16% of the exam;
IV. *Foundations of School Psychological Service Delivery* has approximately 44 questions or 31% of the exam.

The Praxis School Psychologist Exam's Role in Credentialing, Certification, and Licensure

The Praxis® Subject Assessment School Psychologist exam now serves as the requirement for 22 state certification/licensure standards (see Table 1.1). Each state determines its own cutoff score, and this information is available on each individual state department of education's website.

TABLE 1.1
Praxis Series: Testing Requirements for School Psychology Certification by State Boards of Education and Boards of Psychology

STATE BOARDS OF EDUCATION	Alabama	Missouri	Oregon	Vermont
	Arkansas	Mississippi	Pennsylvania	Washington
	Colorado	North Carolina	Rhode Island	Wisconsin
	Kansas	North Dakota	South Carolina	West Virginia
	Kentucky	New Mexico	Tennessee	
	Maryland	Ohio	Utah	
BOARDS OF PSYCHOLOGY	Florida	Ohio	Wisconsin	
	Massachusetts	Texas	British Columbia	
	NASP			

Source: Retrieved from http://www.ets.org/s/praxis/pdf/passing_scores.pdf, August 21, 2014.

TABLE 1.2
Praxis Series: States That Use the NCSP in the State Credentialing of School Psychologists

Alabama	Kentucky	North Dakota
Alaska	Louisiana	Oklahoma
Arizona	Maine	Oregon
Colorado	Maryland	South Dakota
Delaware	Massachusetts	Texas
Florida	Michigan	Utah
Georgia	Minnesota	Vermont
Hawaii	Montana	Virginia
Idaho	Nevada	Washington
Indiana	New Jersey	
Iowa	New Mexico	

Source: Retrieved from http://www.nasponline.org/certification/statencsp.aspx, August 21, 2014.

In a few states, certification in school psychology comes under the auspices of boards of psychology, rather than under the state departments of education. In these cases, the Praxis® Subject Assessment is required by boards of psychology for credentialing. For example, the state of Massachusetts's Board of Psychology requires the Praxis® Subject Assessment for school psychology licensure. Table 1.1 provides a listing of boards of psychology testing requirements. Included in this category are the National Association of School Psychologists and the British Columbia Association of School Psychologists.

The Praxis® Subject Assessment School Psychologist exam also plays a role in national certification. At the national level, a passing score on the Praxis® Subject Assessment School Psychologist exam is required to earn the NCSP credential (see Table 1.2). Thirty-one states recognize the NCSP as one avenue to securing state licensure in school psychology, and in many states those school psychologists who hold the NCSP are being considered for and awarded additional monetary stipends by state-level educational credentialing agents and/or local and county school districts. Thus, in response to the national school reform movement and the need to establish qualified professionals, the Praxis® Subject Assessment School Psychologist exam has become the hallmark of competency in the field of school psychology.

What's Ahead: Organization of This Book

The purpose of this book is to provide the reader with information and strategies to help you PASS—that is, prepare, assist, survive, and succeed on the Praxis® Subject Assessment School Psychologist exam. The preparation model included in this book was originally designed as a course for advanced school psychology candidates who were completing their internships and preparing to take the Praxis® Subject Assessment in school psychology. You will be reading about a model that has been successful in preparing graduate students for the last 20 years or so. Many of these students have agreed to share their personal reflections about the exam preparation model, and these are included in Chapter 11.

Organizationally, the book is divided into three parts. In Part I, the process of preparing for the test is discussed. This includes an orientation to the Praxis® Subject Assessment using ETS materials from the website, learning about the general content (domains), and preparing review materials to share with classmates. Also included are the basic logistics of Praxis® Subject Assessment registration and study skills. Finally, Part I ends with suggestions for beginning to develop your own study strategies.

In Part II, the current subject matter for the four exam content categories and 10 practice domains are outlined. These are directly aligned with the NASP Practice Model. The content categories include: (a) Professional Practices That Permeate All Aspects of Service Delivery; (b) Direct and Indirect Services for Children, Families, and Schools (Student-Level Services); (c) Direct and Indirect Services for Children, Families, and Schools (Systems-Level Services); and (d) Foundations of School Psychological Service Delivery. Subsumed under the four content categories are the 10 NASP Practice Domains (refer to Table 1.3 for a list of the 10 domains).

The content of this book includes a breakdown of each of the 10 domains into key topics with graphic organizers detailing sample contents in each of the categories. At the end of each section, sample questions are included; however, these are not questions written by ETS, but rather those of the authors and student contributors.

Part III is a collection of testimonials written by students who have experienced the PASS model. We believe you will find it helpful and thought-provoking to read the reflections of other students, like yourself, who have experienced the process of preparing for the Praxis® Subject Assessment School Psychologist exam.

Finally, a new feature of this second edition of the book is information to guide you on the next step of your career as you apply for the NCSP and enter the profession of school psychology.

TABLE 1.3
Praxis Exam Content Categories and Practice Domains

I. **Professional Practices That Permeate All Aspects of Service Delivery**
   Domain 1: Data-Based Decision Making and Accountability
   Domain 2: Consultation and Collaboration

II. **Direct and Indirect Services for Children, Families, and Schools: Student-Level Services**
   Domain 3: Interventions and Instructional Support to Develop Academic Skills
   Domain 4: Interventions and Mental Health Services to Develop Social and Life Skills

III. **Direct and Indirect Services for Children, Families, and Schools: System-Level Services**
   Domain 5: School-Wide Practices to Promote Learning
   Domain 6: Preventive and Responsive Services
   Domain 7: Family-School Collaboration Services

IV. **Foundations of School Psychological Service Delivery**
   Domain 8: Diversity in Development and Learning
   Domain 9: Research and Program Evaluation
   Domain 10: Legal, Ethical, and Professional Practice

Chapter 2

Preparing for the Test

Getting Started

Registering to Take the Exam

You can register for the Praxis® Subject Assessment School Psychologist exam (5402) online, by phone, or by mail. Information about all of these processes is available on the ETS website at https://www.ets.org/praxis/register, or by calling 1-800-772-9476. Please note there have been changes in the registration procedures that accompany the computer-delivered administration. First, you complete and submit the Test Authorization Voucher Request form to ETS with payment. After you receive the completed voucher from ETS, you schedule your test appointment. Remember this voucher is good for 90 days. Test administration is available monthly; you can choose from multiple days within a window of days posted on the website. For example, if you want to take the exam in September, you can choose from a window of approximately 10 days that month. The monthly schedule is available on the ETS website. After you register, you print your admission ticket from your online Praxis® Subject Assessment account. Now you are ready to go.

Test Accommodations and Preparation

Test takers who need accommodations must register by mail and have accommodations approved prior to taking the exam. For more information, see the ETS *Bulletin Supplement for Test Takers With Disabilities or Health-Related Needs* (2015a), available online at https://www.ets.org/praxis/register/disabilities. Please be aware there are multiple steps in this process that will require your attention to detail while reading the ETS procedures. However, by doing so, you will be able to request accommodations and register for the exam.

Once you have completed the test registration process, you should begin to plan for preparing or studying for the exam. This book provides a comprehensive and sequential model for test preparation that will be described in subsequent chapters. Other forms of test preparation materials are also available. For example, the ETS website offers both free and low-cost test preparation materials, the National Association of School Psychologists' website (nasponline.org) has test preparation suggestions and materials, and other forms of commercially prepared publications are available.

On the Day of the Test

Several days prior to your scheduled appointment to take the exam, we suggest you log onto the ETS website to check the location for the testing center and be sure you have exact directions. Many students report that taking the Praxis® Subject Assessment at a familiar location is helpful in order to reduce the anxiety of trying to find a building and parking accommodations in an unfamiliar area.

Be well rested and have something to eat, dress comfortably, and arrive at least a half hour before you are requested to be there. Be aware that personal belongings (e.g., your handbag, electronic devices) will be not permitted inside the testing room. Information on the ETS website warns test takers that possession or use of any electronic devices will result in dismissal from the test and cancellation of all scores, with no refunds of registration fees.

ETS requires you to show two valid and acceptable forms of identification. Examples are a current passport and a government-issued driver's license. These must be original documents (not photocopies) and must match the name exactly as you entered it on your registration form. For further information, carefully review the ETS (n.d.) website at: http://www.ets.org/s/praxis/pdf/praxis_information_bulletin.pdf.

To save yourself any possible angst on the day of the exam, be sure when you register to use the exact first, middle, and last names that appear on your forms of photo identification. If there is a discrepancy in the information (different name or variation), you may not be permitted to enter the test site.

Score Reporting

Your scores will be available online via your Praxis® Subject Assessment account two to three weeks after the testing window closes. You will receive an email when your score is available, indicating the results can be retrieved from your account. These scores will be available for a period of one year. It is important for you to copy and save these results. At the time of your registration, up to four free score recipients may be selected to receive the results. Additional score reporting recipients can be requested for a fee.

If you desire your score to be sent to the institution you are attending, you need to specify this on your registration form. In addition to the three recipients you specify, you can request that your score be sent to your state/agency. If you live in one of the 39 states or the District of Columbia that are listed in the ETS Bulletin, your score will automatically be sent to your state's teacher credentialing agency. The 39 states (and District of Columbia) listed in the ETS Bulletin are: Alabama, Alaska, Arkansas, California, Colorado, Connecticut, Delaware, District of Columbia, Georgia, Hawaii, Idaho, Indiana, Iowa, Kansas, Kentucky, Louisiana, Maryland, Mississippi, Missouri, Montana, Nebraska, Nevada, New Hampshire, New Jersey, North Carolina, North Dakota, Ohio, Oklahoma, Oregon, Pennsylvania, Rhode Island, South Carolina, South Dakota, Tennessee, Utah, Vermont, Virginia, Washington, West Virginia, and Wyoming (p. 14 of 2014–15 ETS Praxis Series Bulletin). If you are planning to apply to NASP for the Nationally Certified School Psychologist credential, at the time of registration, request that your score be reported to NASP. The NASP code is R1549. If you wait until you receive your score and then request that ETS send your score to NASP, there will be an additional charge. Please be aware that NASP does not penalize you for a score that does not meet the qualifying score of 147 on your first attempt. If you must retake the Praxis® Subject Assessment School Psychologist exam additional times to attain the score of 147 or greater, you are not penalized in any way.

Getting Ready to Study

Before we begin discussing any test content preparation, let's pause a moment to consider your assets and what you "bring to the table" as a well-prepared school psychology graduate student. You have completed the majority of your coursework, if not all courses, and you have field experience during your practicum and internship. This is a good time for you to reflect upon what you have learned and take stock of where you are in your preparation to become a school psychologist. You should feel confident in your abilities and enter the Praxis preparation with the belief that you have developed knowledge and competencies in the field. This is the time to integrate and consolidate this information through a systematic test preparation plan.

To begin your review, we recommend you talk to at least one or more persons who have recently taken the exam. What was their experience like when they reported to the testing center? What was it like taking the Praxis® Subject Assessment via the computer-delivered mode? Although your experience may differ, by talking to someone who has taken the Praxis® Subject Assessment, you'll learn more about what to expect and how to avoid common pitfalls. You'll also learn about the testing process.

Students ask speakers who have come to our classes if time management during the test is an issue. Speakers have typically said that there is sufficient time to complete the entire exam and still have a few minutes left. Those students who have taken the computer-delivered Praxis® Subject Assessment School Psychologist exam since September 2014 have not reported that time was a limiting factor.

Exam Categories

Education Testing Service (ETS) states that the Praxis® Subject Assessment School Psychologist test measures subject-area knowledge that a beginning school psychologist should know. Much of this information is covered in school psychology graduate programs. It is important that you check the Praxis® Subject Assessment website for any available information on test contents (http://www.ets.org/Media/Tests/PRAXIS/pdf/0401.pdf). The *Test at a Glance (TAAG)* document has descriptors of the four 5402 Praxis® Subject Assessment School Psychologist categories and 35 sample questions with correct answers and rationale. With the advent of the computer-delivered test, ETS has added two helpful links on its website: a *Computer-Delivered Testing Demonstration*, to familiarize you with the physical conditions and rules in effect when you arrive at the testing center to take the computer-delivered test, and an *Interactive Practice Test*, which will allow you to read and respond to sample questions under the same conditions you will be exposed to during the actual testing day.

Examining the Content

At this point, you should be ready to begin further defining what the four Praxis® Subject Assessment School Psychologist exam content areas are all about. The content areas include the following:

- Professional Practices That Permeate All Aspects of Service Delivery
- Direct and Indirect Services for Children, Families, and Schools (Student-Level Services)
- Direct and Indirect Services for Children, Families, and Schools (System-Level Services)
- Foundations of School Psychological Service Delivery

Now it is important to begin to "drill down" to the more specific topics that make up these content areas. From this point forward, we will be organizing the structure of this book around the specific topics.

The two areas, *Data-Based Decision Making* and *Consultation and Collaboration*, cover a large amount of information (i.e., 30% of the content of the exam). For example, using the *TAAG*, you will see that the topic *Data-Based Decision Making* is divided into (a) problem identification, (b) assessment and problem analysis, (c) knowledge of measurement theory and principles, and (d) assessment considerations and special populations. Each of these four subheadings is further subdivided into specific areas that explicate the topic. By examining the *TAAG*, you can get the full flavor of the content covered on the exam. By dissecting each category, you can begin to conceptualize separate content areas around which you will gather study materials.

As you are developing materials for each area, we recommend you go back to your lecture notes and textbooks from the major courses you took in graduate school. Once you have divided the subject-area knowledge into more manageable segments and you begin to gather study materials, consider working with a study group so you can "divide and conquer." For the purposes of organizing the study material and allowing this to be a more manageable task, each group member can focus on a specific area(s) and collect the material to synthesize and identify major content within his or her specific area. This can provide an excellent framework to organize your study material and make the job of organizing it that much easier. This can be a group process that will save time and allow you to collaborate with others before the actual study process begins. Once your materials are assembled, you can choose to either continue to work as a member of a study group or to study independently—or a combination of both.

The information we have compiled into graphic organizers in Chapters 5 through 9 will also be helpful in your quest to develop the ultimate study guide. However, while we provide you with some review information, we recommend that you also consider expanding topics to include in your personal study guides.

In our study review sessions with our own students, we begin with the graphic organizers provided in Chapters 5 through 9. Then each student assumes responsibility for compiling an expanded outline, a PowerPoint to present to group members, and copies of NASP position papers related to the topic.

The following is an example of an expanded outline based on Table 5.7, which is the graphic organizer for *Data-Based Decision Making*, under the main idea of Problem Identification: Interview Strategies for the topic of Components of Effective Interviewing (see *TAAG*). By examining this outline and comparing it to Table 5.7, you will see that the content has been expanded to include more detailed information around the topic of effective interviewing. This is an example of what you could do within your study group to help each other review the major content surrounding those areas outlined in the graphic organizers.

Components of Effective Interviewing

- Overview of Interviewing
  - The purpose is to obtain information about the interviewee and his or her problems;
  - It is one of the most useful techniques for obtaining information;
  - It allows interviewees to express their views;
  - Interviewing multiple sources: student, teacher and parent/guardian.
- Goals of Interviewing
  - Establish rapport with student/teacher/parent;
  - Identify the major problem areas;
  - Obtain information about student's developmental histories;
  - Learn about student's current family situation;
  - Obtain information about student's academic and behavioral functioning at home, in school, and in community;
  - Generate hypotheses about problems;
  - Integrate information with other sources of data (e.g., referral information, norm-referenced and other assessment data);
  - Arrive at a tentative formulation of the problem.
- General Guidelines for Interviewing
  - Establish rapport based upon mutual respect and acceptance;
  - Explain confidentiality;
  - Know your purpose—that is, formulate appropriate questions;
  - Consider cognitive and developmental levels;
  - Be a good listener;
  - Facilitate communication;
  - Convey your interest to interviewee;
  - Encourage interviewee to elaborate on responses;
  - Ease interviewee's anxiety;
  - Record information;

    - Close interview appropriately;
    - Briefly summarize information;
    - Obtain feedback from interviewee;
    - Discuss future steps and implications.
- Student Interview Content
    - Reason for referral;
    - Confidentiality and other ethical issues;
    - School (perceptions of teacher, peer group, and school environment);
    - Home (perceptions of parents, siblings, and home environment);
    - Interests (leisure time activities, hobbies, recreation, clubs, sports);
    - Friends;
    - Moods and feelings;
    - Fears and worries;
    - Self-concept;
    - Somatic concerns;
    - Obsessions and compulsions;
    - Thought disorders;
    - Aspirations;
    - Other;
    - With adolescents also ask about:
        - Jobs;
        - Sexual relations (sexual identity and peer relationships);
        - Eating habits;
        - Drug and alcohol use (frequency and type);
        - Pregnancy.
- Parent/Guardian Interview Content
    - Introduction;
    - Confidentiality and other ethical issues;
    - Parent's perception of the problem;
    - Home environment;
    - Community;
    - Sibling relations;
    - Peer relations;
    - Child's relations with parents and other adults;
    - Child's interest and hobbies;
    - Child's routine daily activities;
    - Child's cognitive and academic skills functioning;
    - Child's behavior;
    - Child's affective life;
    - Child's health history;
    - Family;
    - Parent's expectations;
    - Concluding questions.
- Teacher Interview Content
    - Confidentiality and other ethical issues;
    - Student's strengths and areas of need;
    - Teacher's perception of student's problem;
    - Reactions to student's problems:
        - Opinion of student's relationships with peers;
        - Assessment of student's strengths and weaknesses;
        - View of student's family;
        - Expectations for the student;
        - Suggestions for helping the student.

Summary

In summary, we are suggesting that you approach your review for the Praxis® Subject Assessment School Psychologist exam by using the graphic organizers contained in Chapters 5 through 9 of this book as a springboard to work with your fellow students from your study group. Together you will be able to use the main ideas in the graphic organizers to expand the details into more comprehensive outlines that will capture the important content you will need to review prior to taking the Praxis® Subject Assessment School Psychologist exam.

Chapter 3

Assisting
Using the PASS Model to Study for the Praxis

By Terry Molony

Study Skills

Studying for a major test like the Praxis obviously requires a great deal of time, dedication, concentration, and motivation. It tests not only your knowledge base regarding the topics on the test, but also your executive functions and your ability to initiate and sustain your study efforts, and to monitor your progress and regulate your emotions. At the same time, you must attempt to maintain a high level of motivation, and avoid feeling bored, anxious, or inattentive. In my work helping graduate and medical students develop better study skills, it was apparent that there was a method to studying strategically, as opposed to just putting in the time staring at the textbook. This chapter will explore the concept of studying and what interferes with it, what strategies work best, the right study environment, and suggestions for test taking.

As school psychologists, we are fortunate that *what* we are required to study often helps provide the answers to *how* to study. As a framework for test preparation, we suggest that you consider the theories of learning and cognitive psychology, both as part of the content that you will consolidate in your memory and as the process of learning that content by using the strategies discussed in this chapter.

Getting Organized

Did you know that expert problem solvers spend more time planning how to solve problems, for example, matching given information to the problem, than do novice problems solvers, and actually spend less time finding correct solutions (Chi, Glaser, & Rees, 1988)? Therefore, if you initially spend some time getting organized, you will probably be more efficient in the time you spend studying. Many students jump into studying without a plan, which can result in wasted time in not having the materials needed, not recognizing how much time to allot for different parts of the task, and needing to redo sections because of not enough review. Therefore, it is important to take steps to create the correct environment for studying and focus on study hygiene.

What is the right study environment? Although the specific location where you are most productive is a personal decision, there are a few general tips to keep in mind as you hunker down with your books. Most people concentrate better in a location that is quiet and free of distractions, although some prefer a location with soft background noise. If you are working at home and there is family to provide unwanted (and maybe some avoidance-motivated wanted) interruptions, it can be helpful to talk to your family and set up some "office hours" when you put a "Do Not Disturb" sign on the door of the room. Although your family might initially think that is funny or unnecessary, it can be a helpful reminder when they want to ask you about something during your study hours. Additional suggestions are provided here for consideration in developing your study space:

- Have a clock or watch available to monitor time or to set limits.
- Keep the room temperature somewhat cool for maximum alertness. Warm rooms often make people feel tired.
- Clear away the visual clutter that can be distracting. It is advised that you keep a calendar of your study schedule in view. If you have an inspirational poster or picture that provides you with motivation, keep it visible. I often keep an old calendar with beautiful views from California's Route 1 that I look at for inspiration when I start to feel discouraged while working on a project.
- Use proper lighting—not too dark and relaxing or too bright and jarring.
- Have all of your supplies available to limit time spent looking for items you need.

Now that you have the proper environment for studying, let's consider some aspects of study hygiene.

Study Hygiene Tips

The important idea about study hygiene is to *study smarter, not harder.* Many students report that they spend many hours of study time with minimal results, in terms of grades or information they can recall and use. In this case, an initial task we ask students to do involves keeping a study journal. Often students will report that they are spending five hours a night in the library studying. However, when they record the actual time and activity in their journals, they realize that much of the five hours was spent talking to friends they ran into, getting snacks, taking breaks, going online, and checking email. When they evaluated the amount of time they were truly focused on studying, they discovered it was only an hour or two.

Remember the research on the difference between mass and distributed practice? One of the reasons why distributed practice works better is because it gives the brain time to consolidate information, or to integrate the new information with stored information. Also, when you study over time, you will have the opportunity to vary the context and to use alternate strategies and cues for the encoding, thus enriching and elaborating the connections between all of the facts and concepts you are reviewing. Look at how we're using the content of cognitive psychology as the process of studying for the Praxis!

Amount of Study Time

Study Intervals

Study for only 25 to 30 minutes and then take a short break (5 to 10 minutes) before getting back to studying for another 30-minute block. Many students think that they have so much information to learn that they need to study for long chunks of time to master it all, and therefore are afraid to try this suggestion. However, it is likely that if you take the breaks, you will be much more efficient in retaining what you have learned and you will develop more study stamina, thereby studying over longer periods of time. Many students with whom I've worked have been able to increase the total amount of study time within a week if they take frequent breaks, as opposed to a decreased total amount of study time within a week when they study for large chunks of time.

Take Breaks

Many students don't like to take breaks because they think they will not return to the work. It may be helpful to make a list of 5- to 10-minute activities that you enjoy. Maybe listen to a song you like, eat a healthy snack or get a drink of water to keep your brain hydrated, or practice a relaxation breath, which can go a long way to helping you stay focused on the task at hand.

Avoid Cyberspace Distractions

When you are studying at your computer, make yourself a promise not to check email or get distracted by other Internet activities. As many have discovered, it is quite easy to lose track of time in cyberspace, so limit the time spent doing online searches.

Get Enough Sleep at Night

In the last 15 years there has been extensive research indicating that during certain cycles of sleep, the brain is active at consolidating information. Therefore, it is suggested that while one can review information before bed, learning difficult new information right before bedtime can interfere with sleep. Also, the benefits of a good night's sleep for concentration, attention, and mood are well documented, as are the negative effects of building a sleep debt. In other words, you can make the most of your study hours if you also respect your body's requirement for a good night's sleep.

Increase Your Positive Affect

Start off your study in a good mood. Research in positive psychology indicates that positive affect facilitates problem solving, attention, and creativity (Isen, Daubman, & Nowicki, 1987; Fredrickson & Branigan, 2005; Fredrickson & Losada, 2005; Isen, 2005). Positive affect is generally easy to induce through physical activity, social interaction, and positive reflections (Watson, 2005). Perhaps when you take a study break, you can visualize yourself achieving the goal that you have set for yourself, passing the Praxis, becoming a school psychologist, and helping children and their families.

Reward Yourself for Your Study Efforts

Give yourself some rewards to reinforce the work that you are doing. Put away some money for every good study session that you have to buy something you would not have otherwise purchased for yourself. Maybe save for a great vacation after you pass the test or a nice dinner out, based on your study hours. Reward yourself by spending time with friends after your study sessions. Remember that rewards and positive reinforcement can increase your positive affect and help you maintain your motivation.

Develop a Flexible Study Schedule

It can be very helpful to evaluate how much material you need to cover, what you need to briefly review, and how much you need to relearn. Then you can estimate how much time you will need to spend to cover all of the material. Sometimes when people develop a schedule, they are unrealistic about the amount of time they will devote to studying, and when they fail to achieve the study goals, they feel less motivated. Saying, "I will study four hours each day, seven days a week until the test" is just like saying, "I will never eat chocolate again." The best strategy is to develop a flexible schedule, determine the total number of hours you must study in a week, and then develop a range of hours that you will study each day.

Procrastination

It is a well-known fact that people tend to remember information when they have studied and reviewed it in several sessions spaced over time, as in distributed practice, as opposed to cramming for a test at the last minute, as in mass practice (Bahrick & Phelps, 1987). That brings us to the biggest obstacle to academic success: *procrastination*. As the saying goes, "Don't put off until tomorrow what you could put off until the next day." Procrastination is considered public enemy number one in relation to successful studying and academic success by students and experts alike. What is procrastination? The definitions vary slightly, but they generally converge on the idea of avoiding something that needs to be done. So does that mean that anytime we engage in something other than the specific required tasks of our daily lives we are procrastinating? Many people draw that conclusion, and, as a result, they often think they are lazy, unproductive, and unsuccessful if they are not working on their top priorities. These negative thoughts work further to drain motivation and increase off-task behavior. As graduate students, you are very busy people with jobs, families, and responsibilities beyond your classes. If you engage in social or leisure activities, perhaps you are engaging in healthy balanced lifestyle behaviors and not simply procrastination. Perhaps engaging in those other behaviors actually helps you to *not procrastinate* in the long run because it helps you to remain motivated and focused on your study goal.

It can be very helpful to identify why you may be procrastinating. It is just like doing a functional behavioral assessment (FBA) on yourself about procrastinating. If you go through the steps of the FBA, you will probably learn more about FBAs, and you will also find out why you procrastinate and what reinforces it!

The first rule in arranging your schedule is to be flexible, and the second is to be realistic. Here are some common reasons that people procrastinate:

- *Clarity of goals.* If you cannot see the purpose in doing a task, it is often difficult to do. For instance, if you think you already have a strong knowledge base required to practice school psychology, and if you resent having to take a test to prove it, studying for the Praxis test may be arduous. However, as we stated in Chapter 1, for you to take and succeed on the Praxis is a requirement in many situations—for example, it is a program requirement for most school psychology programs and a requirement for certification in some states. Therefore, we would recommend you reframe the notion of taking the Praxis as merely an intermediate step (i.e., another hoop to jump through) that you need to accomplish in order to achieve your long-range goal of becoming a school psychologist.
- *Working best under pressure.* Many people believe that they work best under pressure, and in fact they may actually have some evidence that they perform well on tests if they study at the last minute. There are three questions to raise about this: (1) How do you know that you would not have done even better if you were better prepared? (2) Although studying at the last minute might have been a successful strategy for you in the short term (e.g., for tests based on a half or full semester's worth of information), will it also be a successful strategy for a test like the Praxis, which covers information from several years? (3) Do you want to waste the payment for the registration fee for the test if you might be wrong?
- *Preferring exciting activities to studying.* Although most people would state that they would prefer to do something more fun than studying, research has demonstrated that those who enjoy undertaking high-risk activities tend to procrastinate more than those who do not have that need for frequent excitement. Value and goal clarification may help deal with this issue. You might make the decision to hunker down and study, although you might prefer to be skydiving, because passing the test is more aligned with your future goals. It is important for those who think this is their preferred procrastination pattern to reward themselves frequently with excitement for achieving some study goals.
- *Not knowing where to start.* This is my favorite procrastination technique and the one I usually employ when I'm avoiding a task. Not knowing where to start a task is an example of an ill-structured or ill-defined problem (Sternberg, 2003). People often put off tasks that seem overwhelming or too large or too difficult. Recall the statements earlier in the chapter that suggested that expert problem solvers initially spend extensive time in planning how to solve the problems. You can use the content regarding problem solving to develop a plan to make your ill-defined study problem into a well-defined one by developing a study schedule and matching your resources to the problem—that is, allotting more time to study more difficult concepts and less time for reviewing what you know well. Another strategy that is recommended when you do not know where to start is to start anywhere. Often *just jumping in anywhere to begin* helps you over the hurdle. Once you get interested in the task, it is easier to keep going. This might be an opportunity to review information about executive functions and to use examples from your own personal experience about the difficulty of initiating.
- *Doing too many tasks at once.* Sometimes doing less important tasks may make you feel productive, but it does not help you to accomplish your major priority. Often we get involved in many projects and cannot see any of them through. This could easily happen when studying for a large test like the Praxis with all of the different

sections. If you study haphazardly, you may not feel like you have mastered any sections, although you learned a little about several of them. A common example of this is cleaning a room. Many people say that when they are cleaning their bedroom, they put something away in the drawer and then notice that the drawer is disorganized, so they begin to clean the drawer. This leads them to put something away in the closet, which they also notice is disorganized, so they get distracted and begin to clean the closet. After a few hours of hard work, they look around the room and it looks worse than it did before they started! In contrast to this, many people report that if they do a low-priority task that leads to feeling productive, this process often leads to motivation to complete the more difficult task. For instance, some people like to clean and organize before they start to study. I know that I like to get a couple of little things accomplished that might distract me from the larger project. Whether it is procrastination depends on whether it helps you to avoid or tackle the priority task.

- *Fear of failure or success.* Some people study less than they should because they are afraid. Fear of failure interferes with studying in that the individual can blame a poor test score on inadequate study time and not on his or her own competence or ability. Some students feel an internal or external pressure to be perfect, and they avoid confronting the fear of truly testing their ability. Fear of success interferes because of the belief that studying and doing well will raise others' expectations of you and you may not want to meet those rising expectations.
- *Magical thinking.* When tasks are difficult, sometimes students give up and think that simply with the passage of time, concepts will become easier to understand and remember. Of course, this magical thinking rarely works. In fact, it often creates more problems since the amount of time available to study decreases as the test draws near. When we were youngsters, our teachers told us to ask for help if a task was too difficult. Often, graduate students have unrealistic beliefs that they *should* have mastered all of the material and therefore *should* not need help. What have our counseling courses told us about when we find ourselves using the word *should?* Recall that *should* usually has some unrealistic aspects to it and is often related to cognitive distortions. Using some of the strategies that we will discuss later regarding cognitive therapy can be very helpful in dealing with magical thinking. Many graduate students with whom I have worked have felt great relief when they have asked for help, participated in study groups, and acknowledged that they did not know something. It can be very freeing to unleash some mental energy that could be put to a more productive purpose.
- *Losing momentum.* Remember the executive functions involved in monitoring and regulating emotions as you complete a long task? You can brush up on those concepts as you apply them to this problem. What do the problem-solving strategies of cognitive psychology suggest about long tasks? Break them up into smaller chunks so there are more beginnings and ends. This is a very helpful strategy, especially for those of you who like to make lists. For instance, if you are studying about all of the court cases related to special education law, you can list all of them and study them separately. This is also directly related to the study hygiene concept of studying for 30- to 60-minute sessions. Hopefully, learning about procrastination has helped you to figure out the reason for the function of the behavior that has led to some strategies about more adaptive competing behaviors.

Study Strategies

As we mentioned earlier, to be very efficient in our studies, we need to study smarter, not necessarily harder. You may recall that learning depends on linking new information with previously learned information and manipulating it to make deep connections. This next section will explore some specific ways to increase learning through applying some of the concepts of cognitive psychology. Bloom's taxonomy (Bloom & Krathwohl, 1956) provides a framework to understand the cognitive levels needed to process information. The taxonomy delineates six levels of processing: knowledge, comprehension, application, analysis, synthesis, and evaluation. Each level progresses to a higher level of processing to create deeper connections to improve long-term learning. The theme of reviewing will be important throughout all the levels of processing. Studies suggest that students who reviewed material seven days after learning it recalled about 83% of the material, while students who did not review it recalled only about 33%. Furthermore, after 63 days of learning, those who reviewed recalled 70% and those who did not recalled 14% (http://www.brain.web-us.com/memory/memory_and_related_learning_prin.htm). The importance of review cannot be underestimated. You would be probably wasting your time if you studied a concept once without ongoing review. Therefore, we suggest you work ongoing reviews into your weekly study schedule.

Improve Memory

There are a few important rules of memory that will help us understand how we remember and learn. The *law of recency* refers to good performance in remembering items at the end of a list (Anderson, 2000). If we apply this to studying for the Praxis, it suggests that we might recall what we studied recently more than what we studied a year ago—hence the importance for ongoing review. The *law of frequency* also reinforces the need for review by suggesting that we will remember things that we have more experience with. Finally, the *law of vividness* helps us to understand how to use memory techniques that work. The law of vividness suggests that something that is striking (funny, shocking, or emotional) is easier to remember than the mundane. You probably can recall family dinners for holidays like Thanksgiving, but not necessarily dinner every night.

It is important to keep in mind that in order to remember or learn, vivid associations are especially important. Using humorous, silly, or shocking associations often provides the most memorable links. They also must be personal to you. A terrific memory technique for someone else may not resonate with you because it might have a personal connection to them but not to you (Table 3.1).

Using your visual memory can be very helpful, as research shows that information that is visually encoded is often easier to recall. This is often a strategy we use to improve comprehension for children who have reading comprehension difficulties. Making a picture with your brain creates a cross-reference that is rich with associations to make tags or connections.

Mnemonic techniques include methods to add meaning to otherwise meaningless or arbitrary lists of items. *Categorical clustering* uses semantic cues to organize items into meaningful categories. For instance, if you are memorizing a list of drugs, you might organize them into those that treat attention-deficit/hyperactivity disorder (ADHD), those that treat mood disorders, and so on. *Interactive images* include conjuring up pictures in your mind that connect the items to each other in some vivid manner.

The *method of loci* involves interactive images. For this method, you create a pathway with common landmarks that you know very well. Perhaps you select the path you routinely take while shopping in the supermarket, or your routine when you enter your home each day, or even when you get up in the morning. You link the concepts or terms you want to learn to the landmarks on the pathway and develop a vivid interactive image that will help you remember the concept or term. *Acronyms* use the first letters of the words to make a pronounceable word, and *acrostics* also use the first letters to spell out a message. Finally, the *drill sandwich* can be used very effectively to learn lists. For the drill sandwich, make a group of flashcards for the things you must remember. Select about seven that you already know from the group, and use them for the first study pile. Then select three new items that you do not know and shuffle them in the pile. After you learn all 10 words or concepts, take 3 of the original 7 out of the pile and put them in a review pile and add 3 new words. Therefore, you are always working with 10 cards, 7 that you know and 3 new terms. And you are always building your review pile, all of the words that you have mastered and that you are reviewing at the end of each study session. You would be surprised how easy it is to learn three new things when they are combined with seven things you already know.

TABLE 3.1
Memory Techniques

Mnemonics	Add meaning to list of items
Categorical Clustering	Use semantic cues to organize items
Interactive Images	Develop pictures in your mind to connect items

Tips on Organizing Information for Maximum Learning

Learning requires making connections with things you already know. Therefore, it is helpful to manipulate the new information in many ways to increase the connections that we can make with it. This type of deeper processing could be thought of as a file cabinet, in which information is cross-referenced in several different ways, thereby increasing the access to the new information. You can also think of this deeper processing as making deeper grooves in the sand because of the repetition or frequency of making the connections. The following section examines some methods of interacting with the material you need to learn or review. The funnel approach looks at the big picture first, and initially provides the framework for the general concept or overview to then funnel through and delineate the details. Holistic learners are usually drawn to this approach because they see the pattern, rather than the disconnected pieces of details that make no sense individually. Making outlines or graphic organizers is an example of how to use this approach. When studying for the Praxis, if you use the funnel approach for studying the court cases for special education, you might look at them from a historical perspective, thinking about the progression of rights for individuals with disabilities. That historical framework might help you to link the details of the specific cases because they might make more sense from the perspective of a logical timeline.

A final step in keeping the information organized in your mind for easy review is to develop quick-reference graphic representations—for example, large index cards—that you can refer to during the last two weeks before the test. These visual aids should contain the information consolidated in key terms, lists, or other graphic forms. Having these index cards or other quick reference will allow you to conveniently review whenever you want. These can be the finishing touches or the last step in your mental organization of the large volume of knowledge you will need to know for the Praxis or other credentialing tests.

Building the Knowledge Base

This method is in contrast to the one just described in that you pull all of the information together to develop the concept. As mentioned earlier, it is difficult to recall a list of unrelated details, but if you pull the details together by organizing them, you add meaning to them. This organization can involve categorizing, grouping, or chunking the details. Some of the earlier memory techniques are related to this method, in that it is easier to recall a meaningful sentence or word that starts with the initials of the items in a list (acrostics or acronyms) than to recall all the unrelated details.

Active Learning

Increasing your cognition effort is essential in studying smarter, not harder. If you find yourself having spent a half hour reading something and then realize that you cannot recall anything that you have read, then you have not engaged your metacognition. Some of the tips for the proper study environment can help to provide the correct external cues for maximum cognitive efficiency. Monitoring your attention can also be helpful. I worked with a student once who studied all the time but did poorly despite the effort. We devised a plan for her to set a timer to go off to note if she was on task studying and, if not, what she was thinking of. From that exercise, she learned that not only was she frequently not paying attention, but also that she had constant negative thoughts about how she disliked studying and how she was fearful of doing poorly! That awareness helped her to learn more about cognitive behavior therapy. She did some work to replace her distorted cognitions with those that were more in line with facilitating her goal.

When reading study material, we suggest that you employ some of the reading comprehension strategies that we recommend for youngsters with reading disabilities. They work for all ages. The SQ4R (Richardson & Morgan, 1997) and some variations have been around for some time and have proven to be helpful for learning material, in part because they help someone to stay focused. The SQ4R method includes six parts: survey, question, read, recite, record, and review. The *survey* section suggests looking over a chapter's introduction and learning objectives, reading all headings, and looking at pictures, charts, or graphs, as an exercise to prime the brain. The survey helps to activate any background knowledge you have, thereby opening the pathway for connections with what you will learn. Next you make up a *question* that you want to answer regarding each section. This tells your brain to be more active in seeking information as opposed to being passive in just receiving information that may be meaningless to you. Next you *read* the section, highlighting or underlining important points while looking for the answer to the question. Then you *recite* something about what you read, including the answer to the question you asked. You *record* the answer, taking notes on the section. It is generally a good idea to create a written product for future review. Finally, when you finish reading the chapter, you *review* all of your notes for the entire chapter immediately and again within the next 24 hours. The SQ4R method might seem time-consuming and tedious; however, it probably takes less time than rereading sections over and over because of drifting off into daydreams and not staying focused while reading.

A well-organized, focused study group can be very helpful in learning difficult material or just reviewing. Talking out the material and listening to others can also increase the cross-references. Perhaps you can remember information by who said it. Sometimes someone will say something funny in a study group that helps to make the material more vivid. Talking it out also helps you to paraphrase the information, which again increases the associations or connections with the information. As you talk to the members of your study group, they can add missing information or state the concepts in their words, which might also deepen your understanding. To develop even deeper connections, try to teach someone else the material. If you do this, you will be able to discover your weak points or gaps in understanding the concept.

Bloom's taxonomy (Bloom & Krathwohl, 1956) provides an excellent framework to understand the cognitive levels needed to process information. As mentioned, the taxonomy delineates six levels of processing: knowledge, comprehension, application, analysis, synthesis, and evaluation. Each level progresses to higher levels of processing to create deeper connections to improve long-term learning. It helps us to understand the cognitive levels in order to process information deeply.

The knowledge level includes memorizing, or recalling facts, naming items, making lists, enumerating, defining, and identifying. When I was a youngster, I thought that having knowledge was the highest level of learning, but it is actually the first level. Knowledge forms the foundation for the higher stages of learning. The memory techniques described earlier facilitate the accumulation of factual knowledge. The comprehension level of cognitive processing involves understanding the information at a basic level. It involves organizing and reorganizing material, manipulating information by translating it into your own words, and interpreting it. Some activities to enhance comprehension include drawing a picture, giving an example, interpreting and extrapolating through making inferences, explaining how and why, and summarizing.

Application provides the opportunity to use the information, to take the abstract concepts and apply them to a concrete situation. Can you transfer the information to a new situation? We all know that in math, we apply the information by making calculations to solve a problem. Many of the Praxis questions involve application of a principle to the school setting; therefore, relating the material to real-life school situations is essential. Remember the law of vividness? If you can think of a real example for application with people or a situation you have really experienced, then you are probably making a very deep and vivid connection.

Analysis deals with the form of the information. It is related to the funnel approach discussed earlier, in which we put the overall idea through a funnel and disassemble it into the individual elements, relationships, and principles. It can help to determine if there are patterns or themes between the components. Some of the strategies you can use to get to the analysis level include developing a hypothesis, discussing the rationale or logic behind the idea, showing the cause, and tracing the steps or pathway. For example, if you were trying to learn different theories, you could use analysis to compare and contrast.

Synthesis brings together the information in a new way. It creates something new from the previous information. Using synthesis, you can develop your knowledge base as discussed earlier. Using the component parts, you can create a model; you can test a new hypothesis, or design an experiment. Evaluation is the final level of cognition and involves making judgments about the material. If you make something your own by evaluating it, you are most surely making a deep connection. If you take a position on something, you usually have developed a rationale or defense with supporting arguments, which leads to vivid and meaningful associations. This level allows you to discriminate between ideas and to verify evidence regarding the topic.

Test Taking

Many students who do poorly on tests often report that they have studied and that they thought they knew more information than it appeared from their test grade. Often when this happens, the problem might be based on the fact that the student had studied to the level of *recognition*, but not to the level of *recall*. If you need cues to remember something, then you are at the recognition level. We've all experienced the feeling in which we could picture our notebook with the answer to the question on the top right-hand side, but we cannot recall what it says. Maybe if you just glanced at that page, you would be able to recognize the answer without even reading what it says. Sometimes it is said that multiple-choice tests are recognition tests because all of the answers are there. However, many people find that the distracters in multiple-choice tests interfere with the ability to recognize the correct answer. Therefore, knowing the information at the level of recall will generally improve test performance.

If you are at the level of recall, you are able to provide a correct answer without many cues. Many of the study tips discussed earlier are exercises to allow for free recall of materials. The reciting portion of the SQ4R strategy allows you to test your recall. With the book closed, could you recite the answer? Also, the suggestions involving talking out the material facilitate recall of the information. If you are able to state or explain the material in your own words, then you are probably at the level of recall.

Confidence in Test Taking

If you have practiced some of the strategies suggested in this chapter, you are probably studying more effectively than before. For many students, that sense of studying smarter provides some confidence in taking the test. Furthermore, if you have done well in your graduate program and have learned the information along the way, you can also focus on that success to feel confident. As you know, the thoughts that you repeat in your mind can help you to feel motivated and ready or insecure and anxious. It is important that you become aware of any cognitive distortions or negative thoughts to work on changing them. Many students who talk about feeling anxious about tests often think thoughts about the tests "trying to trick them." These students often second-guess themselves because they are constantly vigilant for hidden tricks in the test. In working with graduate and medical students, I have discovered that it is often the student who thinks that the test will be straightforward and therefore an opportunity to demonstrate what he or she knows who does well on the test.

Borrowing a strategy from positive psychology, many students have found it helpful to develop a positivity portfolio about their previous academic or other accomplishments. A positivity portfolio is a concrete or virtual collection of items (e.g., pictures, notes, other artifacts) that elicit the feeling that the portfolio is based on. A couple of weeks before the test, you can spend a few minutes every day exploring your positivity portfolio by carefully examining the items that symbolize your success and remembering how you felt when you received them. The strength of the positivity is in eliciting the powerful feelings and bringing you back to situations where you conquered a goal or overcame an obstacle. Using a positivity portfolio in this way can help decrease your stress level while increasing your feelings of confidence.

Taking the Test

It seems oversimplified to suggest that you read carefully when you are taking the test. Even though we know to read carefully, we often make silly errors in reading. Mark up the test, underlining keywords and crossing off unnecessary words. As you read the questions and possible answers, focus in on keywords. Don't second-guess yourself, although it is always a good idea to check for glaring errors.

Generally there are a few approaches to taking tests: answer-search, elimination, and guessing. If you are currently in a graduate program taking tests, you can examine which of these methods you use and which works best for you. Using the *answer-search* method, you read the question and come up with your own answer, and then look for one that matches your answer. This can be a very effective method, but some students become anxious or fixated if they do not find an answer that is similar to what they think is the correct answer. If this happens, you must think about cognitive flexibility and free your mind from the answer that came to you. You were obviously on a different track of thought than the question is looking for, so you must take a breath and let go of how you were thinking about it. With the *elimination* method, you read the question and then go through the answers to recognize the correct answer. Of course, *guessing* is the least recommended method for taking a test. However, if you have no idea of the answer, look for keywords and try to use your critical thinking skills to guess. Some general test-taking heuristics include using caution with absolute terms (*always*, *never*), recognizing qualifying or clarifying words, and noticing choices that have balanced phrasing. Often those types of wordings can lead to keywords to answer the questions correctly.

For those who think they have test anxiety, there is an *intuitive response* method of test taking. Research has suggested that often our first response to a question is correct, if we have no other information. Most students who are anxious when taking tests often read too much into a question and get lost in all of the words. The intuitive response method suggests that you note your first response to a question quickly without thinking about it too much. Go through the rest of the test and come back to the ones you did not know. If you have remembered some new information at that point, you can change your answer, but if not, go with your intuitive response.

Test Anxiety

It is very natural for most people to feel somewhat anxious when they are taking a test, especially an important one like the Praxis; however, if the anxiety is extreme, you may not be able to study or take the test effectively. There are generally two strategies to help deal with test anxiety: cognitive approaches and physiological approaches.

The cognitive approaches suggest that you take inventory of your anxious thoughts. Do you have concerns about how others view you, about your future security, beliefs about failure, perfectionism, and so on? If so, you might need to explore some of these ideas and work to modify them. You might need to develop more positive self-talk, thinking of statements including "I am well prepared" and "This is an opportunity to demonstrate what I have learned." You might also want to use some imagery, both to help yourself relax and to envision your future after you pass the test.

The physiological approach uses relaxation skills, breathing exercises, and muscle stretches during the test. Physically doing these activities can increase your concentration and focus while studying or taking the test. If you begin to feel fatigued while taking the test, do some shoulder rolls, neck stretches, or other nonobtrusive movements to increase your blood flow and your mental energy. In the end, the best antidote to test anxiety is to be well prepared and well rested for the test. If you are well prepared, you will increase your confidence. If you are well rested, you will be able to maximize your problem-solving skills because your brain will be nourished and ready.

Summary

Studying for an important test such as the Praxis can seem like a daunting task. If you create the right study environment, organize your study schedule, employ effective memory and learning techniques, and remain positive, you can increase your likelihood of doing well when you sit for the test. Being well prepared must, however, be accompanied by effective test-taking strategies. Having confidence, staying relaxed, keeping focused, and knowing your approach to multiple-choice questions will allow you to draw on your knowledge resources and perform effectively.

Terry Molony, PhD, NCSP, earned her doctorate in school psychology from the Philadelphia College of Osteopathic Medicine and her educational specialist degree from Rowan University. She is a nationally certified school psychologist and school psychology practitioner in Cherry Hill Public Schools, Cherry Hill, New Jersey.

Chapter 4

Surviving

Developing Your Own Plan

We are now at the point where we need to talk about developing your own study plan. This chapter will address study preparation, self-care, and management of test anxiety. All three of these areas are important aspects of helping you prepare for and survive the Praxis experience.

Study Preparation

Designing a Study Space

First, consider the physical environment or the location where you are going to study. Is there a place in your home or other environment that you can designate as a study area where you can have materials readily accessible? Some people need a totally silent environment, some need soft music playing in the background, and others work best with an organized and clutter-free workspace. Determine what your individual needs are and create a physical environment that is conducive to your studying needs and preferences.

Selecting Content

In Chapter 2, we discussed the content of the Praxis Exam in School Psychology. In Table 4.1, you will find a list of not only those content areas but also the key topics covered in the exam.

In subsequent chapters, we will provide you with more detailed information for each of these areas. But for now, your next step is to make a list of the specific content you will need to cover for each domain, or, in other words, *what is it that you will need to know?* For example, under the topic "Data-Based Decision Making," assessment of intelligence is a category you will need to address. First, determine if this is an individual area of strength or weakness of yours. Next, we suggest that you should first determine the level of detail and specific information you want to cover—for example, this might include specific norm-referenced tests (e.g., Wechsler scales, Woodcock-Johnson Stanford-Binet V, and other nonverbal measures), with an emphasis on any assessments with which you have less familiarity. What we are suggesting is that you begin with some strategic planning to determine what information is most important to review. As one school psychology graduate student reflected,

> The biggest challenge I faced when preparing for the Praxis was choosing what to study and what not to study. I struggled to weed through thousands of facts, dates, theories, and terms to decide what was worth my time; not to mention wondering how much my brain could actually hold.
>
> (Personal communication, 2008)

TABLE 4.1
School Psychologist Praxis® Subject Assessment Content Areas and Key Topics

Professional Practices, Practices That Permeate All Aspects of Service Delivery

- Data-Based Decision Making and Accountability
- Consultation and Collaboration

Direct and Indirect Services for Children, Families, and Schools (Student-Level Services)

- Interventions and Instructional Support to Develop Academic Skills
- Interventions and Mental Health Services to Develop Social and Life Skills

Direct and Indirect Services for Children, Families, and Schools (System-Level Services)

- School-Wide Practices to Promote Learning
- Preventive and Responsive Services
- Family-School Collaboration Services
- Child and Adolescent Psychopathology

Foundations of School Psychological Service Delivery

- Diversity in Development and Learning
- Research and Program Evaluation
- Legal, Ethical, and Professional Practice

General Knowledge of Psychological Principles and Theories

- Knowledge of Psychological Principles
- Knowledge of Psychological Theory

Source: http://www.ets.org/s/praxis/pdf/5402.pdf. Retrieved June 11, 2015.

Gathering Materials

Next, gather together all your study materials that cover the topics you have listed. This might include study guides and selected textbooks and online resources (e.g., NASP position papers) you may need to refer to when you have a question about some information. It is helpful to have all the materials you will need at your fingertips. Don't forget to visit your local office supply store to pick up some much needed highlighters or other motivating and fun supplies.

Creating Study Guides

In Chapters 5 through 10, you will find prepared graphic organizers that outline the content under each area covered in the Praxis Exam in School Psychology. We suggest that you review the content of the graphic organizers to identify the material that you have achieved mastery of and select those areas where you need to spend time reading and reviewing. Those areas selected for more intense review will be based on your individual background, knowledge, and personal style, and will be different for each person. Next, reread Chapter 3 on study techniques and select those strategies that are a good fit for your learning style and will help you succeed. Remember you are preparing for a standardized, computer-delivered test. Reflect on your past success when you prepared for similar standardized tests—for example, the Scholastic Aptitude Test and Graduate Record Exam—and incorporate those strategies you found to be effective.

When you are creating your personal study guide, consider including content that could be covered in a variety of test items. By this we mean that some questions are based purely on factual knowledge and assess the "low-hanging fruit" of literature in the field of school psychology. If you recall, the content that is described as low-hanging fruit is information that lends itself directly to factual multiple-choice questions. For example, based on the National Association of School Psychologists Graduate Preparation Standards, how many hours of supervision per week does an intern require? The answer is two. This is clear-cut, factual information that can be assessed easily through a multiple-choice question format. On the other hand, there are also questions that require the test taker to synthesize and integrate information in order to respond successfully. And finally, there are questions that are scenario-based and present brief vignettes that require problem solving in order to respond correctly. Thus, remember when you are assembling your study guide to consider material that will assist you with each of these types of questions.

Developing a Schedule

Time management is important. Within your busy schedule, we suggest planning blocks of time to devote to reviewing for the Praxis. If you intentionally set aside Praxis study time, you will be less likely to find yourself caught in the last-minute crunch of having vast quantities of material to review in a very short time. Some of our graduate students have shared that beginning a few months before they are scheduled to take the exam, they have set aside one hour each day to devote to reviewing the materials they have gathered. In addition, the same people found it helpful to schedule blocks of time within their week when they had more time to review larger segments of material. This seems to have worked for them, but you need to determine what will work for you. Remember to make your study schedule realistic and doable for you, since it will be important for you to follow through and remain positive and motivated. Spending time studying for the Praxis is a short-term activity and it won't last forever, so follow through on your plan.

Selecting Study Techniques

Now, go back and (once again) review Chapter 3. Based upon your own personal experience with test preparation, select some strategies that you believe are consistent with your learning style. Try them out to see which ones might be most effective. Continue using those study techniques that help you understand and remember information. Keep in mind, however, that it is important to be flexible enough to make changes if you find that a particular technique is not as effective as you thought. Here is what one graduate student had to say:

> Taking practice tests and answering practice questions were extremely helpful when preparing for the Praxis and simulating the real test-taking experience. As a student who fears multiple-choice tests, answering practice questions allowed me to discover the best strategies to use when I take these kinds of tests. I tried various approaches, including coming up with the answer on my own after reading the question. Preparing this way eased my multiple-choice anxiety and gave me the confidence to take the test in a way that worked best for me.
> (Personal communication, 2009)

As this student reflected, taking practice tests is an excellent method of preparing for the Praxis. You may want members of your study group to develop questions based upon material you are covering and share those questions with members of the group. Another resource is now available from ETS in the form of an Interactive Practice Test for School Psychologist test (5402) that you can access via the NASP website for a fee at http://www.ets.org/praxis/prepare/materials/5402. You may find it helpful to practice this computer-delivered test under timed conditions.

Self-Care

In addition to developing your study guides and selecting study techniques, we believe it is equally important for you to focus some of your time and energy on investing in yourself. Having a mind-set that allows you to be open and receptive to maximizing the time you are devoting to preparing for the Praxis is important.

In order to accomplish this, you should consider developing a personal care plan to address general well-being—for example, diet, sleep, exercise, and fun—and don't forget to reflect on ways to handle anxiety and stress. After reading this section, think about each of the suggested areas and then develop your own plan that will allow you to create balanced care.

Sleep

As you sleep your body rests and restores energy. As a result, sleep facilitates healthy well-being. Sufficient sleep helps you maintain your alertness, memory, thought processes, and coping skills. The National Sleep Foundation states that most adults need between seven to nine hours of sleep per night ("Diet, Exercise and Sleep," n.d.) in order to function at an optional level. A 2003 study completed at the University of Pennsylvania Medical School found that cognitive performance decreases in adults who get less than eight hours of sleep (Van Dongen, Maislin, Mullington, & Dinges, 2003). Based on this information, it is important that as you are preparing for the Praxis and developing a personal care plan, you don't forget to schedule sufficient time for sleep. If you are presently sleep deprived because of a hectic schedule, make a commitment to yourself to allow time in your day for that necessary seven to nine hours of sleep. In other words, as you are developing a schedule to review material, do not plan to study at the expense of your sleep.

Diet and Exercise

As part of your personal plan, examine your eating habits and exercise regime. Ask yourself: *How healthy is my diet? Am I incorporating exercise and physical activity into my daily life?* An important factor to consider as you begin preparing for the Praxis is to be mindful of maintaining a healthy, well-balanced diet and getting regular physical exercise. At a time when you are adding one more item to your busy schedule—that is, Praxis preparation—remember not to sacrifice taking the time to maintain your physical well-being. All of these are important to maintaining a strong mind, healthy body, positive outlook, and alert mood. Taken together, we are suggesting that you strive to establish and maintain improved physical fitness and emotional well-being. The benefits can be incredible.

Pleasure

Now that we have addressed issues of physiological well-being, let's shift our focus to psychological health. We strongly believe that it's important not to forget to plan and schedule opportunities for pleasure. Lunch with a friend, time with your family, a glass of wine with colleagues, and just enjoying a good movie on DVD are examples of ways to relax and experience whatever makes you happy and can serve as a welcomed respite from test preparation. You deserve it!

Balance in your life is important, and it should be no different when you are preparing for the Praxis. As you are developing your study schedule, do not forget to include times when you can relax and recharge. You will find yourself better able to return to your study preparation after you have taken time to clear your head and enjoy the things and people that bring you pleasure. Our motto is work hard, play hard.

Managing Test Anxiety

Test anxiety is a feeling of fear, nervousness, stress, and possible physical symptoms. If you are someone who experiences test anxiety when you are preparing for or taking a standardized test, then you are not alone. In our experience, many students experience some form of test anxiety as they begin to think about preparing for or taking the Praxis Exam in School Psychology. This is a normal reaction when you are faced with the prospect of taking a high-stakes test. The good news is there are a variety of recommendations you can follow to help reduce this form of anxiety.

First, we suggest that you take some time to determine the potential source of the anxiety—for example, you don't consider yourself a good standardized test taker, these experiences trigger feelings of questioning your own competency, or you tend to be an anxious person who expects perfection. And although you recognize that these feelings can all be counterproductive to doing your best on the test, they are difficult for you to control.

Some amount of anxiety may actually serve as a positive motivator. By this we mean your anxieties activate you to make plans and begin the preparation process. While you are taking the test, a small amount of tension can help you achieve a state of arousal that allows you to work at peak performance. We recommend that you review a publication available on the Educational Testing Service (ETS) (2005) website (www.ets.org) entitled "Reducing Test Anxiety." In this brief but valuable document, the authors discuss ways to recognize test anxiety, suggest how to cope with it, and offer recommended strategies to help you succeed.

Relaxation and Other Ways to Reduce Negative Thoughts

Anxiety can affect both the mind and the body. In order to deal more effectively with those racing thoughts and physiological indicators of tension, we suggest that you rely upon your own professional training in anxiety reduction. You might consider exercises such as deep breathing, guided imagery, and relaxation. Based upon your training, determine which of these may be helpful to you and regularly practice them so you can reduce your anxious thoughts and feelings. Many of you will also have to address thoughts and feelings on a cognitive level. Negative thinking can spiral out of control. We recommend you take time to focus on productive strategies that will help you to deal with these nagging thoughts. When you begin thinking or saying negative things about yourself, pay attention to them and reframe them. Counter those negative thoughts with positive statements that are true about you. For example, write down any negative thoughts and challenge or dispute them with positive statements.

Finally, remember what we have learned from Vroom's expectancy theory of motivation (Vroom, 1995): if you develop an expectancy belief that effort will result in attainment of a goal, you are far more likely to achieve that goal. Positive thinking can help you develop improved levels of self-confidence and self-efficacy that can contribute a great deal to your test preparation and success.

The Night Before and the Morning of the Test

Decisions for what to do the night before and the day of the test require planning as well. Determine what you need to do to help you be ready for the upcoming exam. There is no one answer about what is the best routine for you to follow the night before and the day of the test. Make a plan that fits your needs. Your plan may include reviewing material, eating a good meal, getting proper rest, organizing the necessary documentation for test admission, and having directions readily available. All these things will help you to be prepared for the morning that you will be arriving at the test site to take the Praxis. Think about what you need to do to be in the best frame of mind to take the test. Have confidence in your abilities and knowledge, and believe that you will succeed. We wish you well, and remember to stay positive.

Part II

Content of the Exam

Chapter 5

Professional Practices That Permeate All Aspects of Service Delivery

Chapter 5 includes the category of *Professional Practices That Permeate All Aspects of Service Delivery*. This category is divided into two topical areas: (1) *Data-Based Decision Making and Accountability* and (2) *Consultation and Collaboration*. On the following pages, the authors provide an introduction to and description of these two topics. Next, there is a series of graphic organizers that outline the *content knowledge* in these areas. Finally, you will find 15 sample questions on *Data-Based Decision Making and Accountability* and *Consultation and Collaboration*. The correct answers and rationale for each are included.

Data-Based Decision Making and Accountability

Data-Based Decision Making and Accountability encompasses diverse methods and models of assessment in order to conceptualize problems. The four topics included in this area are (1) knowledge of measurement theory and principles, (2) problem identification, (3) assessment and problem analysis, and (4) assessment considerations for special populations.

Knowledge of measurement theory and principles is fundamental to understanding all assessment. Included in this area are understanding the concepts of validity and reliability, various test scores and norms, strengths and limitations of assessment procedures, diversity factors and their impact, and knowledge of test fairness.

Problem identification involves various interview strategies, observation techniques, collection of pertinent background information, including review of previous interventions, and incorporation of any important information from screening measures.

Assessment and problem analysis includes a comprehensive understanding of various measurement tools. Among these methods are measures of intelligence/cognitive abilities, educational achievement, processing, adaptive behavior, social-emotional functioning, and functional behavior. Other types of data collection are performance-based assessment, curriculum-based assessment, and ecological assessment. Through the use of technology to collect data, the effectiveness of interventions can be monitored. The resulting collected data facilitates the understanding of needs, challenges, and strengths of all children and youth, including special populations. By using these various methods and models of assessment, school psychologists are able to identify problems, analyze the needs of all children and youth, and plan evidence-based interventions that follow a problem-solving model to evaluate outcomes of services (see Figure 5.1).

Each of the four components that make up *Data-Based Decision Making and Accountability* (i.e., *Knowledge of Measurement Theory, Problem Identification, Assessment and Problem Analysis, Assessment Considerations for Special Populations*) are further explained in detail in the graphic organizers that follow. Key information is outlined below each main topic. These are the areas that we recommend you review and master. While you are reviewing the key information outlined and answering the sample questions, you may want to add your own information on the graphic organizers to supplement what is provided here.

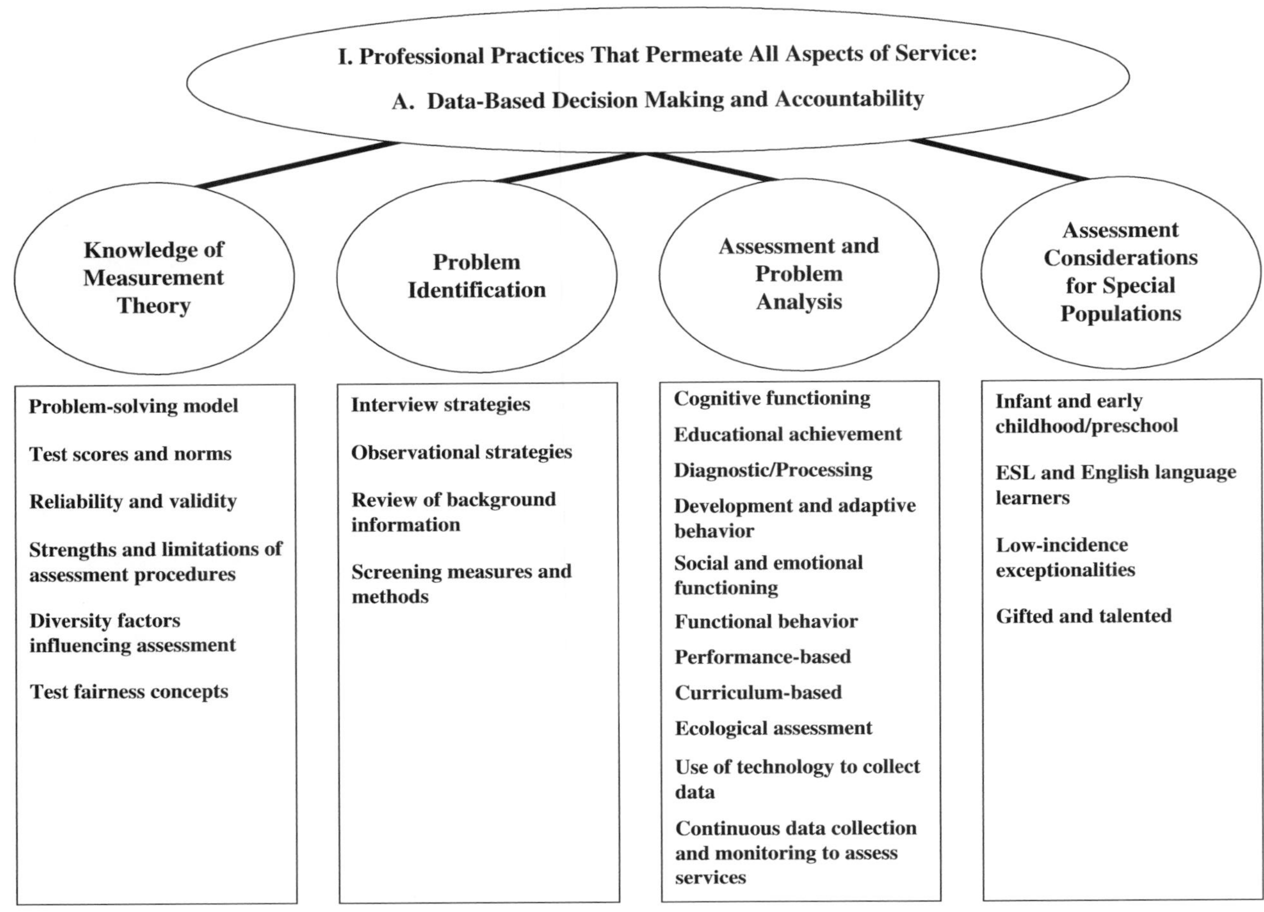

Figure 5.1
Professional Practices That Permeate All Aspects of Service: Data-Based Decision Making

Graphic Organizers for Knowledge of Measurement Theory

TABLE 5.1
Graphic Organizer for Problem-Solving Model

DBDMA: Knowledge of Measurement Theory

Problem-Solving Model

Main idea	Main idea	Main idea	Main idea
Problem Identification	Problem Analysis	Plan Development	Plan Evaluation
• Involves developing a clear, measurable, and operational definition of the problem that clarifies the nature, magnitude, and context of the problem in observable terms • Be sure that addressing the problem presented is the best way to address an underlying concern, which could represent a larger issue • Gap analysis o Team needs to examine the difference in performance between the problem situation and some target that would represent desired performance o Answer two questions: What is the individual/group expected to do? What is the individual/group actually doing?	• Create a hypothesis about why the problem is occurring • Questions to consider: o Is it a skill problem or performance problem? (Can't do/Won't do) o Are there sufficient data to confirm or refute the proposed hypothesis? o Is the hypothesis related to alterable factors with the school's control? o Is there sufficient expertise on the team?	• Team needs to develop a plan or goal statement that clearly defines closing the gap between current and desired performance • Goal statements must be written as a measurable statement of expected outcomes • Develop an effective intervention plan that considers: o Evidence that the intervention is effective for the problem o Treatment acceptability o Data collection planning o Resource allocation that provides sufficient support to the individual who is responsible for implementing the intervention • Schedule regular progress reviews	• Use outcome and fidelity data to determine whether the intervention has resulted in a reduction in the performance gap and a resolution of the problem • If successful: student/group reached the criteria (decision rule) set by the team as the goal for the intervention outcome o Can choose to decrease the intensity or discontinue the intervention • If not successful: team needs to ask additional questions to determine the best course of action to create a plan to improve the outcome o May need to cycle through the problem-solving model again

TABLE 5.1 (Continued)
Graphic Organizer for Problem-Solving Model

DBDMA: Knowledge of Measurement Theory

Problem-Solving Model

Main idea	Main idea	Main idea	Main idea
Data-Based Problem Solving	Data-Based Problem Solving in Schools	Data-Based Problem Solving in Schools (continued)	Data-Based Problem Solving in Schools (continued)
• Defined as using data within a well-defined, systematic problem-solving process to make decisions about continuously improving educational programs and services • Uses data to identify and analyze why problems are happening, to create viable changes to improve system performance that result in improved student outcomes, and to monitor system and student outcomes over time • Four basic questions: What is the problem (problem identification)? Why is it happening (problem analysis)? What should be done about it (plan development)? Did it work (plan evaluation)?	• Critical in meeting the growing demands for increased accountability from public institutions • Key for school systems moving to a multitiered systems of support model (MTSS), also called response to intervention (RTI) In Tier 1 • Data are collected across levels within a school system • Primary considerations: Areas of core instruction, curriculum, and school/classroom environment • Data used for this level include: High-stakes, state-administered, or standardized academic proficiency tests; norm-referenced tests; universal screening measures for academics; and school-wide discipline	In Tier 2 • Can use the same kinds of data used in Tier 1 • Evaluating outcomes for Tier 2 services include: o Mastery measures or formative/summative assessments specifically designed for interventions being used o Diagnostic tools for the purpose of identifying skills that need additional instruction or support to be mastered o Progress monitoring • Tier 2 teams examine small-group data for program evaluation and to identify students who may need more intensive supports	In Tier 3 • Interventions designed for individual students who need intensive instruction and supports or whose academic needs are so significant that they need targeted core replacement • Considers data about student outcomes that examine the intensity of service delivery needed to result in improved performance for students who are not successful with multiple layers of good core instruction and targeted instruction

TABLE 5.2
Graphic Organizer for Test Scores and Norms

DBDMA: Knowledge of Measurement Theory

Test Scores and Norms

Raw Score	Measures of Central Tendency	Measures of Variability	Other
• Most basic level of information provided by a test • Usually out of a numeric tally • Becomes meaningful in relation to norms	• Single measure used to represent all of the score within a sample • Mean: arithmetic average • Median: middlemost score when all of the scores have been ranked; is a better index of central tendency when looking at a skewed sample • Mode: most frequently occurring score	• Statistical index describes the dispersion of scores around the mean • Standard deviation (SD) o Found by taking the square root of variance o Directly relates to normal distribution o The closer the scores to the mean→ smaller the SD o The farther the scores from the mean → larger the SD o Conveys interchangeable information with the variance	

TABLE 5.2 (Continued)
Graphic Organizer for Test Scores and Norms

DBDMA: Knowledge of Measurement Theory

Types of Test Scores and Norms

Percentile and Percentile Ranks	Standard Scores	Standard Scores and Z-scores	T-scores
• Expresses the percentage of people in the standard sample who scored below a specific raw score • Percentile rank is not the percentage correct • Can also be viewed as rank within a group of 100	• Is most desirable psychometric property • Uses the standard deviation of the total distribution of raw scores as the fundamental unit of measurement • Expresses the distance from the mean in standard deviation units • Expresses the magnitude of deviation from the mean and the direction (+ or –) • Distribution of standard scores has exactly the same shape as distribution of raw scores	• Standard score o Some aspects of the Standard score are seen as unnecessary (e.g., decimals, fractions, + or – signs) o Standardized score eliminates fractions and negative signs • Z-score o Useful when attempting to compare items from distributions with different means and SD o Indicates how far and in what direction test score is from its mean expressed in SD	• Mean = 50; SD = 10 • Commonly used on personality test • Can be used with any statistic having a bell-shaped distribution • Central limit theorem states that the sampling distribution of a statistic will be normal if any of the following apply: 1. Population distribution is normal 2. Sampling distribution is symmetric, unimodal, without outliers and the sample size is 15 or less 3. Sampling distribution is moderately skewed, unimodal, and without outliers and sample size is between 16 and 40 4. Sample size is greater than 40 with outliers

TABLE 5.2 (Continued)
Graphic Organizer for Test Scores and Norms

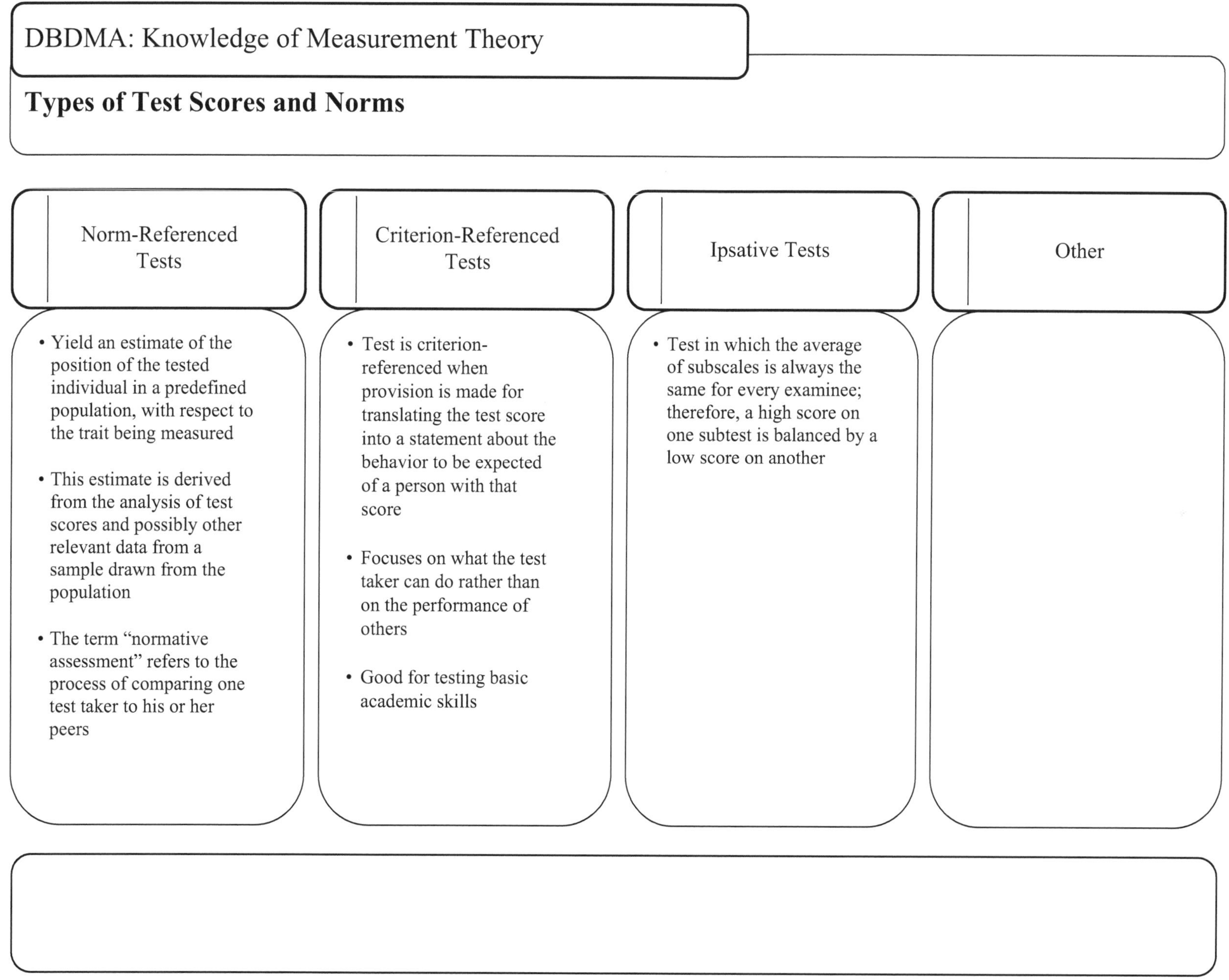

DBDMA: Knowledge of Measurement Theory

Types of Test Scores and Norms

Norm-Referenced Tests	Criterion-Referenced Tests	Ipsative Tests	Other
• Yield an estimate of the position of the tested individual in a predefined population, with respect to the trait being measured • This estimate is derived from the analysis of test scores and possibly other relevant data from a sample drawn from the population • The term "normative assessment" refers to the process of comparing one test taker to his or her peers	• Test is criterion-referenced when provision is made for translating the test score into a statement about the behavior to be expected of a person with that score • Focuses on what the test taker can do rather than on the performance of others • Good for testing basic academic skills	• Test in which the average of subscales is always the same for every examinee; therefore, a high score on one subtest is balanced by a low score on another	

TABLE 5.3
Graphic Organizer for Reliability and Validity

DBDMA: Knowledge of Measurement Theory

Reliability and Validity of Measurement

Reliability-Consistency in measurement	Reliability-Consistency in measurement (continued)	Validity	Validity (continued)
Test-retest • Most straightforward way to measure reliability • Administer identical forms of test to the same people at two different points in time Alternate form • Test incorporates similar content and the same range and level of difficulty in items Split-half reliability • Combination of Test-Retest and Alternate Form • Correlating the pairs of scores obtained from equivalent halves of a test given only once to a representative sample	Interscorer reliability • For tests involving qualitative scoring • Typical degree of agreement between scorers Coefficient alpha • Index of internal consistency of the items and their tendency to correlate positively with one another	Content validity • Determined by the degree to which the questions on a test are representative of the behavior the test was designed to measure • If the sample (specific items on the test) is representative of the population (all possible items), then the test possesses content validity Face validity • Measure of social acceptability (i.e., test appears to be valid to test users, examiners, etc.)	Criterion-related validity • When test is shown to be effective in estimating an examinee's performance on an outcome measure 1. Concurrent: criterion measures are obtained at approximately the same time as the test scores 2. Predictive: measures are obtained for future use Construct validity • Appropriateness of the test-based inferences related to the underlying construct purportedly measured by the test

TABLE 5.4
Graphic Organizer for Strengths and Limitations of Assessment Procedures

DBDMA: Knowledge of Measurement Theory

Strengths and Limitations of Assessment Procedures

Self-Report Tests	Multiple-Choice Tests	Interviews	Inventories
Strengths • Patient fills out without the assistance of a professional • Asks direct questions about symptoms, behaviors • Can be taken within 5 to 15 minutes Limitations • Patients may exaggerate or underreport symptoms in order to make their situation seem worse or to minimize their problems • Should never be solely used to diagnose a mental disorder	Strengths • Are appropriate for use in many different subject areas • Can be used to measure a variety of educational objectives Limitations • Responses are selected from a list of alternatives rather than supplied or constructed by respondent • Do not measure student's ability to: o Articulate explanations o Organize thoughts o Perform a specific task o Provide original ideas	Strengths • Can lead to further research using other methodologies • Can use variety of structures (formal and informal) Limitations • Amount of time needed to collect and analyze the responses • Rarely provides information consistent with other type of data, such as direct observation	Strengths • Examine specific questions • Able to contact large number of people quickly, easily and efficiently • Easy to standardize; very reliable method of research Limitations • Format makes it difficult for the researcher to examine complex issues and opinions • If researcher is not present, it is difficult to ensure that questions are understood properly

TABLE 5.5
Graphic Organizer for Diversity Factors Influencing Assessment

DBDMA: Knowledge of Measurement Theory

Diversity Factors Influencing Assessment

Personal Factors	Social and Environmental Factors	Linguistic Factors	Racial and Cultural Factors
• Carelessness • Anxiety/panic • Ability level • Motivation • Lack of sleep • Negative attitude	Social factors: • How the test is presented • Social anxiety • Incidents that happen prior to testing • Social exposure • Socialization of test taker Environmental factors: • Temperature • Lighting • Number of people around • Seating • Noise • Windows • Distracting events during administration	• Ability to understand questions and directions • Native language vs. second language • Understanding of context • Language ability level • Ability to form or understand concepts	Racial factors: • Biased instruments • Insensitive questions Cultural factors: • Impulse control • Value of education • Norms • Practices • Beliefs

TABLE 5.6
Graphic Organizer for Test Fairness Concepts

DBDMA: Knowledge of Measurement Theory

Test Fairness Concepts

Test Fairness	Test Fairness Three Ethical Positions	Test Bias	
• A broad concept that recognizes the importance of social values in test usage • Ultimately based on society's image of a just society • Even unbiased tests can be deemed unfair because of the way they are being used	1. Unqualified individualism States without exception the best candidates should be selected for employment, admission, or other privileges using factors such as race, age, and gender 2. Quotas Selection procedures should approximate the demographics of the local/supporting population 3. Qualified individualism Rely solely on tested abilities without reference to age, gender, and race	Content bias • When an item or subtest is proven to be more difficult for one group of a population than another Predictive validity bias • An inference drawn from a test score is not made with the smallest error possible or if there is a constant error in an inference or prediction as a function of membership in a particular group Construct validity • When a test is shown to measure a different psychological construct rather than the one intended	

Graphic Organizers for Problem Identification

TABLE 5.7
Graphic Organizer for Interview Strategies

DBDMA: Problem Identification

Interview Strategies

Main idea

Components of Effective Interviewing

- Establish rapport based on mutual respect and acceptance
- Facilitate communication
  - o Convey your interest to the interviewee
  - o Encourage interviewee to elaborate on responses
  - o Ease interviewee's anxiety
- Formulate appropriate questions
- Remain objective, yet empathic
- Be a good listener
  - o Give the interviewee time to share thoughts and feelings
- Close the interview appropriately
  - o Summarize
  - o Obtain feedback from the interviewee
  - o Discuss implications for future

Main idea

Types of Interviews

- Structured interview
  - o Standardized interviews yielding information about presence, absence, severity, onset, and duration of symptoms
  - o Yield quantitative scores in symptom areas or global indices of psychopathology
  - o Disorder-specific under category of DSM-V (ADHD, ODD, major depressive order, eating disorder, etc.)
- Unstructured interview
  - o Interviewee tells his/her story
  - o Interviewer guides interviewee to talk about issues and concerns related to referral problem
  - o Requires good clinical skills
  - o Can be used to identify general problem areas, then follow up with structured interview
- Computer-generated interview
  - o Software used to present uniform questions to all persons
  - o Child/adult sees and hears questions
  - o Can be novel experience
  - o Disadvantages: unfamiliar computer user may become anxious, format is impersonal, may experience technical difficulties

TABLE 5.8
Graphic Organizer for Observational Strategies

DBDMA: Problem Identification

Observational Strategies

Main idea: Purpose of Observations	Main idea: Systematic Observations	Main idea: Types of Observations
• Uses: evaluation, planning intervention, and monitoring progress • Provides an opportunity to see students' spontaneous behaviors in classroom, playground, etc. • Provides systematic record of students' behavior • Provides information about students' interpersonal skills • Provides information about fit of teaching style to students' learning style • Part of functional behavioral assessment	• Define target behavior as clearly and precisely as possible • List examples of target behavior • Observe student's behavior in natural or specifically designed settings • Record data objectively as it occurs • Ensure data are reliable and valid • Understand behavioral codes, if applicable • Sustain attention and focus on details • Identify important behaviors and summarize them according to system	Narrative recording • Anecdotal recording of noteworthy behaviors • No specific timeframes or codes Interval recording • Focuses on selected aspects of behavior as occur within specific time interval • Sample behavior rather than recording every behavior • Useful for overt behaviors • Unit of measure is time Event recording • Record each event of behavior as it occurs during observation period • Frequency count of discrete behavior • Unit of measure is behavior Rating recording • Rating behavior on a checklist or scale • Useful for evaluating global aspects of behavior or for gaining impressions

TABLE 5.8 (Continued)
Graphic Organizer for Observational Strategies

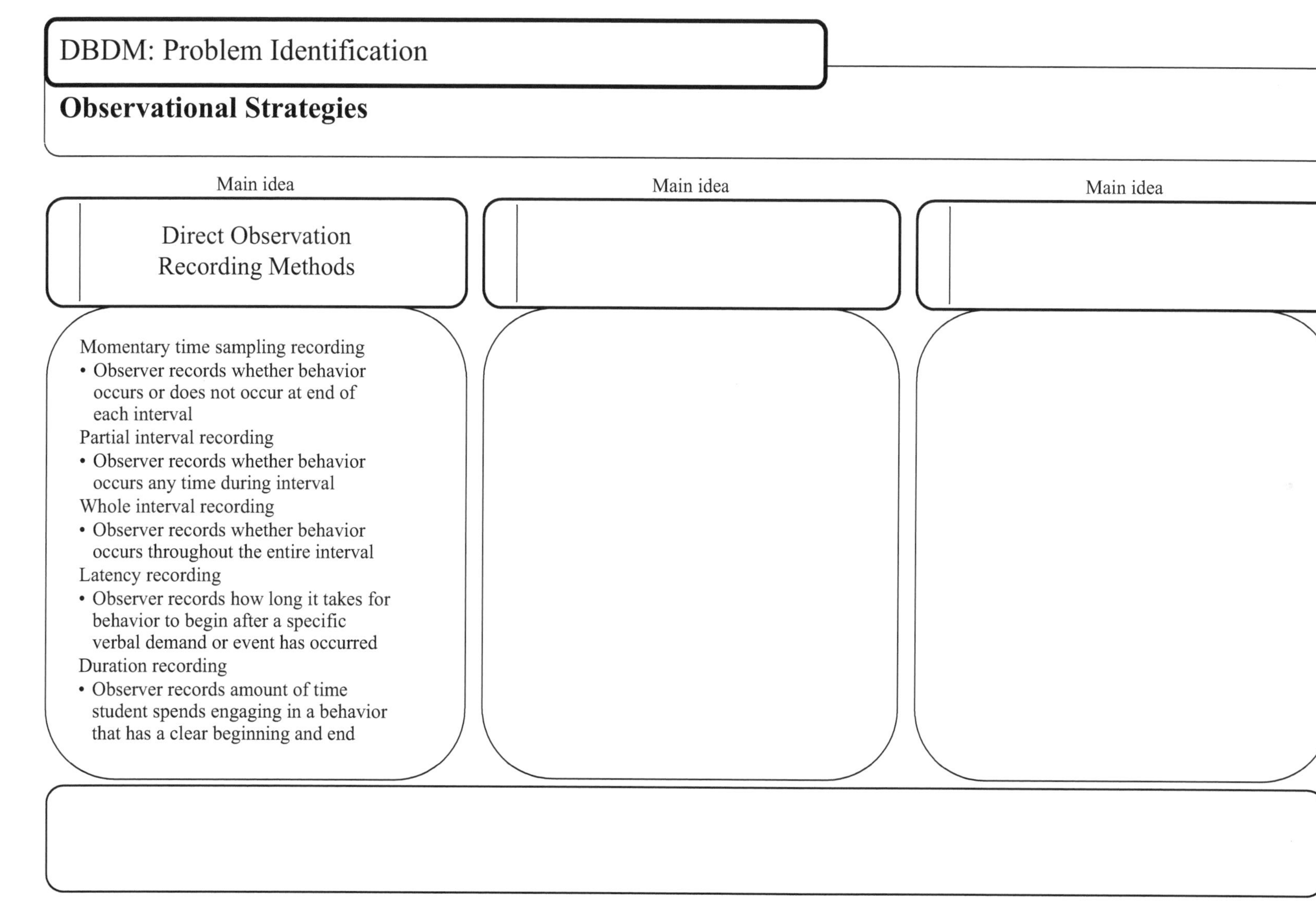

TABLE 5.9
Graphic Organizer for Review of Background Information

DBDMA: Problem Identification

Review of Background Information

Main idea: Cumulative School Records	Main idea: Medical Records and Previous Evaluations	Main idea: Developmental History	Main idea: Review of Previous Interventions
School cumulative records: • Academic grades • Attendance • Discipline referrals • State/district testing results • Health records (nurse's screenings, etc.) Notice any trends in the records	Before beginning intervention or assessment, review any previous reports: • Medical • Psychological • Neuropsychological • Psychoeducational • Psychiatric • Neurological • Neurodevelopmental	• Parent/caregivers • Family history • Brothers/sisters • Child's residence • Family relationships • Pregnancy • Birth • Development • Medical history • Family history • Friendships • Recreation/interests • Behavior/temperament • Educational history	Review documentation on previous interventions including steps: • Problem identification • Problem analysis • Intervention planning • Evaluation-progress monitoring

TABLE 5.10
Graphic Organizer for Screening Measures and Methods

DBDMA: Problem Identification

Screening Measures and Methods

Main idea: Measures	Main idea: Methods	Main idea: Additional Methods
In general, screening assessment is a brief evaluation to indentify students who • are eligible for specific programs • have a weakness in need of intervention • may need more comprehensive assessment Screening assessment, by definition, is a brief evaluation; eligibility for IDEA services should not be made based on screening results.	Curriculum-based measurement is a valuable method of gathering information about student performance • Simple, accurate, fast • Effective indicators of student achievement to guide intervention decisions and check progress • Verify what is working and what is not • Identifies weaknesses and allows instruction to be geared toward strengths	Creating a data-based process • Requires knowledge of effective data-based decision making and problem-solving processes/methods • Is a systematic collection of information to identify and define strengths/needs to be used in a collaborative team process for solving problems using treatment integrity • Decisions made without systematic data collection may result in targeting inappropriate/ineffective interventions

Graphic Organizers for Assessment and Problem Analysis

TABLE 5.11
Graphic Organizer for Cognitive Functioning

DBDMA: Assessment and Problem Analysis

Cognitive Functioning

Main idea	Main idea	Main idea	Main idea
Wechsler Adult Intelligence Scale, 4th Ed. (WAIS – IV)	Wechsler Intelligence Scale for Children, 5th Ed. (WISC – V)	Wechsler Preschool and Primary Scale of Intelligence 4th Ed. (WPPSI – IV)	Wechsler Abbreviated Scale of Intelligence 2nd Ed. (WASI – II)
• Age ranges: 16 yrs–89 yrs • Mean = 100 SD = 15 • 14 subtests: 7 Verbal and 7 Performance Scales 4 Indices: VCI, PRI, WMI, and PSI • Used for assessment of LD, ADHD, MR, and age-related differences in ability of adults	• Age ranges: 6 yrs–16 yrs 11 mos • Mean = 100 SD = 15 • FSIQ + 5 Primary Index Scales: VCI - SI, VC, (IN) and (CO) VSI - BD and VP FRI - MR, FW, (PC), and (AR) WMI - DS, PS, and (LN) PSI - CD, SS, (CA) • Can provide 5 Ancillary Scales: QRI, AWMI, NVI, GAI, and CPI and 3 Complementary Scales: NSI, STI, and SRI • Used for assessment of LD, cognitive impairment, and age-related differences in ability of children	• Age ranges: 2 yrs 6 mos–7 yrs 7 mos 2 batteries: 2:6-3:11 and 4:0-7:7 • Mean = 100 SD = 15 • 2:6-3:11: FSIQ+3 Primary Index Scales VCI - RV, IN and (PN) VSI - BD and OA WMI - PM and ZL • 4:0-7:7: FSIQ+5 Primary Index Scales VCI - IN, SI, (VC), and (CO) VSI - BD and OA FRI - MR and PC WMI - PM and ZL PSI - BS, CA, and (AC) • Can provide 4 Ancillary Scales: VAI, NVI, GAI, and CPI (4:0-7:7 only) • Used for assessment of LD, cognitive impairment, and age-related differences in ability of young children	• Age ranges: 6 yrs–89 yrs • Mean = 100 SD = 15 • FSIQ+ 2 Composite Scores: VCI - VC and SI PRI - BD and MR • Used for a quick screening of LD, ADHD, MR, and age-related differences in ability of children and adults; often useful for research protocols

TABLE 5.11 (Continued)
Graphic Organizer for Cognitive Functioning

DBDMA: Assessment and Problem Analysis

Cognitive Functioning

Main idea	Main idea	Main idea	Main idea
Stanford-Binet Intelligence Scales, 5th Ed. (SB5)	Differential Ability Scales, 2nd Ed. (DAS-II)	Cognitive Assessment System, 2nd Ed. (CAS2)	Kaufman Brief Intelligence Test, 2nd Ed. (KBIT-II)
• Age Ranges: 2 yrs–85 yrs • Mean = 100 SD = 15 • 2 domains (Verbal and Nonverbal); 5 factors in each domain (FR, KN, QR, V-SP and WM) • Used for assessment of LD, developmental delay, brain functionality with neurological impairments, and giftedness • Is effective with low-functioning individuals	• Age Ranges: 2:6–7:11 (2 batteries): Lower: 2:6–3:5; Upper: 3:6–6:11; School Age: 7:0–17:11 • Mean = 100 SD = 15 • 20 total subtests: 4 verbal subtests, 3 nonverbal subtests, 3 spatial subtests, and 11 diagnostic subtests • Used for assessment of LD, intellectual disabilities, giftedness, and neurological impairments • Is appropriate for non-English proficient individuals, individuals with giftedness, and hearing impaired	• Age Ranges: 5:0 yrs–8:11 yrs • Mean = 100 SD = 15 • Full Scale + 13 subtests in 4 categories: planning, attention, simultaneous, successive • Used for assessment of LD, intellectual disabilities, ADHD, giftedness • Is appropriate for individuals with a TBI and with culturally diverse groups	• Age Ranges: 4 yrs–90 yrs • Mean = 100 SD = 15 • 2 subtests: Verbal IQ - vocabulary Nonverbal IQ - matrices • A quick, nonverbal test used for assessment of intellectual and learning abilities; is appropriate for nonreaders and hearing-impaired individuals

TABLE 5.11 (Continued)
Graphic Organizer for Cognitive Functioning

DBDMA: Assessment and Problem Analysis

Cognitive Functioning

Main idea	Main idea	Main idea	Main idea
Woodcock-Johnson Tests of Cognitive Abilities, 4th Ed. (WJ IV)	Kaufman Adolescent and Adult Intelligence Test (KAIT)	Universal Nonverbal Intelligence Test, 2nd Ed. (UNIT 2)	Test of Nonverbal Intelligence, 4th Ed. (TONI-4)
• Age ranges: 2 yrs–90+ yrs • Mean = 100 SD = 15 • Based on CHC theory with 2 batteries Standard: 10 subtests Extended: 8 subtests • Used for assessment of LD, cognitive impairment, and age-related differences in ability of children and adults	• Age ranges: 11 yrs–85 yrs • Mean = 100 SD = 15 • Based on Cattel and Horn, Piaget, and Luria's work o Core battery: Fluid (3 subtests) and Crystallized (3 subtests) o Expanded battery: same as core with 4 additional subtests; Mental Status Exam included • Used for assessment of developmental and neurological changes	• Age ranges: 5 yrs–21:11 yrs • Mean = 100 SD = 15 • 6 subtests: Symbolic Memory, Nonsymbolic Quantity, Analogic Reasoning, Spatial Memory, Numerical Series, and Cube Design • Entirely nonverbal stimulus and response administration format incorporating full-color stimuli, manipulatives, and hand/body gestures • Used for assessment of individuals who have speech, language, or hearing impairments; who are culturally diverse; and/or verbally uncommunicative	• Age ranges: 6 yrs–89:11 yrs • Mean = 100 SD = 15 • Nonverbal, 60 items from easy to difficult; measures intelligence, aptitude, abstract reasoning, and problem-solving abilities • Uses simple oral instructions, and requires test takers to answer with simple but meaningful gestures such as pointing, nodding, or blinking • Used for assessment of individuals who have communication disorders, LD, cognitive impairment, CP, head injury, developmental disabilities, and autism

TABLE 5.12
Graphic Organizer for Educational Achievement

DBDMA: Assessment and Problem Analysis

Educational Achievement

Main idea	Main idea	Main idea	Main idea
Wechsler Individual Achievement Test, 3rd Ed. (WIAT-III)	Woodcock-Johnson Tests of Achievement, 4th Ed. (WJ IV)	Kaufman Test of Educational Achievement, 3rd Ed. (KTEA-III)	Wide Range Achievement Test, 4th Ed. (WRAT4)
• Age ranges: 4 yrs–50:11 yrs; Grades: PreK–12+ • Mean = 100 SD = 15 • 7 composites: Oral Language, Total Reading, Basic Reading, Reading Comprehension and Fluency, Written Expression, Mathematics, and Math Fluency • Empirically linked with WISC-V; large validity study with clinical populations (LD, ADD, language disabled, hearing impaired, gifted)	• Age ranges: 2 yrs–90+ yrs • Mean = 100 SD = 15 • Based on CHC theory with 2 batteries Standard: 11 subtests Extended: 9 subtests • 20 subtests grouped by: Reading Clusters Written Language Clusters Math Clusters Cross-Domain Clusters • 22 total possible clusters	• Age ranges: 4 yrs 0 mos–25 yrs 11 mos (Comprehensive and Brief Form) • Mean = 100 SD = 15 • 19 total subtests make up 3 Core composite scores (Academic Skills Battery): o Reading o Math o Written Language 3 Supplemental composite scores: o Reading-Related o Oral o Cross-Domain	• Age ranges: 5 yrs–94 yrs • Mean = 100 SD = 15 • 4 subtests: Word Reading, Sentence Comprehension, Spelling, Math Computation • 2 forms (Blue Form and Green Form) allow for retesting within short periods of time

TABLE 5.12 (Continued)
Graphic Organizer for Educational Achievement

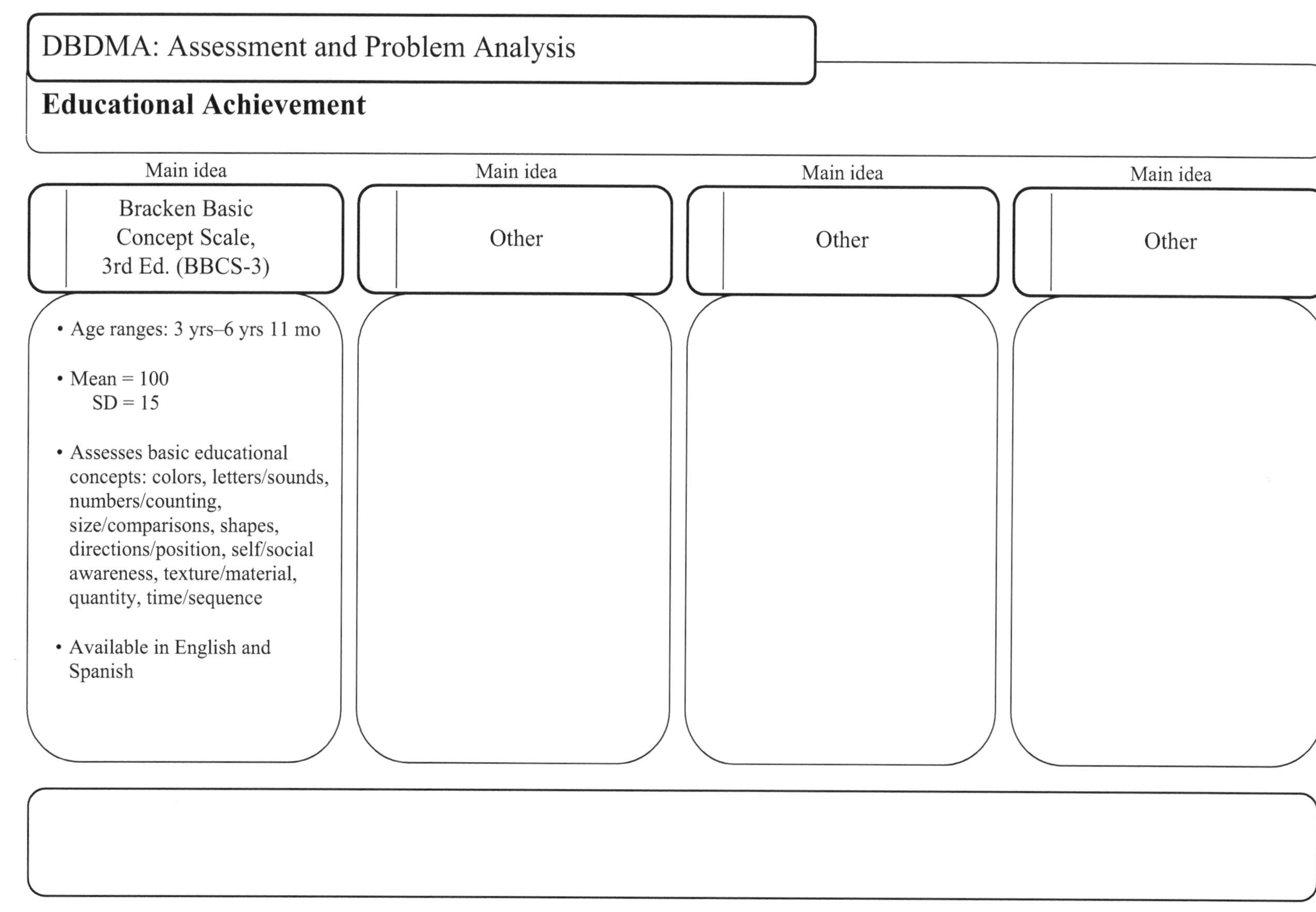

TABLE 5.13
Graphic Organizer for Diagnostic/Processing Measures

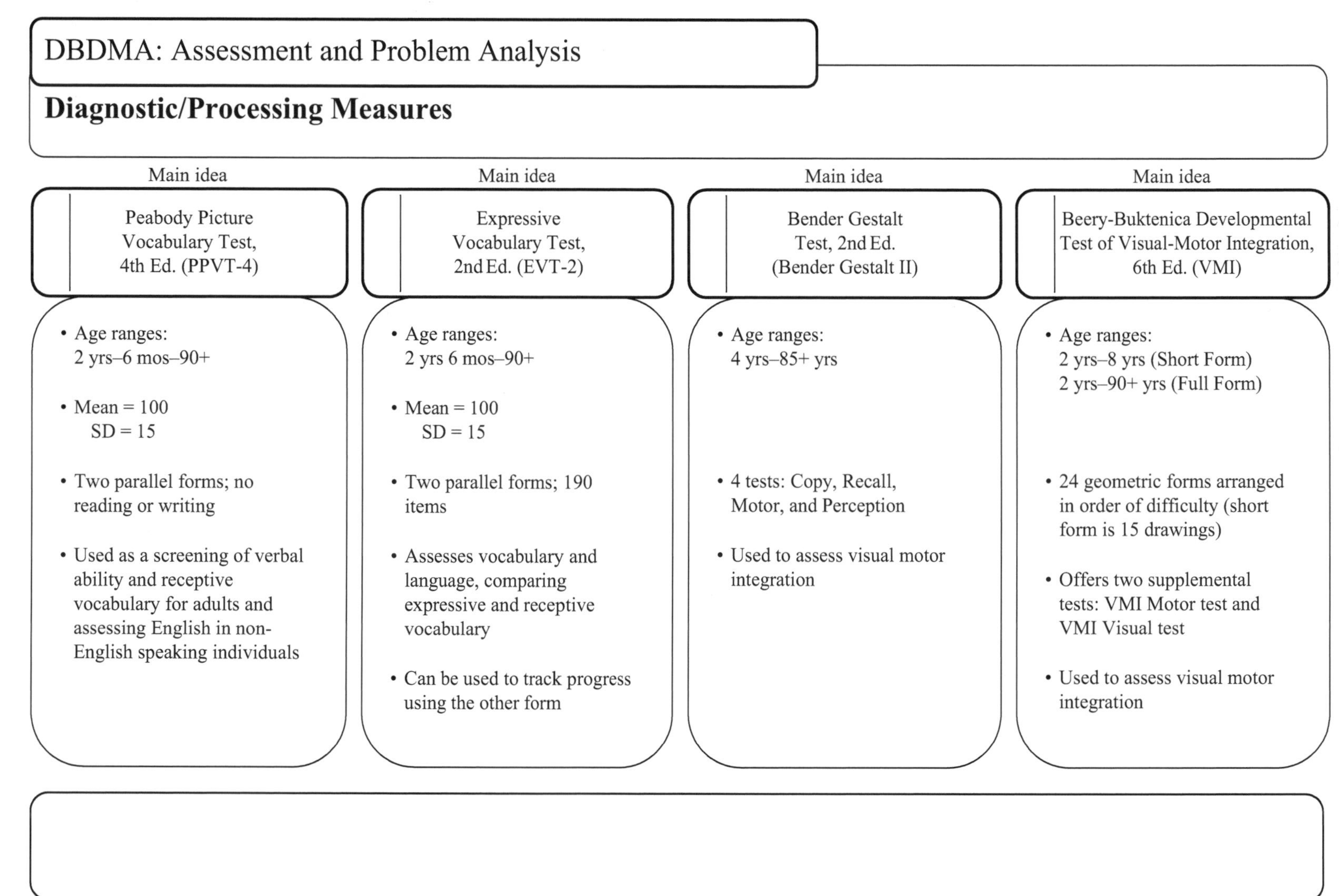

DBDMA: Assessment and Problem Analysis

Diagnostic/Processing Measures

Main idea	Main idea	Main idea	Main idea
Peabody Picture Vocabulary Test, 4th Ed. (PPVT-4)	Expressive Vocabulary Test, 2nd Ed. (EVT-2)	Bender Gestalt Test, 2nd Ed. (Bender Gestalt II)	Beery-Buktenica Developmental Test of Visual-Motor Integration, 6th Ed. (VMI)
• Age ranges: 2 yrs–6 mos–90+ • Mean = 100 SD = 15 • Two parallel forms; no reading or writing • Used as a screening of verbal ability and receptive vocabulary for adults and assessing English in non-English speaking individuals	• Age ranges: 2 yrs 6 mos–90+ • Mean = 100 SD = 15 • Two parallel forms; 190 items • Assesses vocabulary and language, comparing expressive and receptive vocabulary • Can be used to track progress using the other form	• Age ranges: 4 yrs–85+ yrs • 4 tests: Copy, Recall, Motor, and Perception • Used to assess visual motor integration	• Age ranges: 2 yrs–8 yrs (Short Form) 2 yrs–90+ yrs (Full Form) • 24 geometric forms arranged in order of difficulty (short form is 15 drawings) • Offers two supplemental tests: VMI Motor test and VMI Visual test • Used to assess visual motor integration

TABLE 5.13 (Continued)
Graphic Organizer for Diagnostic/Processing Measures

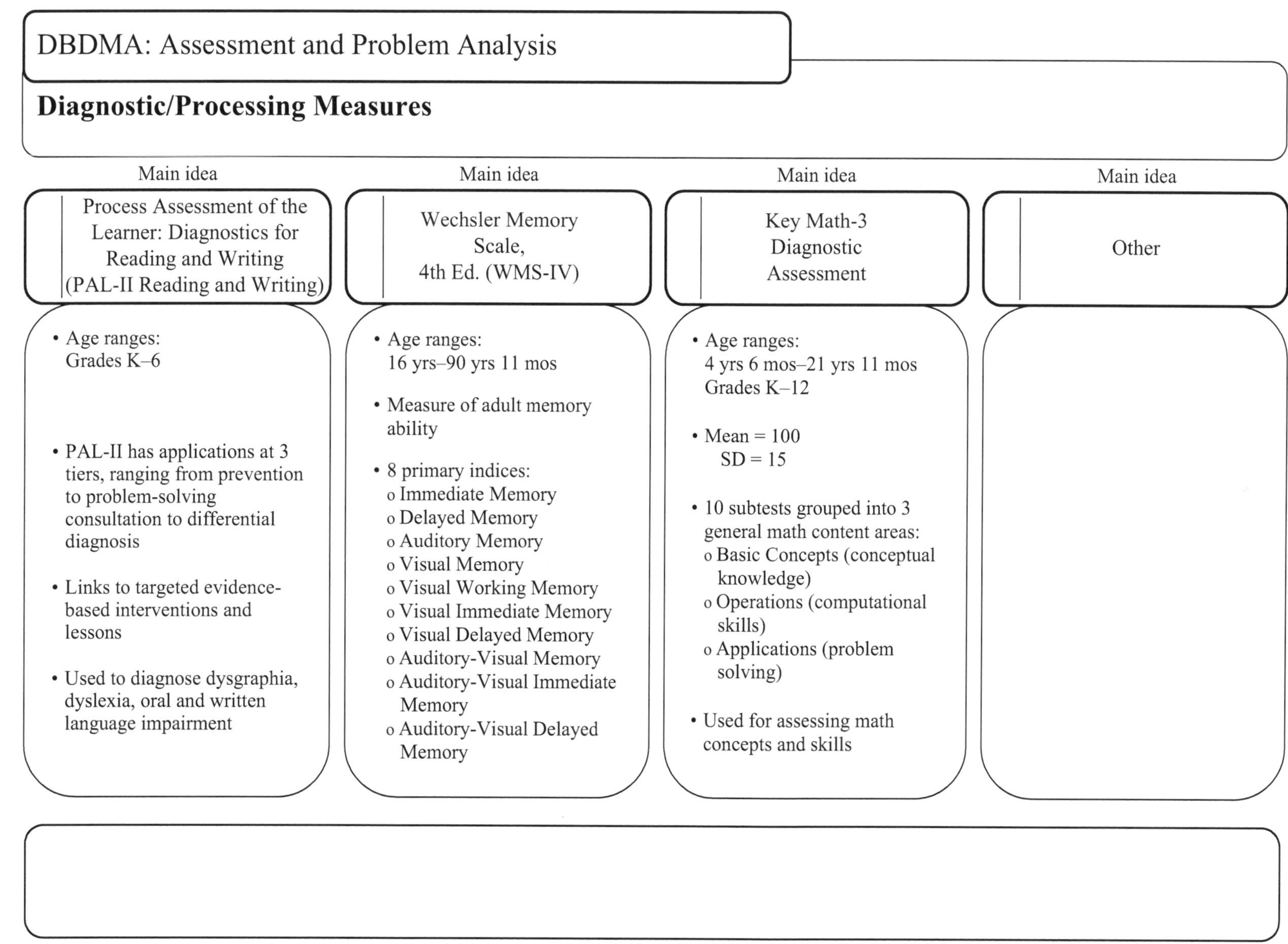

TABLE 5.14
Graphic Organizer for Development and Adaptive Behavior

DBDMA: Assessment and Problem Analysis

Development and Adaptive Behavior

Main idea	Main idea	Main idea	Main idea
Bayley Scales of Infant and Toddler Development, 3rd Ed. (Bayley-III)	Battelle Developmental Inventory, 2nd Ed. (BDI-2)	Scales of Independent Behavior-Revised (SIB-R)	AAMR Adaptive Behavior Scales 2nd Ed. (ABS-2)
• Age range: 1 mo–40 mos • Mean = 100 SD = 15 • 5 subtests: 3 with child—cognitive, motor, and language; 2 with parents–social/emotional and adaptive behavior • Used for measuring developmental delays in very young children	• Age range: Birth–7 yrs 11 mos • Mean = 100 SD = 15 • 5 domains on the long form: Adaptive, Cognitive, Communication, Motor, and Personal-Social; abbreviated form is 100 items from the long form • Used for screening, diagnosis, and evaluation of early development	• Age range: Infancy to 80+ yrs • 14 areas of adaptive behavior and 8 areas of problem behavior • Norm referenced assessment of adaptive behavior and maladaptive behavior	• Age range: 3 yrs–21 yrs • School version: 9 behavioral domains, 7 maladaptive domains related to personality and behavior disorders; also a residential version available • Used to assess ability of individuals with intellectual disability, emotional maladjustment, or development delays to cope with natural and social demands of environment

TABLE 5.14 (Continued)
Graphic Organizer for Development and Adaptive Behavior

DBDMA: Assessment and Problem Analysis

Development and Adaptive Behavior

Main idea	Main idea	Main idea	Main idea
Vineland Adaptive Behavior Scales, 2nd Ed. (Vineland-II)	Adaptive Behavior Assessment System, 3rd Ed. (ABAS-3)	Adaptive Behavior Evaluation Scale Revised 2nd Ed. (ABES-R2)	Other
• Age ranges Parent Form: 0–90 yrs Teacher Form: 3 yrs–21 yrs 11 mos • Mean = 100 SD = 15 • 4 Domains: Communication, Daily Living Skills, Socialization, and Motor Skills; and 1 Maladaptive Behavior Index (Optional) • Used to measure adaptive behavior especially in individuals with ID, ASD, ADHD, or post-traumatic brain injury	• Age ranges 2 Parent Forms: 0–5 yrs and 5–21 yrs; 2 Teacher Forms: 2–5 yrs and 5–21 yrs; and Adult Form: 16–89 yrs • Mean = 100 SD = 15 • 3 Domains: Conceptual, Social, and Practical with 11 Skill areas: Communication, Functional Pre/Academics, Self-Direction, Social, Leisure, Self-Care, Home/School Living, Community Use, Health/Safety, Motor, and Work • Useful when evaluating individuals with ID, ASD, LD, developmental delays, neuropsychological disorders, or sensory/physical impairments	• Age ranges: 4–12 yrs and 13–18 yrs • Mean = 100 SD = 15 • 3 Domains (and 10 subscales) o Conceptual: Communication and Functional Academics o Social: Social, Leisure, and Self-Direction o Practical: Self-Care, Home Living, Community Use, Health/Safety, and Work • Used to measure adaptive behavior especially in individuals with ID, LD, BD, or visual or hearing impairments	

TABLE 5.15
Graphic Organizer for Social and Emotional Functioning

DBDMA: Assessment and Problem Analysis

Social and Emotional Functioning

Main idea	Main idea	Main idea	Main idea
Behavior Rating Scales – General Comments	Behavioral Assessment System for Children – 2nd Ed. (BASC-2)	Child Behavior Checklist (CBCL)/Achenbach System of Empirically Based Assessment (ASEBA)	Conners 3rd Ed. (Conners 3)
Behavior rating scales: • Used to identify student's behavioral strengths and weaknesses • Can be completed by parent, caregiver, teacher, or individual (self-report) • Requires informants to make judgments about child's functioning; subject to bias or distortion • Provides information from a variety of sources (i.e., parent, teacher, student) to obtain comprehensive picture	• Age range: 2–25 yrs • Includes: Teacher (TRS), Parent Rating Scales (PRS), Self-Report of Personality (SRP; ages 8 and up) • Measures problem and adaptive behaviors • Composite scales provide internalized, externalized, and school problems (TRS and SRP); also provides behavioral/emotional symptom index and adaptive behavior composite	• Age ranges Preschool: 1.5–5 yrs School: 6–18 yrs • Includes: Teacher's Report, Youth Self-Report, and Caregiver-Teacher Report Form • Measures internalized/externalized problems • Includes DSM-oriented scales	• Age ranges: 6–18 yrs for parent/teacher report; 8–18 yrs for self-report • Includes: Parent, Teacher, and Self-Report Forms (all available in long and short form) • Assesses ADHD and comorbid disorders, such as ODD and CD • DSM and IDEA-oriented scales

TABLE 5.15 (Continued)
Graphic Organizer for Social and Emotional Functioning

DBDMA: Assessment and Problem Analysis

Social and Emotional Functioning

Main idea	Main idea	Main idea	Main idea
Conners Comprehensive Behavior Rating Scales (CBRS)	Devereux Scales of Mental Disorders (DSMD)	Revised Behavior Problem Checklist (RBPC)	Behavior Dimensions Scale 2nd Ed. – School and Home Versions (BDS-2 HV and BDS-2 SV)
• Age ranges: 6–18 yrs for parent/teacher report; 8–18 yrs for self-report • Provides comprehensive overview of child and adolescent concerns and disorders; assesses emotions, behavior, academic, and social problems • DSM and IDEA-oriented scales	• Age ranges: 5–12 yrs (child) and 13–18 yrs (adolescent) • Used to identify behavioral or emotional problems in children and adolescents • Completed by parent or teacher; both use same form (different norms) • Effective for treatment planning and outcome evaluation	• Age range: 5–18 yrs • 89 items that make up 6 scales: Conduct Disorder, Socialized Aggression, Attention Problems-Immaturity, Anxiety-Withdrawal, Psychotic Behavior, and Motor Tension-Excess; Teacher and Parent Forms available • Used to screen for behavioral disorders in schools • Does not provide specific diagnostic formulation	• Age range: 5–15 yrs (both versions) • Teacher and parent forms • 6 subscales measuring ADHD, ODD, Conduct Disorder, Avoidant Personality Disorder, Generalized Anxiety Disorder, Major Depressive Disorder

TABLE 5.15 (Continued)
Graphic Organizer for Social and Emotional Functioning

DBDMA: Assessment and Problem Analysis

Social and Emotional Functioning

Main idea	Main idea	Main idea	Main idea
Personality Assessment – General Comments	Minnesota Multiphasic Personality Inventory – Adolescent (MMPI-A)	Million Adolescent Clinical Inventory (MACI)	Piers-Harris Children's Self-Concept Scale, 2nd Ed. (Piers-Harris 2)
Personality assessment: • Are primarily self-report measures • Can be designed to identify (a) pathological states, (b) normal personality traits, or (c) normal and abnormal dimensions of personality • Validity of scores may be affected by readability or misinterpretation of items • Are subject to response bias—e.g., faking good, faking bad, acquiescence/ social desirability, or deviance response sets	• Age range: 14–18 yrs • Based upon MMPI items • Helps identify personal, social, and behavioral problems in adolescents • 10 basic clinical scales—e.g., hypochondriasis, depression, hysteria; 7 validity scales; and 15 content scales • Suggested seventh-grade reading level	• Age range: 13–19 yrs • Replaces Million Adolescent Personality Inventory • 160-item self-report scale measuring personality characteristics and clinical syndromes in adolescents • Suggested sixth-grade reading level	• Age range: 7–18 yrs • Self-report measure of self-concept • Assesses issues of physical appearance and attributes, intellectual and school status, happiness and satisfaction, freedom from anxiety, behavioral adjustment, and popularity • Can be administered in groups; used as screen to identify children in need of additional evaluation

TABLE 5.16
Graphic Organizer for Functional Behavior Assessment

DBDMA: Assessment and Problem Analysis

Functional Behavior

Main idea: FBA Process	Main idea: FBA Process	Main idea: Conducting an FBA	Main idea: Conducting an FBA (continued)
• FBA is required under IDEA when student's disability impedes learning, i.e., destructive, aggressive, noncompliant, or disruptive behaviors directed toward self, others, or objects; and/or when student's disability becomes subject of school discipline proceedings • FBA must be performed when either (a) change of placement for the student is being considered and/or (b) when the IEP team determines that student's behavior is a manifestation of student's disability; a behavior intervention plan (BIP) must also be implemented	• It is important to involve informants (parent, teacher, etc.) from beginning of FBA through design, implementation, progress monitoring, and program modification phases • FBA can be used during intervention process (prior to referral) and in determination of eligibility for special education • The FBA process is designed to be an accumulation of information collected at each stage	1. Describe problem behavior in observable, measureable terms 2. Perform assessment—e.g., review of records; conduct systematic behavioral observations; interview student, parents, and teachers; and use other assessments as necessary 3. Evaluate assessment results to identify patterns that may indicate purpose or cause of behavior problem	4. Develop hypothesis to explain relationship between problem behavior and situations in which problem occurs 5. Formulate a behavior intervention plan (BIP); implement the plan; assess for treatment fidelity 6. Evaluate the effectiveness of intervention plan; periodically interview, observe, and assess to determine if plan is working

TABLE 5.17
Graphic Organizer for Performance-Based Assessment

DBDMA: Assessment and Problem Analysis

Performance-Based Assessment

Main idea	Main idea	Main idea	Main idea
How is performance assessed?	How is performance assessed? (continued)	Why use performance-based assessment?	Other
• Performance may result in a ***product***—e.g., painting, portfolio, paper, or exhibition OR it may consist of ***performance***—e.g., speech, athletic skill, musical recital, or reading • Students should produce evidence of the accomplishment of curriculum goals to demonstrate achievement • Products or performances are judged on an agreed-upon set of criteria	• Tasks can include: writing an essay that requires student to rethink and apply info, giving an oral presentation, solving open-ended problems, participating in real-life simulations, designing and carrying out experiments, working in groups to perform a task • Tasks are concerned with problem solving and demonstrating understanding; they are meaningful and authentic	• It actively involves students in process of assessment • Evidence (product or performance) can be maintained for later use • Used as method of state testing for students with severe disabilities (alternative proficiency assessments)	

TABLE 5.18
Graphic Organizer for Curriculum-Based Assessment and Curriculum-Based Measurement

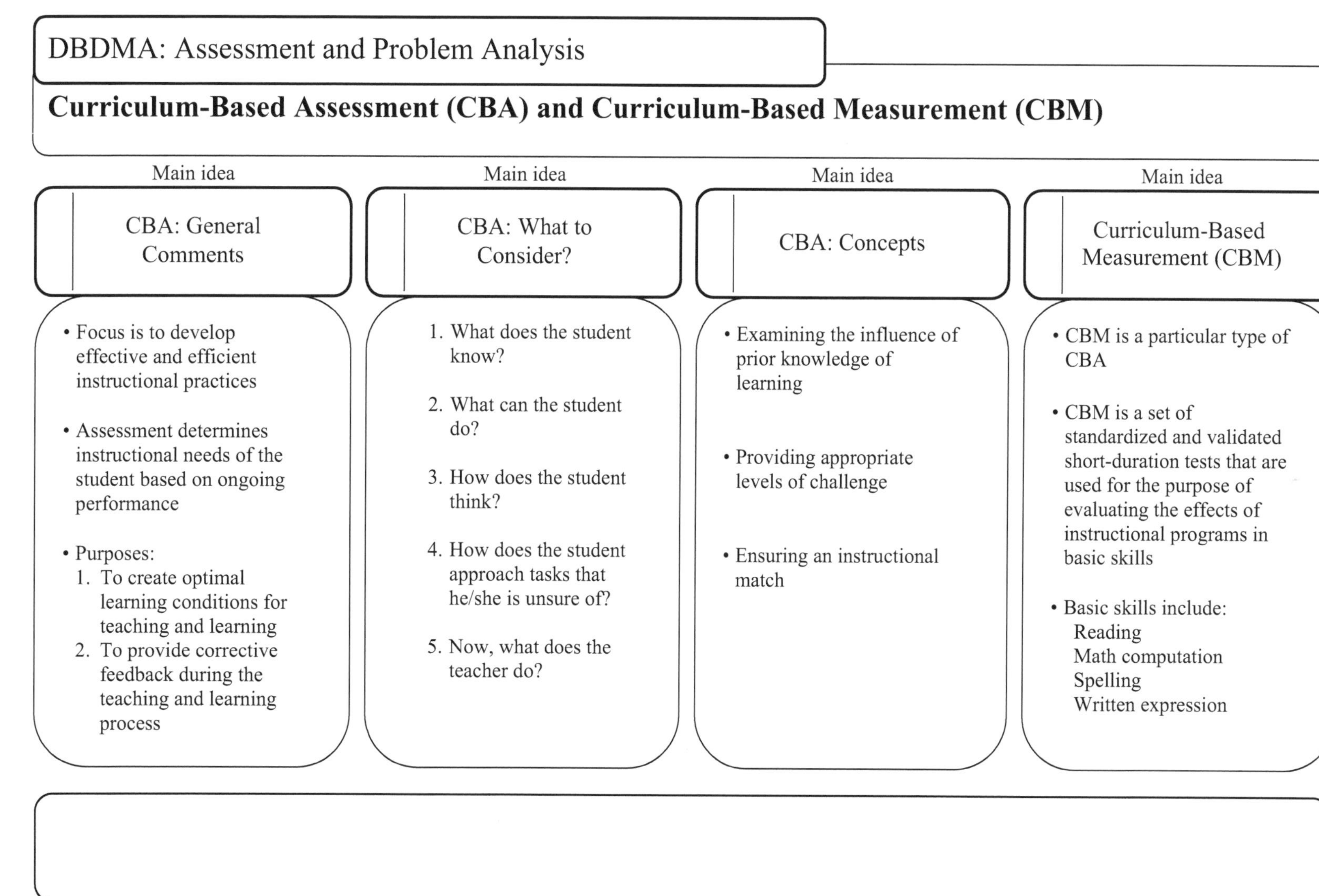

TABLE 5.18 (Continued)
Graphic Organizer for Curriculum-Based Assessment and Curriculum-Based Measurement

DBDMA: Assessment and Problem Analysis

Curriculum-Based Assessment (CBA) and Curriculum-Based Measurement (CBM)

Main idea	Main idea	Main idea	Main idea
CBM: Measuring Basic Skills	Dynamic Indicators of Basic Early Literacy Skills, 6th Ed. (DIBELS-6th)	DIBELS – 6th Ed. (continued)	DIBELS – 6th Ed. (continued)
• Reading – students read aloud for one minute; score is number of words read correctly • Spelling – students write words that are dictated at specific intervals; score is number of letter sequences (pairs of letters) spelled in correct order • Writing – students write a story for 3 minutes based on a story started; score is number of correct word sequences (pairs of words that are grammatically and semantically correct and spelled correctly) • Math – students are given two 5-minute probes on math computation; score is number of correct answers	• DIBELS was developed to monitor growth of acquisition of critical early reading and literacy skills • Is used to identify children in need of intervention and evaluate the effectiveness of intervention strategies • Results can indicate those children who will have significant difficulty learning essential literacy skills unless instructional support is provided	• Foundational reading and literacy skills measured: o Phonological awareness o Alphabetic principle and phonics o Accuracy and fluency with connected text o Comprehension o Vocabulary and oral language • DIBELS – 6th Ed. subtests: 1. Initial Sound Fluency 2. Phoneme Segmentation Fluency 3. Nonsense Word Fluency 4. Letter Naming Fluency 5. Oral Reading Fluency 6. Retell Fluency 7. Word Use Fluency	• Benchmark goals = minimal level students need to achieve to be confident they are on track • If students do not meet benchmarks, they need strategic support or intensive support • Interventions are developed based on area of need • Progress-monitoring materials are available

TABLE 5.19
Graphic Organizer for Ecological Assessment

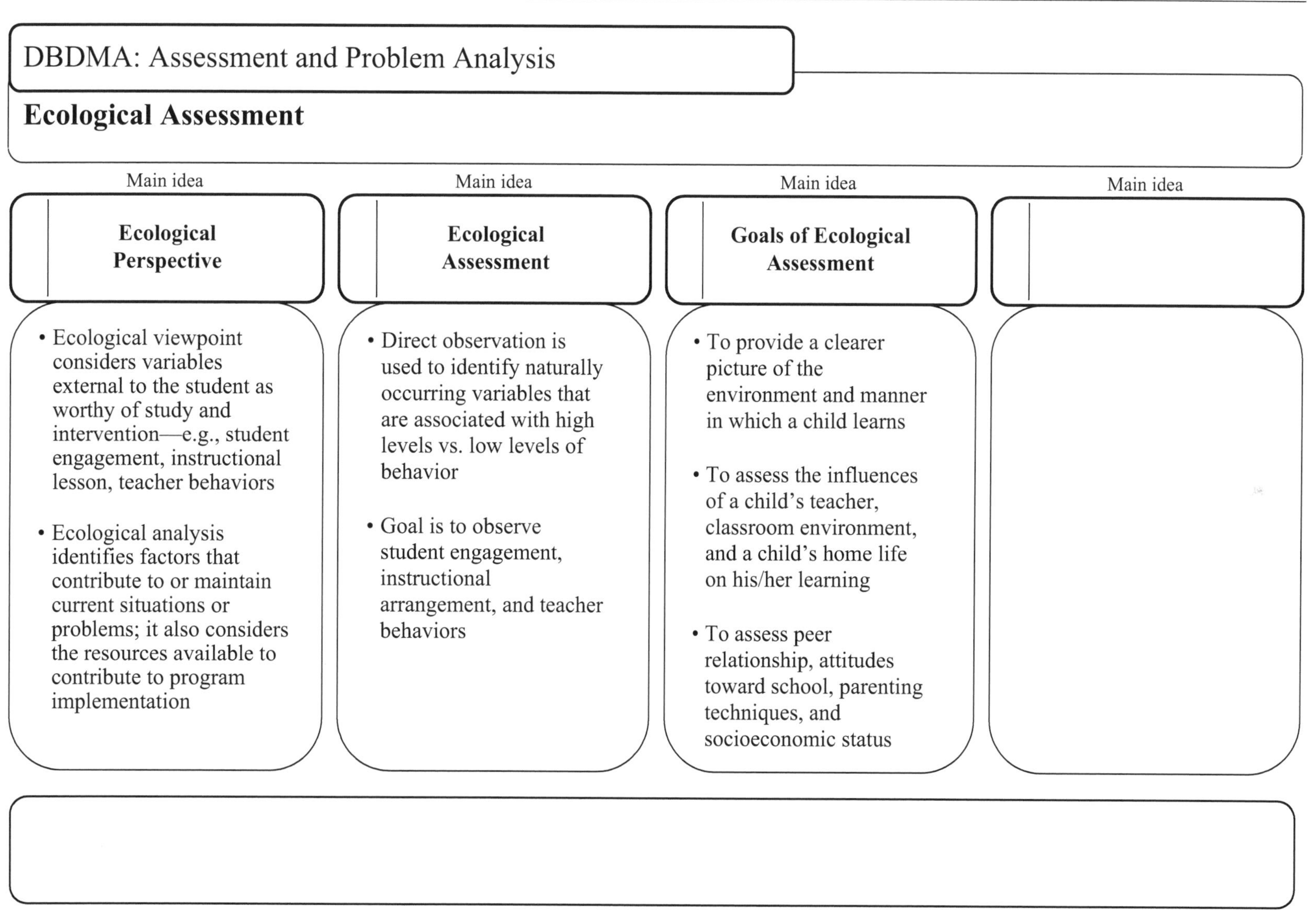

TABLE 5.20
Graphic Organizer for Use of Technology to Collect Data

DBDM: Assessment and Problem Analysis

Use of Technology to Collect Data

Main idea	Main idea	Main idea	Main idea
Technology	Managing Data	Report and Communicate Data	Setting Performance Expectations
• Supports the implementation of the problem-solving model and multitiered systems of support • Has the capability to enforce consistency • Can be used for strong data management of student academic and behavioral performance and for tracking of supports put in place • Many quickly emerging technologies in portable note-taking tools, cloud computing software, webinars, podcasts, supplemental content/interventions are becoming readily available, but have limited research and evaluation of their effectiveness	• Most schools have a technology plan, but should also include a data management plan • Management programs and techniques can include spreadsheet software, relational database software, single function software, and data warehouse technology • The future of managing data is interoperability, which is the ability of these systems to effectively communicate	• Critical in guiding to whom and how the data are displayed • Consider the visual display of information • Use the problem-solving model for data-storytelling • Include percentages	• Use technology tools that are sufficiently flexible to set growth goals properly • Predictive analytics: process of leveraging statistical analysis to make predictions about future behavior based on past and current information • Target-setting approach provides context for performance on screening and progress monitoring assessments that is directly relevant to key outcomes • Future for target setting is use of data mining

TABLE 5.20 (Continued)
Graphic Organizer for Use of Technology to Collect Data

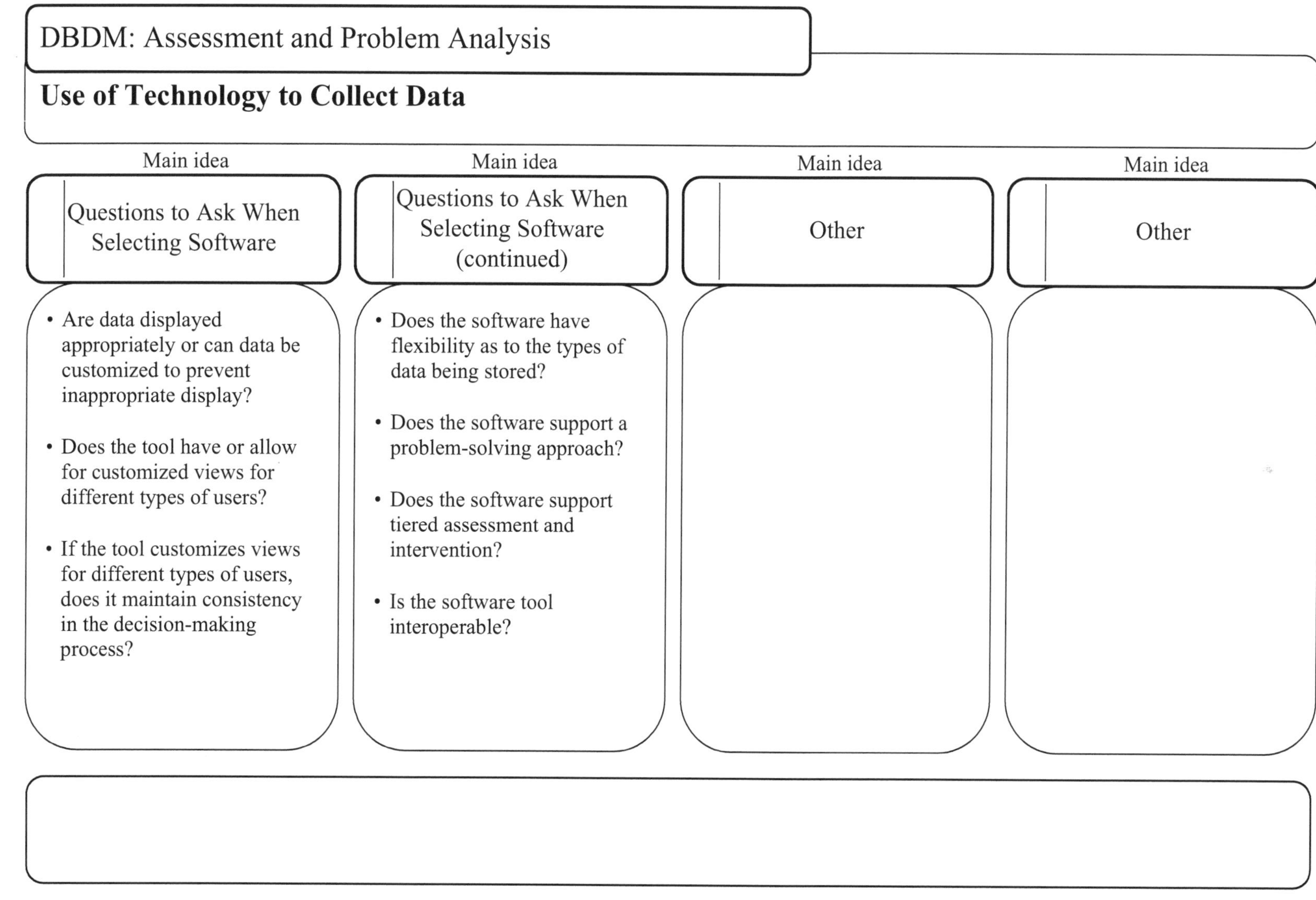

TABLE 5.21
Graphic Organizer for Continuous Data Collection and Monitoring to Assess Services

DBDMA: Assessment and Problem Analysis

Continuous Data Collection and Monitoring to Assess Services

Main idea	Main idea	Main idea	Main idea
Progress Monitoring	Validity and Reliability	Display of Progress Monitoring Data	Analysis and Decision Making
• Essential component of data-based decision making within a problem-solving model • Progress monitoring data are collected repeatedly over time for systematic interpretation • Research on certain types of data for progress monitoring is still evolving, so specific best practice guidelines are not always available • School psychologists need to be aware of issues related to interpreting and analyzing progress monitoring data	• Define behavior in observable terms • Measurement should take place at the appropriate time and place • Interrater reliability (or interobserver agreement) is most relevant type of reliability • Requires measurements that are approximately parallel across time	• Displayed graphically and interpreted through methods of visual analysis • Graphic displays provide clear presentation of behavior change over time and allow for quick and easy interpretation of many different sources of information • Many formats available including: bar graphs, scatterplots, tables, and most commonly used line graphs • Include goal lines, trendlines, level lines, and envelopes of variability	• Characteristics of progress monitoring data are level, trend, and variability o Level: average performance within a condition o Trend: systematic increases or decreases in behavior over time o Variability: how much a student's data deviate from the level or trendline • Student performance data should be evaluated in relation to the specific goal

TABLE 5.21 (Continued)
Graphic Organizer for Continuous Data Collection and Monitoring to Assess Services

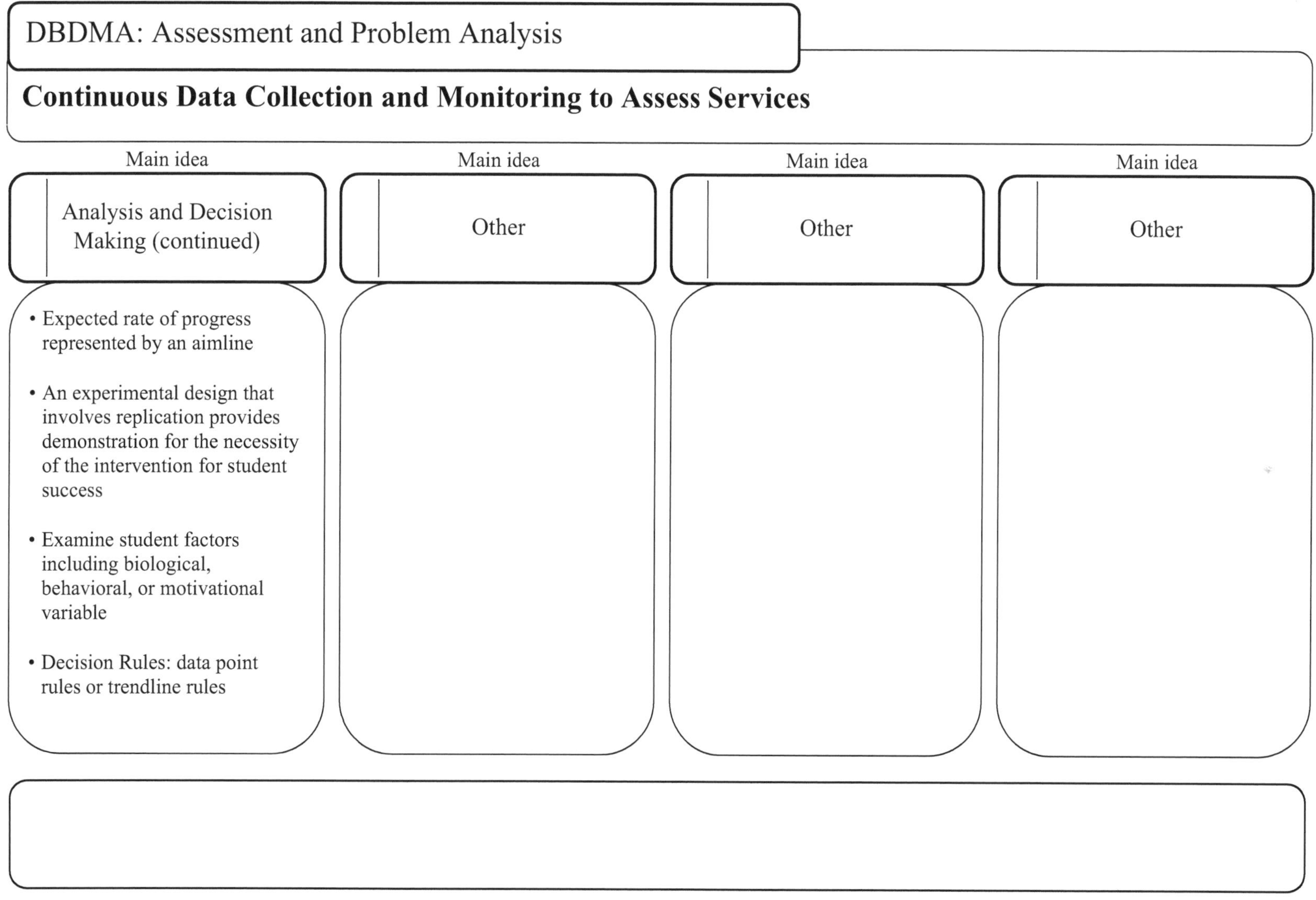

Graphic Organizers for Assessment Considerations for Special Populations

TABLE 5.22
Graphic Organizer for Infant and Early Childhood/Preschool

DBDMA: Assessment Considerations for Special Populations

Infant and Early Childhood/Preschool

Main idea: Wechsler Preschool and Primary Scale of Intelligence 4rd Ed. (WPPSI – IV)

- Age ranges: 2 yrs 6 mos–7 yrs 7 mos; 2 batteries: 2:6-3:11 and 4:0-7:7
- Mean = 100; SD = 15
- 2:6-3:11: FSIQ+3 Primary Index Scales
  - VCI - RV, IN, and (PN)
  - VSI - BD and OA
  - WMI - PM and ZL
- 4:0-7:7: FSIQ+5 Primary Index Scales
  - VCI - IN, SI, (VC), and (CO)
  - VSI - BD and OA
  - FRI - MR and PC
  - WMI - PM and ZL
  - PSI - BS, CA, and (AC)
- Can provide 4 Ancillary Scales: VAI, NVI, GAI, and CPI (4:0-7:7 only)
- Used for assessment of LD, cognitive impairment, and age-related differences in ability of young children

Main idea: Stanford-Binet Intelligence Scales, 5th Ed. (SB5)

- Age ranges: 2 yrs–85 yrs
- Mean = 100; SD = 15
- 2 domains (Verbal and Nonverbal); 5 factors in each domain (FR, KN, QR, V-SP, and WM)
- Used for assessment of LD, developmental delay, brain functionality with neurological impairments, individuals with giftedness
- Is effective with low-functioning individuals

Main idea: Bayley Scales of Infant and Toddler Development, 3rd Ed. (Bayley-III)

- Age range: 1 mo–40 mos
- Mean = 100; SD = 15
- 5 subtests: 3 with child—cognitive, motor, and language; and 2 with parents—social/emotional and adaptive behavior
- Used for measuring developmental delays in very young children

Main idea: Battelle Developmental Inventory, 2nd ED. (BDI-2)

- Age range: Birth–7 yrs 11 mos
- Mean = 100; SD = 15
- 5 domains on the long form: Adaptive, Cognitive, Communication, Motor, and Personal-Social; abbreviated form is 100 items from the long form
- Used for screening, diagnosis, and evaluation of early development

TABLE 5.22 (Continued)
Graphic Organizer for Infant and Early Childhood/Preschool

DBDMA: Assessment Considerations for Special Populations

Infant and Early Childhood/Preschool

Main idea	Main idea	Main idea	Main idea
Woodcock-Johnson Tests of Achievement, 4th Ed. (WJ IV)	Woodcock-Johnson Tests of Cognitive Abilities, 4th Ed. (WJ IV)	Denver Developmental Screening Test II (DDST-II)	Other
• Age ranges: 2 yrs–90+ years • Mean = 100 SD = 15 • Based on CHC theory with 2 batteries Standard: 11 subtests Extended: 9 subtests • 20 subtests grouped by: Reading Clusters Written Language Clusters Math Clusters Cross-Domain Clusters • 22 total possible clusters	• Age ranges: 2 yrs–90+ yrs • Mean = 100 SD = 15 • Based on CHC theory with 2 batteries Standard: 10 subtests Extended: 8 subtests • Used for assessment of LD, cognitive impairment, and age-related differences in ability of children and adults	• Age ranges: 2 yrs–90+ yrs 2 mos–6 yrs • 4 areas: Fine-motor function, gross-motor function, personal-social, and language skills • Used for examining developmental progress of children • Can use for screening purposes and progress monitoring	

TABLE 5.23
Graphic Organizer for English as a Second Language and English Language Learners

DBDMA: Assessment Considerations for Special Populations

English as a Second Language and English Language Learners

Main idea: Components of Assessment	Main idea: Components of Assessment (continued)	Main idea: Sequence of Steps When Assessing	Main idea: Sequence of Steps When Assessing (continued)
Pre-referral documentation • Examination of instructional program • Dynamic assessment of skills/abilities Language Assessment • Level of native language • Level of English language Assessment of Literacy • Oral and written skills in native language • Oral and written skills in English language	Formal Assessment • Must use reliable and valid psychometric measures • Most cognitive assessments are bias for ELL due to a heavy language load • Consider use of non-standardized measures • Administration of tests in native language is preferred	1. Language and Culture • Child's language proficiency is assessed with formal and informal measures • Acculturation data is collected through interviews 2. Achievement • Assessed in each language exposed to or had formal instruction in • If LD is suspected, the academic achievement must be present in both languages	3. Cognitive Abilities • Use appropriate language • More than one battery may be used • Nonverbal measures may be more appropriate 4. Adaptive Behavior • As appropriate to referral question or if intellectual disability is suspected, assess adaptive behavior at home and in school • If the home language is not English or Spanish, conduct parent interview Both must be interpreted with the student's cultural experiences in mind

TABLE 5.23 (Continued)
Graphic Organizer for English as a Second Language and English Language Learners

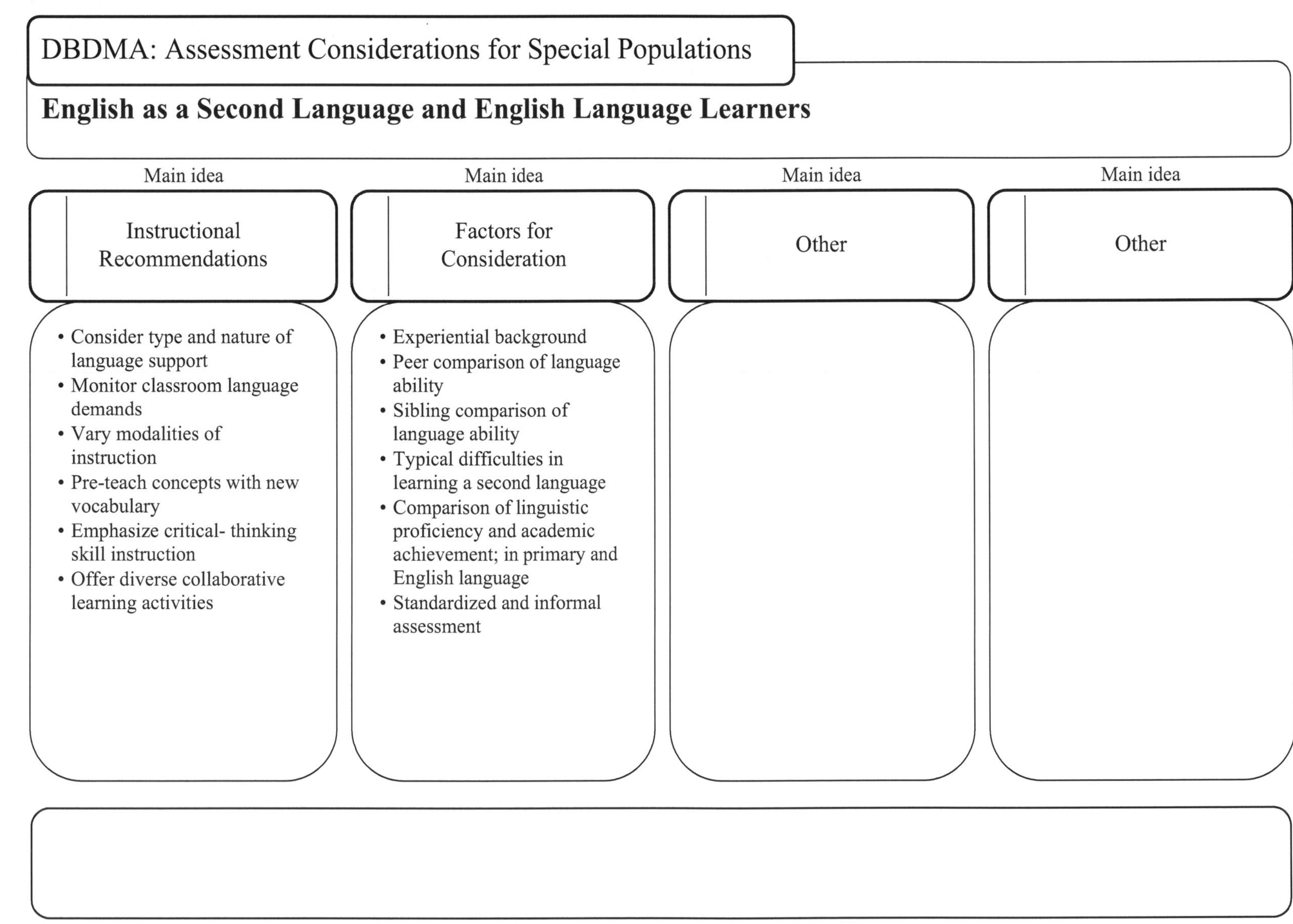

TABLE 5.24
Graphic Organizer for Low-Incidence Exceptionalities

DBDMA: Assessment Considerations for Special Populations

Low-Incident Exceptionalities

Autism Spectrum Disorders

- Child exhibits impairments in the areas of social interaction, communication, and behavior
- Assessments should include: interviews, observations, checklists/rating scales for parents and teachers, review of medical history, skill deficit assessment, and formal IQ tests
- Formal assessments may include: Universal Nonverbal Intelligence Test; Wechsler Nonverbal Intelligence Scale; Leiter International Performance Scale–Revised, or other measure
- About 40–69% of children with autistic spectrum disorders fall into the cognitively impaired range. However, even high-functioning children with autism have difficulty with executive functioning

Hearing Impairments

- When planning assessment, determine student's preferred mode of communication (sign language, speaking) and determine if a sign language interpreter is necessary
- Test administration can be modified for students with hearing impairments by omitting verbal tests, adding printed or signed words, using pantomime, demonstration, and manual communication
- Recommended assessments include: Nonverbal subtests of WISC-V, Performance scales of WPSSI-IV and WAIS-IV, and Nonverbal subtests of SB5

Visual Impairments

- Verbal tests are used to assess students with visual impairments
- Assessments should include information about the student's functional vision
- Using general test such as the WISC-IV, necessary accommodations must be made to help the child feel comfortable; this may include administering only the verbal and some nonverbal portions of the test
- Assessment and academic planning must be multidisciplinary and include the use of visual aids, such as magnifiers, large print, and book stands
- Thorough review of background information and previous evaluations, especially visual exams, prior to assessment is key

Chronic Health Impaired/Severe Physical Disability

- Assessment of students with a chronic health impairment and/or severe physical disability should be tailored to the individual student and include the necessary accommodations to help the child feel comfortable and to support success
- For more severe disabilities (moderate to severe/profound cognitive impairment, Down's syndrome, cerebral palsy), assessment may be geared toward determining adaptive behaviors and functional abilities

TABLE 5.25
Graphic Organizer for Gifted and Talented

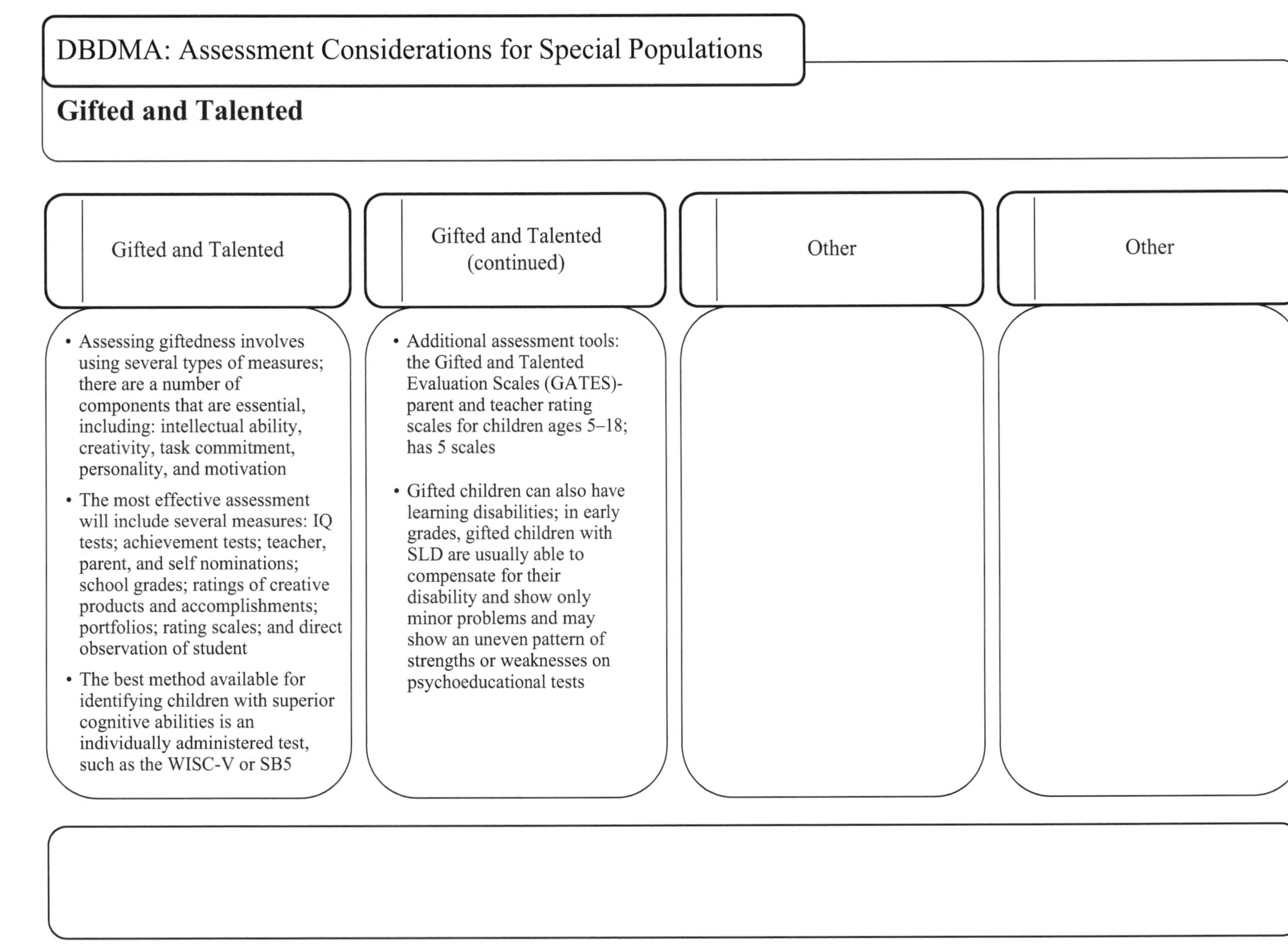

DBDMA: Assessment Considerations for Special Populations

Gifted and Talented

Gifted and Talented	Gifted and Talented (continued)	Other	Other
• Assessing giftedness involves using several types of measures; there are a number of components that are essential, including: intellectual ability, creativity, task commitment, personality, and motivation • The most effective assessment will include several measures: IQ tests; achievement tests; teacher, parent, and self nominations; school grades; ratings of creative products and accomplishments; portfolios; rating scales; and direct observation of student • The best method available for identifying children with superior cognitive abilities is an individually administered test, such as the WISC-V or SB5	• Additional assessment tools: the Gifted and Talented Evaluation Scales (GATES)- parent and teacher rating scales for children ages 5–18; has 5 scales • Gifted children can also have learning disabilities; in early grades, gifted children with SLD are usually able to compensate for their disability and show only minor problems and may show an uneven pattern of strengths or weaknesses on psychoeducational tests		

Consultation and Collaboration

The topic, *Consultation and Collaboration*, encompasses two areas: (1) models and methods of consultation, and (2) home/school/community collaboration. Through the use of the problem-solving perspective, models and methods of consultation in psychology and education include behavioral, mental health, instructional, and organizational. Each process focuses on promoting collaborative decision making among school personnel, families, and others. Included in this area are practices and methods that foster communication between home, school, and community settings with sensitivity and appreciation of diverse characteristics (see Figure 5.2).

The two components that make up *Consultation and Collaboration* (i.e., models and methods of consultation and home/school/community collaboration) are further explained in detail in the graphic organizers that follow. Key information is outlined below each main topic. These are the areas that we recommend you review and master. While you are reviewing the key information outlined and answering the sample questions, you may want to add your own information on the graphic organizers to supplement what is provided here.

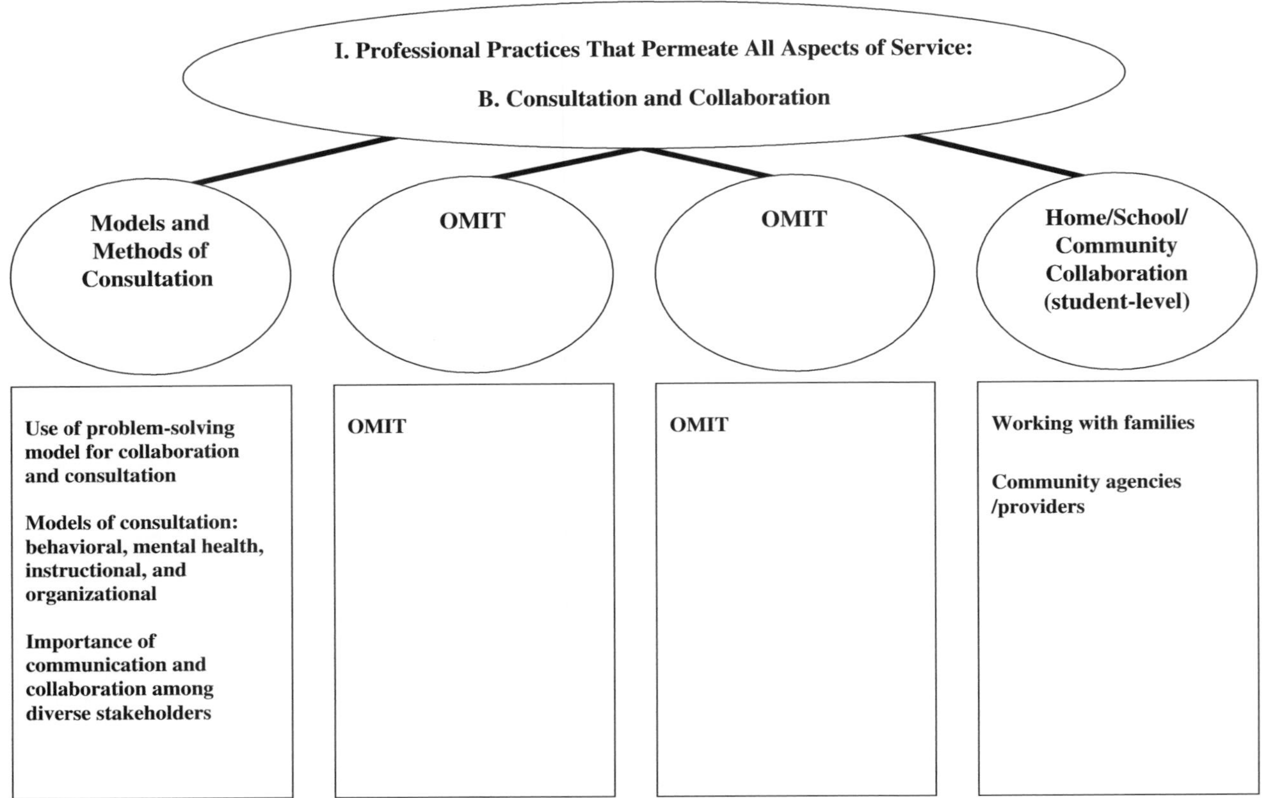

Figure 5.2
Professional Practices That Permeate All Aspects of Service Delivery: Consultation and Collaboration

Graphic Organizers for Models and Methods of Consultation

TABLE 5.26
Graphic Organizer for Problem-Solving Model for Consultation and Collaboration

C and C: Models and Methods of Consultation

Problem Solving Model for Consultation and Collaboration

Main idea	Main idea	Main idea	Main idea
Stage 1: Establishing of Relationships	Stage 2: Problem Identification	Stage 3: Problem Analysis	Stage 3: Problem Analysis (continued)
• The relationship between school psychologist and consultee can and does play a major role in the use and effectiveness of consultative services • Developing positive relationships may lead to less resistance to the consultative process and intervention, suggestions more readily accepted by consultee, increased probability that consultee will follow through on an intervention, and increased effectiveness of the consultative process • Resistance is anything that impedes problem solving or plan implementation and ultimately problem resolution • Two general tactics to respond to resistance: "joining the consultee" and "emphasizing referent power"	• Operationally define the problem through interviews, tests, rating scales, checklists, functional assessments, and direct observations • Define current and desired levels of performance to outline goals of the consultation • "Outcomes: Planning, Monitoring, Evaluating" is a tool that can help establish goals/benchmarks • Together the consultee and consultant agree on the type of measure to be used, what will be recorded, and how this process will be implemented • Establishing time, dates, and formats for subsequent interviews/contacts with consultee	• Focuses on the variables that are hypothesized to influence both the system and/or child's prosocial and challenging behaviors, and establishing functional relationships of the behavior • After baseline data are collected, the consultant and consultee engage in problem analysis interview, including: choosing analysis procedures, determining conditions and/or skills analysis, developing plan strategies, developing plan tactics, and establishing procedures to evaluate performance during implementation of any intervention program	• Determine whether the goal of intervention is to increase, decrease, or maintain conditions of target issue • Identify setting events and antecedent/consequential conditions associated with conditions • Plan for the intervention/s • Establish performance and assessment objectives that will be used during the next stage

TABLE 5.26 (Continued)
Graphic Organizer for Problem-Solving Model for Consultation and Collaboration

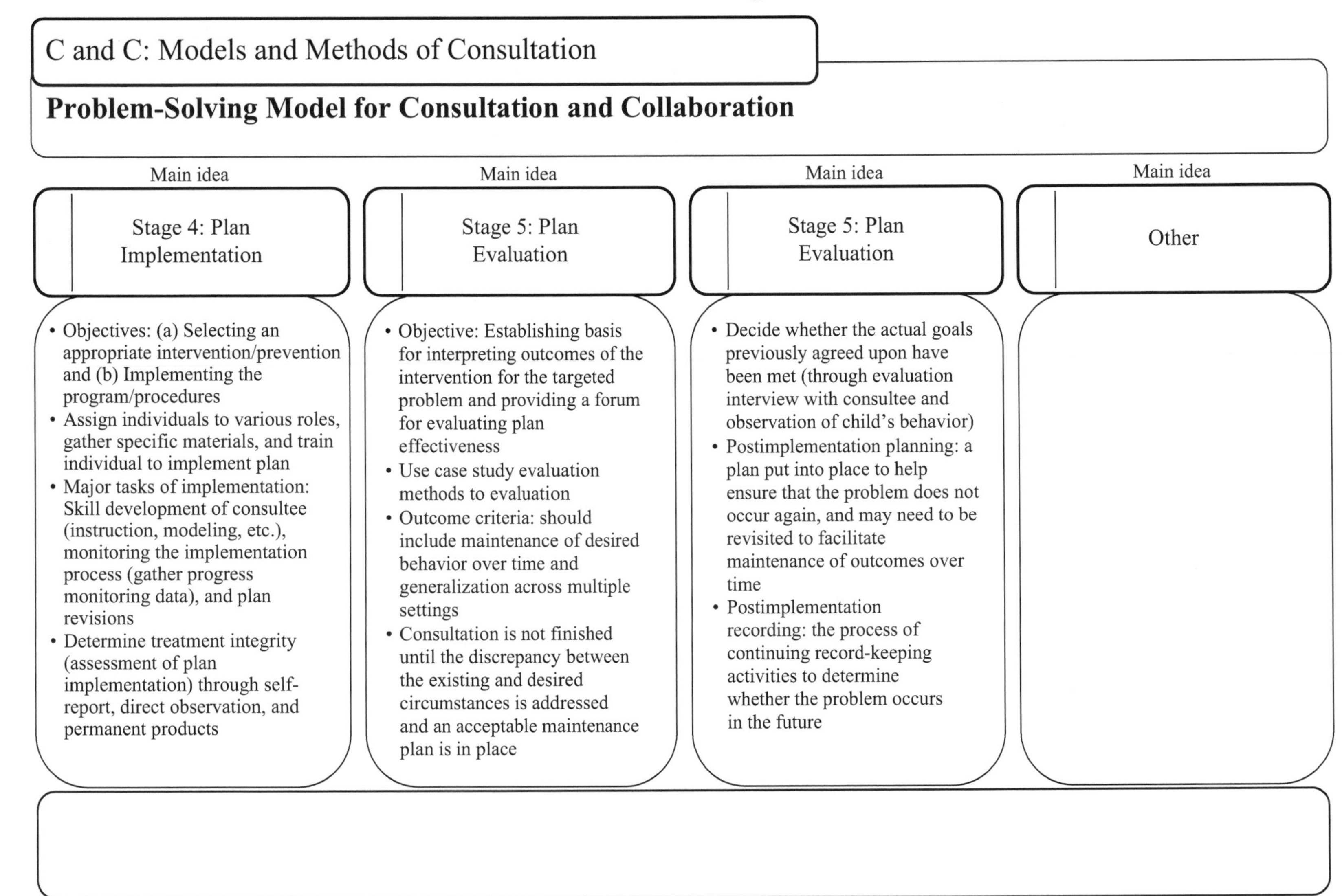

TABLE 5.27
Graphic Organizer for Models and Methods of Consultation

C and C: Models and Methods of Consultation

Models of Consultation

Behavioral Health (Bergen and Kratochwill)	Mental Health (Caplan) (Myers)	Instructional (Rosenfeld)	Organizational
• An indirect service in which the consultant and consultee participate in a problem-solving process to help the client • Built on social-learning and behaviorist theories of learning (Skinner, Bandura, Meichenbaum) • Assumes that all behavior is functional; it serves a purpose • Uses ABC model: behaviors are functions of contingencies (antecedents and consequences) • Major steps: 1. Problem identification 2. Problem analysis 3. Plan implementation 4. Plan evaluation	• Primary focus is on the consultee (nonhierarchical exchange between the consultant and the consultee) • Uses a psychodynamic theoretical framework • Types: o Client-centered o Consultee-centered o Program-centered administrative o Consultee-centered administrative	• Was developed for consultants working in the school to provide framework for working with teachers with concerns about students and classroom management • Assumes instructional mismatch between learner's capabilities and curriculum • Focus is to restructure the setting and instruction to facilitate students' growth, academically, socially, and/or behaviorally • Major steps: 1. Entry and contacting 2. Problem identification 3. Intervention planning 4. Intervention 5. Implementation 6. Resolution/termination	• This model focuses on issues relating to groups, organizations, and systems rather than to individuals • Assumes that conflict among individuals and groups is the basic barrier to effective and efficient organizational functioning • Major steps: 1. Pre-entry 2. Entry, problem exploration 3. Info gathering/problem confirmation 4. Solution searching/ intervention selection 5. Evaluation 6. Termination

TABLE 5.28
Graphic Organizer for Importance of Communication and Collaboration Among Diverse Stakeholders

C and C: Models and Methods of Consultation

Importance of Communication and Collaboration Among Diverse Stakeholders

Main idea	Main idea	Main idea	Main idea
Collaboration	Communication	Benefits of Communication and Collaboration	Common Barriers to Communication and Collaboration
• Consultation is seeking the opinion, advice, or expertise of another; it is an *indirect* process that empowers the consultee • Collaboration is an interactive, planning, and decision-making process involving two or more team members; it is a *direct* process • The relationship between the consultant and the consultee is: cooperative, mutually respectful, collegial, voluntary, and confidential • Individuals within the group (as well as the group as a whole) should fulfill a relevant, meaningful role and receive individual tasks that contribute to interactive group work	• Five basic principles of effective communication: complete, concise, concrete, clear, and accurate • Effective communication skills: written communication, face-to-face communication, professional investment, jargon-free and clear language, vocal tone and speech, repetition of key words, nonverbal communication, and listening skills • Use culturally competent practices	• Stakeholders have the best interest of the child in mind, but may differ with respect to how best to manage those interests • School psychologists are in a unique position to serve as the child's advocate • Effective collaboration and consultation are essential in problem solving and multitiered service delivery	• Human factors: attitudes, cultural or linguistic differences, stress, fatigue, and verbal or nonverbal messages conveyed • Institutional/contextual factors (role definition, organizational culture of the school, etc.) • Fundamental attribution error and elaboration likelihood model

Graphic Organizers for Home/School/Community Collaboration (Student-Level)

TABLE 5.29
Graphic Organizer for Working With Families

C and C: Home/School/Community Collaboration

Working With Families

How to Involve Families	Four Components for Building Effective Partnerships	Benefits	Other
• Partnership is a guiding philosophy for educators and parents as they attempt to build a meaningful long-term relationship • Four components for building meaningful partnerships include: o Approach o Attitude o Atmosphere o Actions	• Approach: interacting in a way that respects values of both home and school in contributing to educational experiences of students • Attitudes: perceptions that families and schools have regarding each other; positive attitudes identify and focus on strengths and assume dual responsibility • Atmosphere: overall climate set for families and educators • Actions: strategies for building long-term partnerships; include activities to include families and to facilitate their active participation in educational process, to break down barriers and to establish trust; accommodate for work schedules; make parents feel welcome	• For students o Develop a more positive attitude toward school o Boost achievement • For parents o Become more supportive of their children o Learn how to help children o Gain more positive views of teachers and school • For schools o Improve teacher morale o Improve student achievement o Increase parent support for schools and bond/budget issues	

TABLE 5.30
Graphic Organizer for Community Agencies/Providers

C and C: Home/School/Community Collaboration

Community Agencies/Providers

Involving families	Interagency Collaboration	Teaming With School Personnel and Resources	Other
• Need broader and more meaningful opportunities for parents to participate • Need to build positive and lasting relationships with parents in order to support student growth and performance • The more positive families' past experiences are the more likely they will feel welcomed as a partner in their child's education • Barriers: o Cultural and language barriers o Negative attitudes o Childcare o Transportation	• School psychologists can work with existing community agencies to provide family support services • Also provide information regarding physical and mental health services, enrichment programs, and other family learning opportunities • Interagency collaboration is one of the keys to promoting a smooth transition from: o Preschool to school-age o School to adulthood o Hospital to school o Juvenile justice system to school	Approach • Deals with interacting with families in a way that respects the values of both the home and the school in constructing the educational experiences of the students Attitudes • The perceptions that families and schools have of one another Atmosphere • The overall climate is set for families and educators Actions • Component involves strategies for building long-term partnerships • Activities that include families and facilitate their active participation in the educational process	

Sample Questions for Professional Practices That Permeate All Aspects of Service Delivery

1. Ms. Norman has been consulting with the school psychologist for the past three weeks regarding one of her students, Cory. Under the behavioral consultation model, the school psychologist has asked Ms. Norman to collect data on the frequency, duration, and intensity of Cory's identified problematic behaviors. Ms. Norman has also contacted Cory's parents and the school counselor to get more information about his behavior. After collecting the data for the past week, Ms. Norman shares it with the school psychologist at their next consultation session. After reviewing the data, what is most likely to be the next step at this consultation session?
   a. Continue to collect more data to see if Cory's problematic behaviors diminish on their own.
   b. Brainstorm possible interventions that Ms. Norman can implement in the classroom to decrease Cory's problematic behaviors.
   c. Interpret the collected data and develop a hypothesis regarding what function the problematic behaviors serve for Cory.
   d. Ask Ms. Norman to describe Cory's behavior in specific, observable, and measurable terms.
   e. None of the above.

2. A school psychologist conducts a direct observation of a student with behavioral difficulties within the classroom and collects data using narrative recording techniques. To obtain narrative recordings, an observer writes a description of events that occurred within a given time frame. Which of the following is NOT a technique or method used for a narrative record?
   a. Daily log
   b. ABC analysis
   c. Descriptive time sampling
   d. Continuous recording
   e. Behavior intervention plan

3. The *Wechsler Preschool and Primary Scale of Intelligence—IV* (*WPPSI-IV*) is an individually administered test of cognitive ability with two core batteries based on the child's age. The battery intended for the younger population is used for children ranging in age of:
   a. 3 years, 0 months to 5 years, 0 months
   b. 2 years, 6 months to 3 years, 11 months
   c. 4 years, 0 months to 7 years, 7 months
   d. 2 years, 0 months to 4 years, 6 months
   e. 2 years, 6 months to 7 years, 7 months

4. A teacher is implementing a new behavioral intervention for a particular student within her class at the school psychologist's request. The intervention is started on the first day of the month and is designed to run for 30 days. The school psychologist periodically steps into the classroom to observe the teacher's implementation of the intervention. After 15 days, the teacher sits down with the school psychologist to discuss the organization of the program, procedures, and her technique in order to improve her delivery of the program to the student. This is an example of:
   a. Consumer-oriented evaluation
   b. Formative evaluation
   c. Participant-oriented evaluation
   d. Survey evaluation
   e. Summative evaluation

5. Preschool-aged children often exhibit deficits in one or multiple areas that may be a precursor to a possible learning disability. Which of the following deficits is NOT a possible precursor for a learning disorder in preschool-aged children?
   a. Difficulty with balance and walking
   b. Inability to follow or remember one-step directions
   c. Delayed physical growth
   d. Difficulty focusing attention or sitting still
   e. Inability to use words such as "yes" or "no" when appropriate

6. Ms. Hernandez, a novice teacher, is having difficulty establishing a classroom-wide behavioral management plan for her third-grade class. Although she has a basic understanding of behavioral management plans and has a current plan established in the class, she does not feel fully confident in her ability to implement the class-wide plan. She has solicited help from the school psychologist, and together they scheduled weekly consultation sessions to discuss this issue. Which approach is the school psychologist most likely to utilize in this consultative relationship?
   a. Client-centered case consultation
   b. Consultee-centered case consultation
   c. Program-centered administrative consultation
   d. Consultee-centered administrative consultation
   e. None of the above

7. After collecting data from several informants for a functional behavior assessment, the school psychologist determines that the information is insufficient for hypothesis generation. Which best describes what the school psychologist should do next?
   a. Conduct a student file review
   b. Identify other informants to interview
   c. Use another form of data collecting with the same informants
   d. Conduct a direct observation
   e. Interview the student

8. Which of the following statements about the *Wechsler Abbreviated Scale of Intelligence—II* (*WASI-II*) is most accurate?
   a. It is an effective screening measure of verbal and nonverbal abilities.
   b. It is linked to the *Wechsler Intelligence Scale for Children—IV* (*WISC-IV*) and the *Wechsler Preschool and Primary Scale of Intelligence—IV* (*WPPSI-IV*).
   c. It does not have satisfactory reliability and validity.
   d. It is able to be used with a broad range of individuals from age 2 years, 6 months to 90 years, 11 months.
   e. It is an acceptable substitute or replacement for a comprehensive measure of intellectual abilities.

9. A student with a documented visual impairment is recommended for reevaluation. The school psychologist completes the assessment of the student but later finds out that the student is required to wear prescription glasses. What should the school psychologist do?
   a. Throw out the assessment and retest using the same assessment tool, making sure the student wears his glasses the second time.
   b. Keep the original assessment and make a note in the report that the student was not wearing his glasses during testing.
   c. Keep only the parts of the assessment where the student did not have to read or view anything in order to answer the item.
   d. Reassess the student using a new assessment tool, making sure the student wears his glasses during testing.
   e. Throw out the original assessment and complete your evaluation without using a new formal evaluation tool.

10. The systematic collection of data is crucial in developing appropriate interventions that help students in the classroom. Decisions made without gathering this information may result in implementing inappropriate interventions. The process begins with problem identification, and the steps include all of the following EXCEPT which method?
    a. Observation techniques
    b. Teacher interviews
    c. Review of previous interventions
    d. Curriculum-based measurements
    e. Peer-based interviews

11. You are evaluating a first-grade student who is hearing impaired, and his family just recently moved to the United States. Which assessment instrument should you use?
    a. *Test of Early Language Development–Third Edition* (*TELD-3*)
    b. *Universal Nonverbal Intelligence Test* (*UNIT*)

   c. *Cognitive Assessment System (CAS)*
   d. *Wide Range Achievement Test (WRAT-4)*
   e. *Kaufman Assessment Battery for Children (KABC-II)*

12. What are the four A's in the framework for effective family-school collaboration?
   a. Appeal, actions, aptitude, and agreement
   b. Actions, agreement, attitude, and alliance
   c. Approach, actions, agreement, and atmosphere
   d. Appeal, alliance, atmosphere, and aptitude
   e. Approach, attitudes, atmosphere, and actions

13. The director of special education of Middletown School District has hired an outside consultant to evaluate the school district's process to identify students who may have educational disabilities. This is an example of which consultation model?
   a. Mental health (consultee-centered)
   b. Behavioral
   c. Organizational
   d. Empirical
   e. Instructional

14. Mrs. Smith, the school psychologist, was asked to work with the language arts department to strengthen the curriculum for the district. The current curriculum does not emphasize and focus on the state standards, and there have been complaints that the students are not prepared when they enter into the district's high school. With the team, Mrs. Smith has been analyzing and critiquing the current curriculum in order to highlight its strengths and weaknesses. They are trying to figure out why the current curriculum does not prepare their students for what is expected of them in high school. Possible hypotheses are developed, confirmed, or rejected. Mrs. Smith and her team are in which stage of the problem-solving model of systems theory?
   a. Intervention
   b. Collaboration
   c. Problem identification
   d. Problem analysis
   e. Evaluation

15. Mrs. Barnard has been asked to develop an academic intervention for a fourth grader, Johnny, as a result of a recent building-based problem-solving team meeting. She has been told by a member of the team that Johnny is displaying oppositional behaviors when asked to complete any reading assignments. Mrs. Barnard decides to administer the DIBELS to Johnny. According to Bergan and Kratochwill's four-step problem-solving process, Mrs. Barnard is pursuing which of the following steps?
   a. Problem identification
   b. Problem evaluation
   c. Problem solving
   d. Problem implementation
   e. Problem analysis

Answers With Rationale

1. The best answer is ***c***. According to the behavioral consultation problem-solving model, the next step after collecting data is to accurately interpret the data. Together, the school psychologist and the classroom teacher hypothesize on the function(s) the behaviors serve for Cory. Choice *b* is inaccurate, because one would not list possible interventions until after the perceived function is determined. The interventions developed are guided by this hypothesis. Choice *d* is inaccurate because identifying the student's behavior in specific, observable, and measureable terms is one of the first steps in the behavioral

consultation model. Choice *a* is inaccurate because the purpose of the consultation is to diminish problematic behaviors through a problem-solving model.

Reference: Hughes, T.L., Kolbert, J.B., & Crothers, L.M. (2014). Best practices in behavioral/ecological consultation. In P. Harrison & A. Thomas (Eds.), *Best practices in school psychology VI: Data-based and collaborative decision making* (pp. 483–492). Bethesda, MD: National Association of School Psychologists.

2. The best answer is ***e***. If an observer is tracking target behaviors in the classroom, it would be most beneficial to record the behaviors to check the frequency, duration, and intensity. Therefore, ABC analysis, time sampling, and continuous recordings would be valuable methods to implement for gathering observational information. In addition, a daily log would show how often the behaviors are occurring over time and whether the student is progressing. Although the behavior intervention plan is a valuable strategy to implement after the data has been gathered, it is not useful in tracking and recording observable behavior.

   Reference: McConaughy, S.H., & Ritter, D.R. (2014). Best practices in multimethod assessment of emotional and behavioral disorder. In P. Harrison & A. Thomas (Eds.), *Best practices in school psychology VI: Data-based and collaborative decision making* (pp. 367–390). Bethesda, MD: National Association of School Psychologists.

3. The best answer is ***b***. Option *e* is the full range of age of administration for the *WPPSI-IV.* Option *c* is the range for the upper-level battery of the *WPPSI-IV.* The age ranges for the WPPSI-IV, a description, core subtests, supplemental and optional subtests, and interpretation can be found in either the *Essentials of WPPSI-IV Assessment* by Raiford and Coalson (2014) or in the WPSSI-IV administration manual.

   Reference: Raiford, S.E., & Coalson, D.L. (2014). *Essentials of WPPSI-IV assessment.* Hoboken, NJ: Wiley.

4. The best answer is ***b***. The evaluation conducted between the teacher and school psychologist is being done before the end of the intervention. They are using the information gathered about program delivery, organizational context, personnel, and procedures in order to strengthen and improve the quality of the intervention. These are all aspects of a formative evaluation.

   Reference: Gibbons, K., & Brown, S. (2014). Best practices in evaluating psychoeducational services based on student outcome data. In P. Harrison & A. Thomas (Eds.), *Best practices in school psychology VI: Foundations* (pp. 357–358). Bethesda, MD: National Association of School Psychologists.

5. The best answer is ***c***. Precursors of learning disabilities at preschool age include delays in motor functioning (walking and balance), behavior (impulsivity and inattention), cognitive/executive functioning, memory (difficulty remembering directions or facts), communication (speech and language delays), perceptual ability, and social/emotional regulation. Poor growth is not a precursor of a learning disability but may contribute to the development of a disability later in life if the delay continues.

   Reference: Lichtenstein, R. (2014). Best practices in identification of learning disabilities. In P. Harrison & A. Thomas (Eds.), *Best practices in school psychology VI: Data-based and collaborative decision making* (pp. 331–354). Bethesda, MD: National Association of School Psychologists.

6. The best answer is ***b***, consultee-centered. This choice is the correct answer because the main focus of consultation between Ms. Hernandez and the school psychologist is to improve Ms. Hernandez's understanding of class-wide behavioral management plans. Incorrect answers: Option *a*. Client-centered is not the correct option because the consultation process does not directly focus on the client (students). Option *c*. Program-centered administrative is not the correct option because the consultation process does not focus on developing a new program for the school. Option *d*. Consultee-centered administrative is not the correct option because the consultation process does not focus on the administrative level.

   Reference: Sandoval, J. (2014). Best practices in school-based mental health/consultee-centered consultation by school psychologists. In P. Harrison & A. Thomas (Eds.), *Best practices in school psychology VI* (pp. 493–507). Bethesda, MD: National Association of School Psychologists.

7. The best answer is ***d***. In general, when data collected primarily through informant methods is insufficient for hypothesis generation, school psychologists should move to the next stage of information gathering—that is, descriptive or direct observation.

Reference: Steege, M.W., & Scheib, M.A. (2014). Best practices in conducting functional behavioral assessments. In P. Harrison & A. Thomas (Eds.), *Best practices in school psychology VI: Data-based and collaborative decision making* (pp. 273–286). Bethesda, MD: National Association of School Psychologists.

8. The best answer is ***a***. The WASI-II was linked to the *WISC-IV* but not the *WPPSI-IV*, so option *b* is incorrect. Option **c** is incorrect because research has shown the *WASI-II* has satisfactory reliability and validity. The range of ages for the WASI-II is from 6 years, 0 months to 90 years, 11 months, so option *d* is incorrect. Option *e* is also incorrect because the *WASI-II* is not meant to replace more comprehensive measures of intelligence. Instead, it is intended to be used for quickly measuring an individual's verbal, nonverbal, and general cognitive functioning when appropriate.

Reference: Maccow, G. (2011). *Overview of WASI-II.* Retrieved from http://images.pearsonclinical.com/images/PDF/Webinar/WASI-IIHandoutOct2011.pdf

9. The best answer is ***d***. Prior to assessing a student with a visual impairment, review his or her records to determine if the student needs any type of visual device (if the student has low vision) or if the student is totally blind. If an assessment is administered without the student wearing the required and prescribed device, the test is invalid. Because tests cannot be repeated on the same student for a minimum of nine months, a new assessment tool must be used. It is not ethical to keep the original invalid assessment as a means of determining a child's ability, and a formal assessment tool must be used.

Reference: Bradley-Johnson, S., & Cook, A. (2014). Best practices in school-based services for students with visual impairments. In P. Harrison & A. Thomas (Eds.), *Best practices in school psychology VI: Foundations* (pp. 243–256). Bethesda, MD: National Association of School Psychologists.

10. The best answer is ***e***. The data-based decision-making process uses interviews, observations, review of records, and curriculum-based measurements (CBMs) to make informed decisions about interventions for students. During the interview process, a parent, teacher, or the child in question may be interviewed, but peers are not part of the process.

Reference: Christ, T.J., & Arañas, Y.A. (2014). Best practices in problem analysis. In P. Harrison & A. Thomas (Eds.), *Best practices in school psychology VI: Data-based and collaborative decision making* (pp. 87–98). Bethesda, MD: National Association of School Psychologists.

11. The *Universal Nonverbal Intelligence Test* is appropriate for culturally diverse populations. The response administration involves hand/body gestures, making it appropriate for individuals with speech, language, or hearing impairments. The correct answer is ***b***.

Reference: Sattler, J.M., & Hoge, R.D. (2001). *Assessment of children: Behavioral, social, and clinical foundations.* San Diego, CA: Author.

12. The correct answer is ***c***, approach, attitudes, atmosphere, and actions. Approach: the way of interacting should respect values of how both home and school contribute to the educational experience of students. Attitudes: how families and school personnel perceive one another. Atmosphere: the overall climate for educators and families to interact in. Actions: strategies for building long-term partnerships.

Reference: Sheridan, S.M., Clarke, B.L., & Christenson, S.L. (2014). Best practices in promoting family engagement in education. In P. Harrison & A. Thomas (Eds.), *Best practices in school psychology VI: System-level services* (pp. 439–453). Bethesda, MD: National Association of School Psychologists.

13. The best answer is ***c***. The organizational consultation process evaluates the whole system. Option *a* is not the correct answer because the mental health model is child-centered, focusing on one particular child. Option *b* is not the correct answer

because the behavioral model is consultee-centered, where the focus is on the consultee's skill sets. Option *d* is not the correct answer because instructional consultation focuses on the instructional setting and its match to the client (student).

Reference: Kratochwill, T. R., Altschaefl, M. R., & Bice-Urbach, B. (2014). Best practices in school-based problem-solving consultation: Applications in prevention and intervention systems. In P. Harrison & A. Thomas (Eds.), *Best practices in school psychology VI: Data-based and collaborative decision making* (pp. 461–482). Bethesda, MD: National Association of School Psychologists.

14. The correct answer is ***d***, problem analysis stage. Hypotheses are developed to explain why the problem is occurring throughout the second stage in systems theory, problem analysis.

Reference: Pluymert, K., (2014). Problem-solving foundations for school psychological services. In P. Harrison & A. Thomas (Eds.), *Best practices in school psychology VI: Data-based and collaborative decision making* (pp. 25–39). Bethesda, MD: National Association of School Psychologists.

15. The best answer is ***a***. As a part of the problem identification step, one should obtain the current level of functioning in order to provide a baseline, which is useful in evaluating the existence of the problem, the effectiveness of the intervention, and the degree of student progress.

Reference: Pluymert, K. (2014). Problem-solving foundations for school psychological services. In P. Harrison & A. Thomas (Eds.), *Best practices in school psychology VI: Data-based and collaborative decision making* (pp. 25–39). Bethesda, MD: National Association of School Psychologists.

Chapter 6

Direct and Indirect Services for Children, Families, and Schools (Student-Level Services)

Chapter 6 includes the category of *Direct and Indirect Services for Children, Families, and Schools (Student-Level Services)*. This category is divided into two topical areas: (1) *Interventions and Instructional Support to Develop Academic Skills* and (2) *Interventions and Mental Health Services to Develop Social and Life Skills*.

The authors first provide an introduction to and description of the two topics. Next, there is a series of graphic organizers that outline the *content knowledge* in these two areas. Finally, you will find 15 sample questions with correct answers and rationale included.

Key information is outlined below each main topic. These are the areas that we recommend you review and master. While you are reviewing the key information outlined and answering the sample questions, you may want to add your own information on the blank graphic organizers to supplement what is provided here.

Interventions and Instructional Support to Develop Academic Skills

Interventions and Instructional Support to Develop Academic Skills refer to effective instructions for individual students and groups, as well as issues related to academic success and failure. Methods of effective instruction (e.g., cooperative learning, differentiated instruction, scaffolding, and engagement time) are designed to be embedded within a classroom environment that promotes learning. Academic success and failure include evidence-based instructional strategies and the influence of cultural context, families, and student motivation.

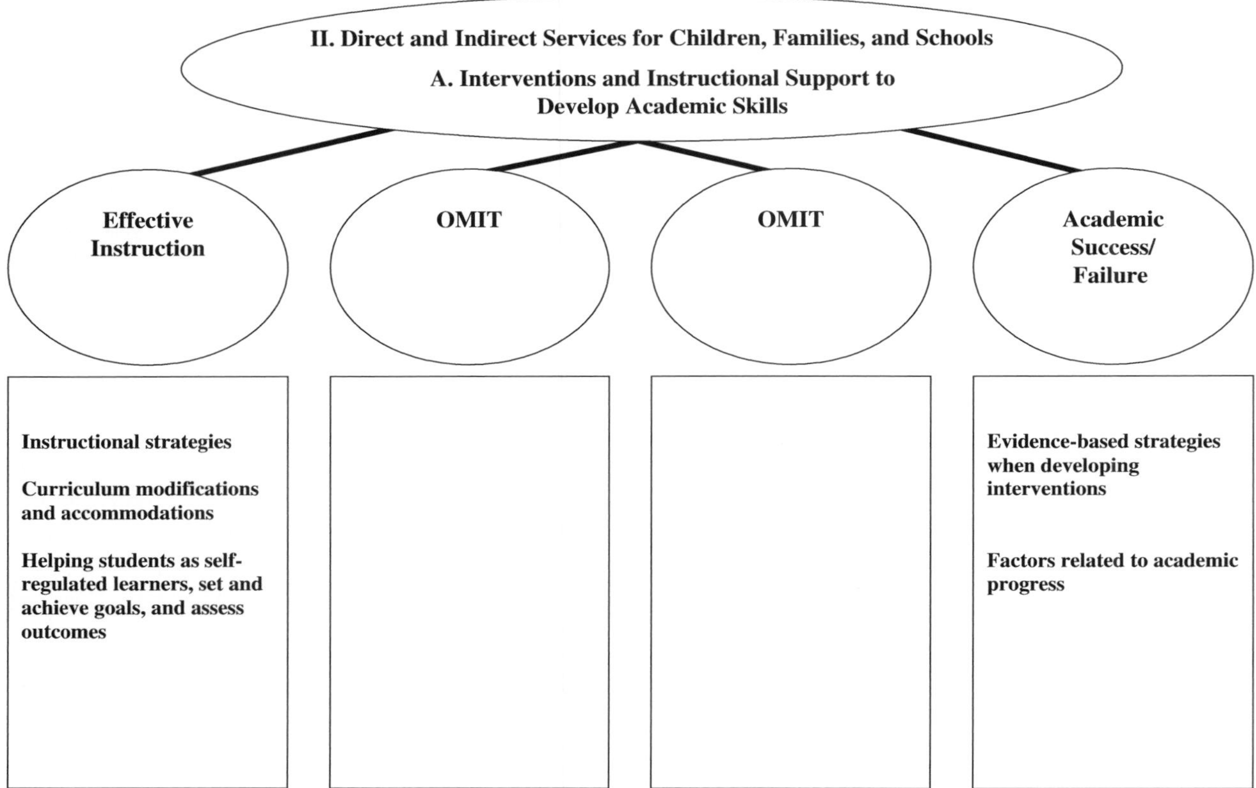

Figure 6.1
Direct and Indirect Services for Children, Families, and Schools: Interventions and Instructional Support to Develop Academic Skills

Graphic Organizers for Effective Instruction

TABLE 6.1
Graphic Organizer for Instructional Strategies

I and ISDAS: Effective Instruction

Instructional Strategies

Cooperative Learning	Differentiated Instruction	Engagement Time	Scaffolding
• Simultaneously addresses academic and social skill learning by students • Student groups are small (2–6), heterogeneous with respect to student characteristics; group members share the various roles and are interdependent in achieving the group learning goal • 5 elements: 1. Positive interdependence 2. Promotive interaction 3. Individual accountability 4. Interpersonal skills 5. Group processing	• Recognizes students' varying background knowledge, readiness, language, preferences in learning, and interests • Intent is to maximize each student's growth and individual success by meeting each student where he/she is and assisting in the learning process • Teachers create different pathways that respond to the needs of diverse learners • Enables teachers to put research-based best practices into a meaningful context	• Portion of the instructional time during which students are engaged in learning, as evidenced by paying attention, completing written work, and/or interacting with peers about assigned work • Four categories: 1. Available time 2. Scheduled time 3. Instructional time 4. Engaged time • 3 factors that produce low rates of engagement: 1. Poor instructional design 2. Ineffective classroom management 3. Poor student self-regulation	• Adequate support needs to be given to a child and gradually faded away once the child approximates independent functioning while completing task • Verbal scaffolding: writing prompts, paraphrasing, pairing oral text with written text • Procedural scaffolding: 1:1 teaching, pairing and grouping students, personalizing information, "jigsawing," use of routines, role playing • Instructional scaffolding: using graphic organizers, word walls, manipulative and visual cues, posting schedules

TABLE 6.2
Graphic Organizer for Curriculum Modifications and Accommodations

I and ISDAS: Effective Instruction

Curriculum Modifications and Accommodations

Assistive Technology	Examples of Assistive Technology	Specially Designed Instruction	Specially Designed Instruction: Accommodations and Modifications
• Any tool that helps students with disabilities do things more quickly, easily, or independently; can be elaborate and expensive or simple and low-cost • Can provide accommodations, modifications, or adaptations made to environment, curriculum, instruction, or assessment practices	• Physical disabilities: o Wheelchairs, walkers, standing aids • Nonverbal concerns: o Remote controls, modified keyboards, head pointers • Hearing impairments: o FM units, hearing aids, CCTVs • Mobility impairment: o Wheelchairs, recreational vehicles like bikes or scooters, drawing software • Information technology: o iPads, computer applications, text-to-speech software, speech recognition software	• IDEA definition: adapting content, methodology, or delivery of instruction to: o Address the unique needs that result from the child's disability o Ensure child has access to the general education • Instruction is implemented in accordance with the IEP process	• Accommodations are key things we can do in class that will allow the student successful access to the day-to-day classroom activities; they do not change the standard or core content of the work • Modifications must be designed by a special education teacher; they are specially designed, direct instruction where standard or core content is modified; performance modifications allow the student to work at his/her own level

TABLE 6.3
Graphic Organizer for Helping Students as Self-Regulated Learners Set and Achieve Goals and Assess Outcomes

I and ISDAS: Effective Instruction

Helping Students as Self-Regulated Learners Set and Achieve Goals and Assess Outcomes

Main idea	Main idea	Main idea	Main idea
Self-Regulation	External Motivators	Internal Motivators	Assessing Outcomes
• 23 self-regulation executive functions capacities that are responsible for day-to-day routines • Capacities occur both consciously and unconsciously • Interventions exist on a severity continuum dependent upon executive functions and developmental levels	• Provide predictable and consistent structure to environment • Provide prompts and cues • Provide time management aids: calendars, clocks, schedules • Allow self-selection on assignments and high-interest material • Provide immediate and frequent feedback • Use rewards to align internal desires with external demands • Use of mild forms of punishment to obtain compliance	• Increase student awareness of expectations, goals, personal strengths and weaknesses • Model appropriate use of self-regulation capabilities • Teach capabilities as specific skill routines • Develop vocabulary and nonverbal symbols for describing and signifying capacities and their use • Model and encourage "self-talk" • Model and teach self-administered reward routines	• Intervention goal: to teach the child to be conscious of the executive functions and how to engage them • Observation forms and scales can progress monitor and provide feedback to teachers and parents

Graphic Organizers for Academic Success/Failure

TABLE 6.4
Graphic Organizer for Evidence-Based Strategies When Developing Interventions

I and ISDAS: Academic Success/Failure

Evidence-Based Strategies When Developing Interventions

Main idea	Main idea	Main idea	Main idea
Goal Setting	Plan Development	Measurement Strategy	Treatment Integrity and Decision-Making Plan
• 3 purposes of goal development: 1. Direct teaching and intervention 2. Focus plan on student outcomes 3. Structure methods for assessment and evaluation • Goal statements: written in a clear and measurable way to explain what student's performance will look like if the intervention is effective • Four components of goal statement(s): 1. Time frame 2. Condition 3. Behavior 4. Criteria	• Serves as a guide for intervention implementation for school psychologists and other parties involved • Plan must be written clearly enough for anyone to implement • Must include how each step will be completed, materials needed, and responsibilities of persons involved	• Measurement strategy should remain the same as when baseline data was collected • Allows for accurate comparisons between baseline performance and progress-monitoring data • Six components to data collection to include in strategy: 1. Method 2. Materials needed 3. Setting 4. Person(s) 5. Time frame 6. Frequency	• Treatment integrity: the degree to which the intervention is implemented as planned • 3 approaches to assess: 1. Self-report 2. Permanent products 3. Direct observation • 4 components in determining effectiveness of an intervention: 1. Frequency of data collection 2. Strategies to summarize data for evaluation 3. When will data be analyzed 4. Decision rule

TABLE 6.5
Graphic Organizer for Factors Related to Academic Progress

I and ISDAS: Academic Success/Failure

Factors Related to Academic Progress

Skills of Teachers	School Conditions	Family Involvement	Language Proficiency
Variables to monitor and address: • Student interruptions • Teacher interruptions • Visitors to the class • Transitions/wait time Academic learning time: • Portion of time allocated to a content area during which students are actively and productively engaged in learning • Assess ALT→ Teacher self-analysis	• Safe schools promote optimal academic achievement for all • Teach school staff crisis management and intervention techniques • Foster caring and supportive relationships between students and staff • Crowd control • Improve lighting • Enforce dress codes • Post signs that communicate zero tolerance for prohibited behaviors • Personalize schools to motivate students	• Family involvement in student educational experience is negatively related to student age • Shared responsibility between schools and home • Collaboration between home/school influenced by: o Family characteristics o Child characteristics o School personnel characteristics o Neighborhood characteristic o Time constraints	• Levels of proficiency affect achievement for English Language Learners Basic Interpersonal Communication Skills (BICS): • Skills first acquired when learning a new language Cognitive/Academic Language Proficiency (CALP): • Ability to manipulate language in decontextualized academic situations • Important to understand how acculturation may affect achievement

Interventions and Mental Health Services to Develop Social and Life Skills

Interventions and Mental Health Services to Develop Social and Life Skills refer to the content areas of prevention, school-based intervention, and psychopathology. Preventive strategies are targeted at primary, secondary, and tertiary levels to address classroom organization and management techniques, as well as small-group and individual needs. In addition, school psychologists utilize their knowledge of child and adolescent psychopathology to design and implement interventions.

Each of the three components that make up interventions and mental health services to develop social and life skills is explained in greater detail in the following graphic organizers. Important information is included in each main topic. These are the areas we recommend you review and master. Finally, sample questions for each topic are included at the end of the section. While you are reviewing the key information outlined and answering the sample questions, you may want to add your own information to supplement what is provided in the table.

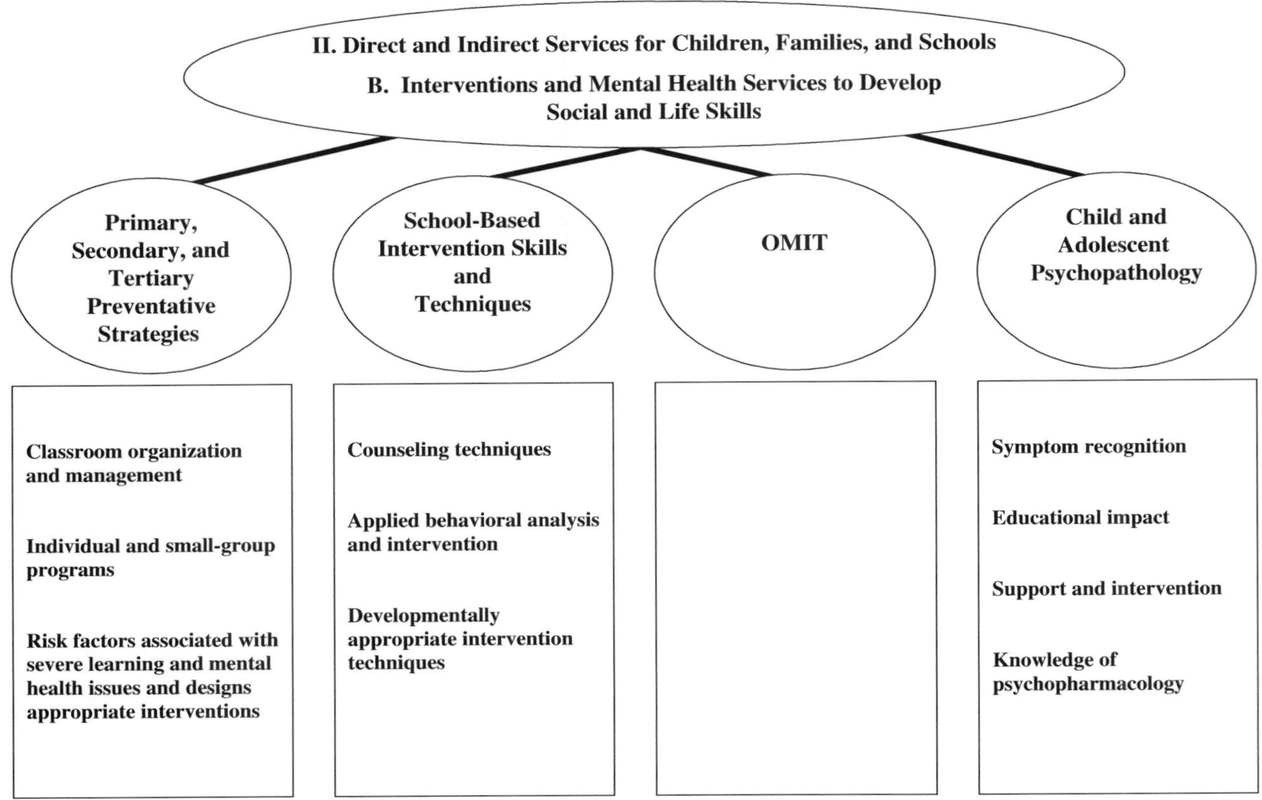

Figure 6.2
Direct and Indirect Services for Children, Families, and Schools: Interventions and Mental Health Services to Develop Social and Life Skills

Graphic Organizers for Primary, Secondary, and Tertiary Preventive Strategies

TABLE 6.6
Graphic Organizer for Classroom Organization and Management

I and MHSDSLS: Primary, Secondary, and Tertiary Preventive Strategies

Classroom Organization and Management

Classroom Design	Classroom Expectations	Classroom Routines	Classroom Consequences
• Design room to stimulate learning and to accomplish instructional goals and objectives • Keep high-traffic areas free of congestion • Make commonly used materials easily accessible • Ensure all students can see and hear presentation and displays • Provide study carrels for students who may need extra help	• Expectations set the stage for leaning and behavioral control • Expectations should: o Be limited in number (3–5) o Be observable and measurable o Be stated explicitly in positive terms o Be taught using standard instructional practices o Extend school-wide expectations to the classroom	• Routines are specific procedures used for the day-to-day running of the class • Routines need to be taught using standard instructional practices • Routines should be implemented during noninstructional times as well • Goal is for students to follow the routines independently	• Positive consequences: o Provide immediate feedback that behavior is acceptable or desired o Increase likelihood behavior will be repeated o Examples include: praise, positive feedback, privileges, breaks • Negative consequences: o Provide immediate feedback that behavior is unacceptable o Increase the likelihood that behavior will not be repeated o Examples include: time out, loss of attention or praise, loss of privilege

TABLE 6.7
Graphic Organizer for Individual and Small-Group Programs

I and MHSDSLS: Primary, Secondary, and Tertiary Preventive Strategies

Individual and Small-Group Programs

Main idea: Social Skills

- Focus for students with difficulties in peer relationships, antisocial and/or aggressive behavior
- Four common features:
  1. Facilitate the initiation and maintenance of positive relationships
  2. Promote peer acceptance and friendship development
  3. Increase positive school outcomes
  4. Help students adapt and adjust to their social environments
- Components of effective social skills development:
  - o Modeling skills
  - o Practicing skills within a group setting
  - o Providing corrective feedback and reinforcement in the moment
  - o Generalization of skills
  - o Discuss and review skills often

Main idea: Conflict Resolution

- Skills may not be acquired incidentally
- Unresolved conflict outcomes include:
  - o Poor academic performance
  - o Low self-esteem
  - o Social-behavioral problems, such as violence
- School-based programs:
  - o Conflict resolution teaching curricula
  - o Anger management skills
  - o Peer mediation

Main idea: Study Skills

- Best practice: for skills to be taught by general educator within the current curriculum for skills to transfer
- Home and school relationship is crucial for generalization
- Through observation and interviews, the school psychologist should develop an implementation plan focused on:
  - o Organization
  - o Comprehending directions
  - o Note taking
  - o Previewing
  - o Reading comprehension
  - o Test preparation
  - o Test taking
  - o Self-management
  - o Motivation and affect

Main idea: Self-Control Training

- Self-control training: strategies for managing and controlling behavior and implementation of these skills
- Types of training:
  - o Relaxation training
  - o Coping self-statements
  - o Anger management
- Class-wide interventions:
  - o Good Behavior Game
  - o Second Step program
  - o Fast Track program

TABLE 6.8
Graphic Organizer for Risk Factors Associated With Severe Learning and Mental Health Issues and Design Interventions

I and MHSDSLS: Primary, Secondary, and Tertiary Preventive Strategies

Risk Factors Associated With Severe Learning and Mental Health Issues and Design Interventions

Main idea	Main idea	Main idea	Main idea
Severe Learning	Anxiety	Depression	Attention Problems
• Risk factors: o Falling below grade level o Dropping out in later grades o Decreased motivation and engagement o Negative attitudes toward school • Skill-by-treatment interaction interventions: o Explicit Instruction o Appropriate instructional level o Frequent opportunities to respond o Targeted intervention based on student skill o Feedback	• Risk factors: o Academic: difficulties with attention, concentration, memory, and problem solving o Social: difficulties in social situations, often become victims of bullying and harassment • School-based interventions: o Develop consistent and predictable routines o Provide opportunities for practice and rehearsal o Use positive approaches o Pair with a peer to help socialization skills o Teach self-relaxation and self-talk strategies	• Risk factors: o Academic: difficulties with task selection and completion, problem-solving skills, reasoning, concentration, memory, and attention; risk of dropping out o Social: difficulties in social situations, having quality interpersonal relationships, and a negative attributional style • School-based interventions o Improve social skills o Avoid negative language o Develop a success-oriented approach using a strengths-based strategy o Emphasize positive effort and production	• Risk factors: o Defiance toward authority figures o Poor relationships with peers o Antisocial behavior (lying, stealing, fighting) o Low academic engagement o Inconsistent work productivity • Interventions: o School-wide positive behavior support o Systematic academic strategy instruction o Assessment-based behavioral strategies o Self-monitoring

Graphic Organizers for School-Based Intervention Skills and Techniques

TABLE 6.9
Graphic Organizer for Counseling Techniques

I and MHSDSLS: School-Based Intervention Skills and Techniques

Counseling Techniques

Ethics of Counseling

- Obtain parental consent if a student is receiving mental health services
- Students should be informed of exceptions to confidentiality from the onset of services
- A school psychologist is obligated to share confidential information when:
  - Student requests it
  - Student may hurt self or others
  - Legal obligation to testify in court

Individual Counseling

Cognitive behavior therapy
- Increase the child's ability to think before acting

Play therapy
- Developmentally appropriate way to provide counseling to students in the elementary school level

Bibliotherapy
- Children can obtain problem solving skills, relate to characters who are having the same struggles

Reality therapy
- Based on forming connections between behaviors and consequences

Group Counseling

- Positive way of addressing students' academic, career, and personal/social/emotional developmental issues
- Provides an atmosphere to develop and establish social skills
- Can help address:
  - Behavior adjustment
  - Self-esteem
  - Coping skills
  - Children of alcoholics
  - Children of divorced families

Multicultural Awareness

- Important to develop multicultural competence when working with ethnically and culturally diverse populations
- Involves understanding:
  - Family systems
  - Cultural values
  - Nonverbal communication

TABLE 6.10
Graphic Organizer for Applied Behavioral Analysis and Intervention

I and MHSDSLS: School-Based Intervention Skills and Techniques

Applied Behavioral Analysis and Intervention

Principles and Methods of ABA	DTI and Verbal Behavior	Task Analysis and Prompts	PECS and Functional Assessment
• Motivation • Reinforcement • Discrete trial instruction (DTI) • Functional assessment • Verbal behavior • Positive behavior support • Task analysis and chaining • Shaping • Prompting • Modeling • Picture exchange communication system (PECS) • Incidental teaching activity schedules • Generalization and maintenance	• Discrete trial instruction (DTI): a systematic way of teaching involving a series of repeated trials to teach and maintain cognitive, behavioral, or social skills until the skill is mastered • Verbal behavior: a framework for thinking about the development of language and its application. Involves: o Echoic: mimic word o Mand: request or demand o Tact: label or identify o Intraverbal: reciprocal conversation	• Task analysis: involves breaking down a skill into smaller steps that are easy to teach; uses forward and backward chaining procedures • Prompts: used to guide learners to make correct responses when teaching tasks; in the beginning, prompts are more obvious and then gradually fade away; types of prompts: o Physical (hand over hand) o Gestural (pointing) o Modeling o Visual	• Picture exchange communication system (PECS): a communication system in which pictures are used by an individual to express what he may need; used with learners who have difficulty with social communication; allows students to make requests, comments, or answers • Functional assessment: a system wherein a behavior analyst collects/records data in order to determine the function of a behavior and what is reinforcing/ maintaining that behavior; uses Antecedent-Behavior-Consequence (A-B-C) charts

TABLE 6.11
Graphic Organizer for Developmentally Appropriate Intervention Techniques

I and MHSDSLS: School-Based Intervention Skills and Techniques

Developmentally Appropriate Intervention Techniques

Aptitude/Intelligence and Intervention	Behaviorist Model vs. Cognitive Behavioral Model	Developing Interventions According to Needs and Abilities	Other
• Aptitude-treatment interaction (ATI): individual differences in abilities need to be taken into account when interventions or treatments are being planned • There are child characteristics that are assumed to be relevant to the extent to which a child benefits from one type of intervention over another • Using testing in conjunction with other cognitive educational methods can be a good cognitive assessment of a child's developmental level (strengths and weaknesses) and lend information leading to the construction of appropriate interventions	• Behaviorist model: o Deals with how the teacher structures the environment and provides reinforcement and punishment o Takes the position that a child learns from practice and reinforcement o Best used with younger students • Cognitive behavioral model: o Deals with how students' cognitive processes dictate behavior o Takes the position that a child learns from gaining knowledge or modifying existing knowledge o Best used with older students	• Use information from functional assessment and list all interventions that seem appropriate to decrease maladaptative behavior and replace it with alternate adaptive behavior • Select an intervention based on resources, treatment acceptability, and strengths/abilities of child • Design and apply interventions according to the hierarchical needs of the child, the unique features of the case, and the current function of behavior	

Graphic Organizers for Child and Adolescent Psychopathology

TABLE 6.12
Graphic Organizer for Symptom Recognition

I and MHSDSLS: Child and Adolescent Psychopathology

Symptom Recognition

Autism Spectrum Disorders	ADHD	Depression	Intellectual Disability
• Impaired social interaction (shows little or no interest in people in their surroundings) • Impaired communication (may not initiate communication for social purposes) • Repetitive behaviors and stereotyped patterns of behavior (ritualistic motor movements) • Preoccupation with an object • Impaired cognition (difficulty in coding and categorization) • Abnormal sensory perceptions (hyper- or hypo-responsive to specific stimuli) *Autistic savant*: advanced skills in a particular area	• Poor attention span o May ignore details, make careless mistakes, have difficulty following directions and listening. o May appear to be forgetful, distracted, and disorganized • Hyperactivity/impulsivity o May be fidgety, have difficulty sitting still, talk excessively, and interrupt others o May be in constant motion and display a general sense of physical restlessness	• Increased moodiness, irritability, self-criticism, and argumentativeness • Poor concentration • Sleep and appetite changes • Increased feelings of despair, sadness, emptiness • Loss of energy • Lack of interest in usual activities and friends • Increased talked of death and dying • Threats of suicide	• Onset prior to age 18 • Psychosocial development does not match same age peers • Significantly subaverage intellectual functioning (IQ of 70 or below) • Deficits in adaptive functioning • Difficulties with social, communication, and functional academic skills • Tendency to be aggressive, demonstrate self-injurious behaviors

TABLE 6.13
Graphic Organizer for Educational Impact

I and MHSDSLS: Child and Adolescent Psychopathology

Educational Impact

Autism Spectrum Disorders	ADHD	Depression	Intellectual Disability
• Poor social interaction with peers; tend to play alone • Trouble expressing wants and needs • Need structure and routine in order to function • Benefit from visual support of verbally presented information • Sensitivity to specific sensory stimuli	• Academic underachievement • Problems with reading, spelling, and written language • Difficulty conforming to rules and behavior expectations • Difficulty with social relationships • Peer rejection	• Poor performance in school • Frequent absences from school • Decreased interest in school activities • Persistent boredom • Skipping class • Social isolation; extreme sensitivity to rejection • Poor communication • Low self-esteem	• Typically have difficulties with social, communication, and functional academic skills; learning these skills takes longer than with a typically developing child • Decreased access to normative peer functions • May be teased or bullied

TABLE 6.14
Graphic Organizer for Support and Intervention

I and MHSDSLS: Child and Adolescent Psychopathology

Support and Intervention

Autism Spectrum Disorders	ADHD	Depression	Intellectual Disability
• Use direct/small group instruction to teach: o Age-appropriate social skills o Behaviors that can be used to replace problem behavior o Cognitive skills that can apply to everyday life • Useful strategies: o Present information in small steps o Provide reinforcement o Develop an extremely structured and consistent environment o PECS o Social stories	• Use behavior management interventions linked to FBA data • Develop self-monitoring and self-evaluation strategies • Useful strategies: o Social skills training o Peer mediation o Response cost systems o Contingency contracts o Frequent breaks o Assignment books to help with organization o Study skills and time management training • Consider use of medications	• Cognitive behavior therapy (CBT) focuses on challenging automatic thoughts, identifying negative thinking, and restructuring negative thoughts • Useful strategies: o Provide study skills and time management training o Teach coping skills and strategies that will assist in battling depressive episodes o Increase social, communication, and problem-solving skills o Increase pleasant activities to decrease anxiety o Avoid negative approaches, such as punishment or sarcasm • Consider use of antidepressants	• Provide early identification/ intervention programs • Develop parent training programs to transfer behavioral programs to the home and community setting • Useful strategies: o Behavioral methods o Token economy systems o Behavior chaining o Contingency programs to reduce excess behaviors while increasing preferred behaviors o Social skills training o Focus on increasing adaptive behaviors

TABLE 6.15
Graphic Organizer for Knowledge of Psychopharmacology

I and MHSDSLS: Child and Adolescent Psychopathology

Knowledge of Psychopharmacology

Medications

- **Depression** (SSRIs):
  - o Fluoxetine (*Prozac*)
  - o Sertaline (*Zoloft*)
  - o Paroxetine (*Paxil*)
  - o Duloxetine (*Cymbalta*)
  - o Escitalopram (*Lexapro*)
  - o Fluvoxamine (*Luvox*)
- **Bipolar disorder** (mood stabilizers):
  - o Lithium
  - o Divalproex (*Depakote*)
  - o Carbamazepine (*Tegretol*)
  - o Lamotrigine (*Lamictal*)
- **Obsessive compulsive disorder** (SSRIs and antidepressants):
  - o Clomipramine (*Anafranil*)
  - o Fluvoxamine (*Luvox*)
  - o Fluoxetine (*Prozac*)
  - o Sertraline (*Zoloft*)

Medications (continued)

- **Seizure Disorders:**
  - o Antiepileptic drugs (AEDs)
  - o Valproic acid (*Depakote*)
  - o Carbamazepine (*Tegretol*)
  - o Lamotrigine (*Lamictal*)

Autism Spectrum Disorder

Serotonin medications	SSRIs and clomipramine (*Anafranil*)
Atypical antipsychotics	Risperidone (*Risperdal*)
Beta-blockers	*Clonidine*
Mood stabilizers	Lithium Valproate Carbamazepine (*Tegretol*)
Stimulants	Methylphenidate (*Ritalin, Concerta*)

Medications (continued)

ADHD

Stimulant	Methylphenidate (*Ritalin, Metadate, Daytrana, Concerta*) Dexmethylphenidate (*Focalin*) Dextroamphetamine (*Adderall, Dexedrine*)
Anti-depressants	Bupropion (*Wellbutrin SR/LA*), Atomoxetine (*Strattera*)
Alpha-2 adrenergic agonists	Clonidine (*Kapvay*) Guanfacine (*Tenex*)

Medications (continued)

Psychotic Disorders

Antipsychotics/ neuroleptics	Chloropromazine (*Throazine*) Mesoridazine (*Serentil*) Haloperidol (*Haldol*) Pimodine (*Orap*) Fluphenazine (*Prolixin*)
Atypical antipsychotics	Aripiprazole (*Abilify*) Clozapine (*Clozaril*), Olanzapine (*Zyprexa*) Risperdone (*Risperdal*) Quetiapine (*Seroquel*)

Sample Questions for Direct and Indirect Services for Children, Families, and Schools (Student-Level Services)

1. Ms. Gardiner, a third-grade teacher, had difficulty encouraging one of her students, Maria, to complete written assignments. Maria generated good ideas, but had trouble transferring her ideas onto paper. Therefore, Ms. Gardiner decreased the demands of the task by allowing Maria to provide her answers orally and write a one-sentence summary. As Maria's written expression improved, Ms. Gardiner gradually reduced her support until Maria gained independence during written assignments. This instructional strategy is best known as:
   a. Engagement time
   b. Flexible grouping
   c. Independence training
   d. Scaffolding
   e. Differentiated instruction

2. As defined by IDEA, "specially designed instruction" includes all of the following EXCEPT:
   a. Requiring classroom accommodations to be used for students.
   b. Adapting the content, methodology, or delivery of instruction.
   c. Addressing the unique needs of the child that result from his or her disability.
   d. Ensuring access to the general curriculum in order for each child to meet the educational standards.
   e. Being a required part of the IEP document.

3. Academic learning time (ALT) is defined as the portion of instructional time that the teacher allocates for which of the following?
   a. Each content area throughout the students' instructional day.
   b. Content areas during which students are actively and productively engaged in learning.
   c. Specially designed, direct instruction within the classroom.
   d. Teaching students based upon their varying background knowledge, readiness, language, and preferences in learning.
   e. Lesson plans and structured instructional activities.

4. Mr. Hunter, a school psychologist, has been using the school district's study skills curriculum to help students improve their time management. Initially, Mr. Hunter asked each student how much time he or she is spending on each assignment. After teaching various time management techniques over a period of six weeks, Mr. Hunter asked students to keep a record of the techniques that did or did not work well for them; these findings were discussed with the group. Now, Mr. Hunter is working on having the students recognize when and where to apply the strategies that best work for them. Which of the following best describes the instructional strategy being used by Mr. Hunter?
   a. Externalizing strategy
   b. Internalizing strategy
   c. Metacognition
   d. Knowledge of strategies
   e. Cooperative learning

5. For students who have social communication deficits, an alternative communication system, in which pictures are used by an individual to express what he or she wants or needs, is called?
   a. Discrete trial instruction (DTI)
   b. Social stories
   c. Verbal behavior system
   d. Picture exchange communication system (PECS)
   e. Token economy

6. Applied behavior analysis is:
   a. A systematic way of teaching involving a series of repeated trials to teach cognitive, social, and behavioral skills.
   b. A framework for thinking about the development of language and its application.
   c. A framework in which the science and principles of behavior are applied to develop procedures to improve socially significant behavior.
   d. The way in which behavior analysts determine the function of a behavior and determine how it is reinforced and maintained.
   e. A program in which skills are broken down into smaller steps that are easy to teach.

7. Mark is a student showing classical symptoms of oppositional defiant disorder. He constantly defies and talks back to teachers, deliberately does things to annoy other students, and is extremely spiteful and vindictive. His behaviors are causing significant impairments in his social and academic functioning. Which intervention is most likely to be effective?
   a. Train Mark's parents to pinpoint problem behaviors as well as model appropriate modes of responding.
   b. Every time Mark breaks a classroom rule, reprimand him and make him face his desk toward the wall.
   c. Get Mark's family involved. Every time he disrupts the classroom, call home and tell his parents about his inappropriate behavior. Inform them he may need more rules enforced at home.
   d. Whenever Mark acts up and talks back, instead of taking him aside and talking to him one-on-one, send him to the vice principal's office.
   e. None of the above.

8. Which of the following is NOT a best practice of implementing negative consequences?
   a. Removing a privilege that the student has previously earned.
   b. Calling the parents to inform them of the student's behavior.
   c. Withholding an extrinsic motivator until the student corrects his or her behavior.
   d. Referring the student to an administrator.
   e. None of the above.

9. The use of time management aides, classroom management techniques, feedback, rewards, and modeling is an effective tool for increasing _______ in students.
   a. Motivation
   b. Positive behavior
   c. Study skills
   d. Self-regulation
   e. Self-awareness

10. Which of the following types of medications can be used to manage attention-deficit/hyperactivity disorder (ADHD) behaviors?
    a. Stimulants
    b. Antidepressants
    c. Alpha-2 adrenergic
    d. Answers A and C
    e. All of the above

11. Anna, a third grader, has struggled to make close friends since kindergarten. Her teacher, Mrs. Bailey, has noticed this and talked to the school psychologist about ways to help Anna. Which type of intervention will best help Anna?
    a. Giving Anna a peer mentor from an older grade.
    b. A class-wide intervention working on social skills.
    c. A group counseling intervention working on social skills.
    d. Giving Anna a peer mentor from the same grade.
    e. Individual counseling sessions to work on social skills.

12. When Alex was six, his family immigrated to the United States from Ukraine. Now 12, he is able to hold in-depth conversations with classmates and friends on topics such as hockey, skateboarding, and video games. Alex is in which stage of language acquisition?
    a. Cognitive/academic language proficiency (CALP)
    b. Acculturation
    c. Beginning fluent
    d. Basic interpersonal communication skills (BICS)
    e. Speech emergence

13. An intervention plan is established for Conner, a third grader with difficulties in reading fluency. The plan states Conner will receive the Wilson Reading System for 60 minutes, five times a week. The reading specialist implements the plan and begins providing Conner the intervention for 60 minutes, two times a week. In which of the following is the reading specialist deviating from evidence-based practice?
    a. Decision-making plan
    b. Plan integrity
    c. Treatment integrity
    d. Formative evaluation
    e. Measurement strategy

14. Before reenacting a scene from Hamlet, Mrs. Rodriguez allows Samantha to work with a classmate to recite her lines. Mrs. Rodriguez is employing an intervention strategy for which mental health issue?
    a. Attention-deficit/hyperactivity disorder
    b. Anxiety
    c. Autism
    d. Oppositional defiant disorder
    e. Depression

15. Which of the following is a situation where the school psychologist is NOT required to breach confidentiality from counseling sessions with a student?
    a. The student says he/she wants to hurt his/her teacher.
    b. The student writes a letter saying he/she wants to hurt himself/herself and has developed a plan.
    c. The student requests for the school psychologist to help disclose confidential information to his/her parent.
    d. The parent requests weekly reports on what is being discussed during counseling sessions.
    e. None of the above.

Answers With Rationale

1. The best answer is ***d***. Scaffolding is an instructional strategy, which emphasizes the gradual removal of support to help students gain independence. Answers *a*, *b*, and *c* are all examples of instructional strategies, but the key point to this question was the gradual removal of support, which can best be covered by the scaffolding strategy.

   Reference: August, D., McCardle, P., & Shanahan, T. (2014). Developing literacy in English language learners: Findings from a review of the experimental research. *School Psychology Review, 43*(4), 490–498.

2. The best answer is ***a***. Accommodations allow the student successful access to the day-to-day classroom activities, but do NOT require specially designed instruction. Thus, the word "accommodation" makes this answer incorrect. If it had read "modifications," rather than "accommodations," then this statement would have also been true. All other statements are true of specially designed instruction.

   Reference: Individuals With Disabilities Education Act, 20 U.S.C. § 1400 (2004).

3. The best answer is ***b***. The key to measuring academic learning time is looking at the time where students are active and productive participants during the learning process. Answer *a* is the definition for scheduled time, answer *d* exemplifies differentiated instruction, and answer *e* describes the term allocated time.

    Reference: Gettinger, M., & Miller, K. (2014). Best practices in increasing academic engaged time. In P. Harrison & A. Thomas (Eds.), *Best practices in school psychology VI: Student-level services* (pp. 19–35). Bethesda, MD: National Association of School Psychologists.

4. The best answer is ***c***. In this example, Mr. Hunter uses the three main components of metacognition to help students learn different time management techniques (knowledge of person, knowledge of task, and knowledge of strategies). Answer *e* is not correct because cooperative learning targets both academic and social skills simultaneously and, in this example, only social skills are targeted. Answers *a* and *b* are not examples of research-based instructional strategies. Answer *d* is only one component of metacognition; therefore, answer ***c*** is the best answer for this example, as it encompasses all three components used by Mr. Hunter.

    Reference: Dawson, P. (2014). Best practices in assessing and improving executive skills. In P. Harrison & A. Thomas (Eds.), *Best practices in school psychology VI: Student-level services* (pp. 269–285). Bethesda, MD: National Association of School Psychologists.

5. The best answer is ***d***. Children with social communication deficits can use PECS to substitute pictures to communicate in order to answer questions, make requests, and make comments about things in their environment. Choice *a* is inappropriate because it is a method for helping students master cognitive, behavioral, and social skills. Choice *b* is incorrect because it is a method for teaching social skills using models of appropriate social exchanges in a story format. Choice *c* is incorrect because this system is based on the development of vocal communication (sounds/words) or nonvocal means (gestures/pointing). Choice *e* is incorrect because token economy is more of a reinforcement system than communication system.

    Reference: Hallahan, D. P., Kauffman, J. M., & Pullen, P. C. (2012). *Exceptional learners: An introduction to special education*. Upper Saddle River, NJ: Pearson Education.

6. The best answer is ***c***. Choice *a* is incorrect because although it is often mistaken as ABA, this is considered to be a method based on the principles of ABA. Choice *b* is incorrect because it is considered verbal behavior and focuses mainly on language. Choice *d* is functional assessment and analysis and is a method of ABA that aids in increasing appropriate behavior. Choice *e* is task analysis and chaining and is incorrect because it is also another method of ABA. Choice *c* is correct because ABA is not a program, but the science applied to develop programs to improve socially significant behavior.

    Reference: Ormrod, J. E. (2012). *Human learning* (6th ed.). New York, NY: Pearson.

7. The best answer is ***a***. According to Bandura's social learning theory, our behavior is influenced by the information we process from observing other people, things, and events. Choices *b* and *d* are incorrect because these answers represent punishment and do not allow learning from his mistakes. Mark is more likely to act out if he knows he will be sent out of the classroom and can avoid class work. Choice *c* is incorrect because children with ODD are prone to actively defy rules and imposing more rules upon him will increase negative behaviors.

    Reference: Wicks-Nelson, R., & Israel, A. C. (2009). *Abnormal child and adolescent psychology* (7th ed.). Upper Saddle River, NJ: Pearson Education.

8. The best answer is ***a***. Negative consequences are delivered to provide immediate feedback that a behavior is unacceptable and to increase the likelihood that the behavior will not be repeated. All of the other answers are examples of negative consequences. Answer *a* is not an example of best practice in implementing negative consequences because students should not have a privilege removed that they have previously earned for positive behavior.

    Reference: Bear, G. G., & Manning, M. A. (2014). Best practices in classroom discipline. In P. Harrison & A. Thomas (Eds.), *Best practices in school psychology VI: Student-level services* (pp. 251–267). Bethesda, MD: National Association of School Psychologists.

9. The best answer is ***d***. Although all answers can be increased through these interventions, students with trouble self-regulating benefit the most from these external interventions. Students with executive functioning difficulties struggle with self-regulation, and interventions to help these students fall along a continuum, depending on the severity.

   Reference: McCloskey, G., Perkins, L., & Van Divner, B. (2009). *Assessment and intervention for executive function difficulties*. New York, NY: Routledge.

10. The best answer is ***e***. Stimulants, antidepressants, and alpha-2 adrenergic medications can be used to manage the behaviors associated with ADHD. It is important to note that the same medication will not work for all students and it may take time to find the correct medication and dosage for each student. The student's teacher(s), school nurse, parent(s)/guardian(s), school psychologist, and physician(s) should have an open dialogue about changes in behavior, mood, and affect when a student is taking medication.

    Reference: Hale, J. B., Semrud-Clikeman, M., & Kubas, H. A. (2014). Best practices in medication treatment for children with emotional and behavioral disorders: A primer for school psychologists. In P. Harrison & A. Thomas (Eds.), *Best practices in school psychology VI: Systems-level services* (pp. 347–360). Bethesda, MD: National Association of School Psychologists.

11. The best answer is ***c***. For students having difficulty developing peer relationships, creating a counseling group is the most beneficial. In the group, students can learn social skills, practice with other members of the group, and receive feedback from the group facilitator and group members before generalizing the skills with peers. After generalization, the students can evaluate the effectiveness and make changes, if necessary.

    Reference: Frey, J. R., Elliott, S. N., & Miller, C. F. (2014). Best practices in social skills training. In P. Harrison & A. Thomas (Eds.), *Best practices in school psychology VI: Student-level services* (pp. 213–224). Bethesda, MD: National Association of School Psychologists.

12. The best answer is ***a***. Cognitive academic language proficiency (CALP) is the advanced stage for second language acquisition and takes approximately five to seven years to develop, possibly longer. Alex has reached this stage because he has been in the United States for six years and has developed the ability to communicate with clarity and efficiency. He is also able to hold in-depth conversations with friends about topics requiring specific terminology, which means he has progressed from option *c*, beginning fluent, which is a component of CALP.

    Reference: Ortiz, S. O. (2004). *Comprehensive assessment of culturally and linguistically diverse students: A systematic, practical approach for nondiscriminatory assessment* [PDF file]. Retrieved from www.nasponline.org/resources/culturalcompetence/ortiz.pdf

13. The best answer is ***c***. The intervention plan was developed to have Connor receiving the Wilson Reading System for 60 minutes, five times a week. With the reading specialist changing the amount of time and days Connor is receiving the intervention, the true effectiveness of the intervention cannot be determined. As a result, the reading specialist compromised treatment integrity as the intervention was not implemented as planned to determine its effectiveness.

    Reference: Upah, K. (2008). Best practices in designing, implementing, and evaluating quality interventions. In A. Thomas & J. Grimes (Eds.), *Best practices in school psychology V* (pp. 209–203). Bethesda, MD: National Association of School Psychologists.

14. The best answer is ***b***. By using the interventions of working with a partner, practicing, and rehearsing, Mrs. Rodriguez is helping Samantha with anxiety. Along with the mentioned interventions, Mrs. Rodriguez is also using in vivo desensitization, where Samantha is addressing her anxiety in a real situation, acting in a scene in front of the class.

    Reference: Huberty, T. J. (2014). Best practices in school-based interventions for anxiety and depression. In P. Harrison & A. Thomas (Eds.), *Best practices in school psychology VI: Student-level services* (pp. 349–363). Bethesda, MD: National Association of School Psychologists.

15. The best answer is ***d***. NASP's Principles for Professional Ethics states that a school psychologist is obligated to share confidential information when a student requests for it to be disclosed, it is determined that the student may be at risk of hurting him- or herself or others, or there is a legal obligation to testify in court.

Reference: Jacob, S. (2014). Best practices in ethical school psychological practice. In P. Harrison & A. Thomas (Eds.), *Best practices in school psychology VI: Foundations* (pp. 437–448). Bethesda, MD: National Association of School Psychologists.

Chapter 7

Direct and Indirect Services for Children, Families, and Schools (System-Level Services)

Chapter 7 focuses on the broad area of *Direct and Indirect Services to Children, Families, and Schools* (System-Level Services). This category is divided into three topics: (1) *School-Wide Practices to Promote Learning*; (2) *Preventive and Responsive Services*; and (3) *Family-School Collaboration Services.*

The authors first provide an introduction to and description of the three topics. Next, there is a series of graphic organizers that outline the *content knowledge* in these three areas. Finally, there are 15 sample questions on this category, with correct answers and rationale included.

School-Wide Practices to Promote Learning

School-Wide Practices to Promote Learning refer to an understanding of school systems as a whole, with an emphasis on the school systems' structure and organization. Included are evidence-based practices implemented within the school system to promote learning and mental health, within both a general education and a special education setting. An understanding of the role of technology within these school-wide practices is also necessary.

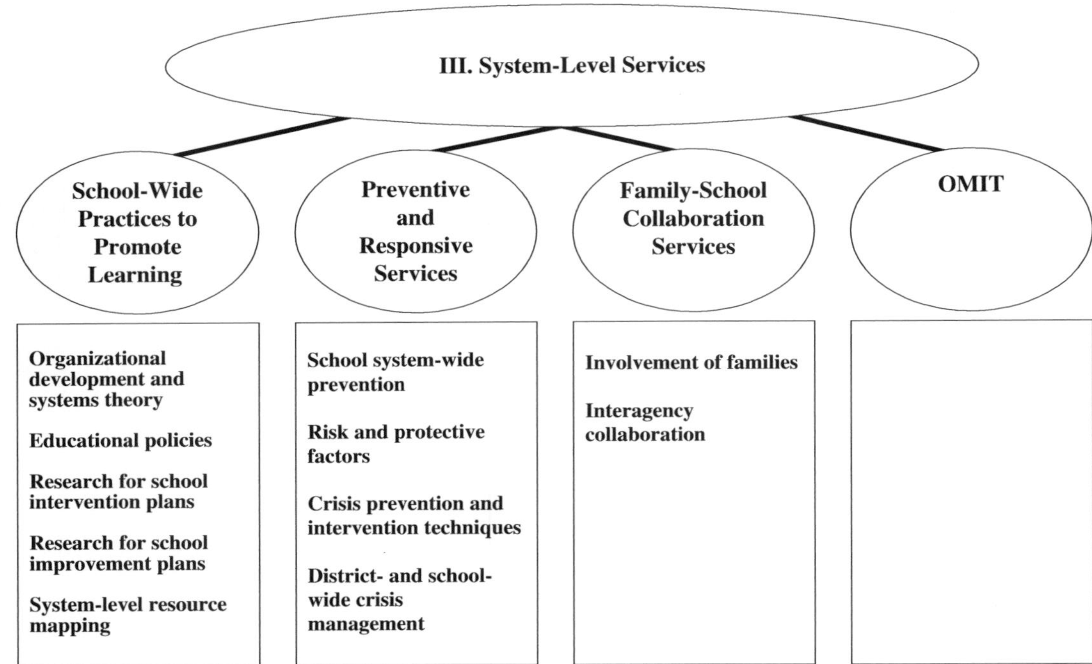

Figure 7.1
Direct and Indirect Services for Children, Families, and Schools (System-Level Services)

Graphic Organizers for School-Wide Practices to Promote Learning

TABLE 7.1
Graphic Organizer for Organizational Development and Systems Theory

System-Level Services: SWPPL

Organizational Development and Systems Theory

Organizational Chart of School District	Limitations of Organizational Chart	Other	Other
• Shows Board of Education members, superintendent, directors, supervisors, specialty teams or groups, and teachers • Line: direct relationship between superior and subordinate • Lateral: relationship between different departments on same hierarchical level • Staff: relationship between supervisor and other areas • Functional: relationship between specialist positions and other areas	• Only shows formal relationships and tells nothing of pattern of social relationships that develop • Shows nothing about managerial style adopted (autocratic or democratic) • Best type of structure varies from district to district—e.g., size of district		

TABLE 7.1 (Continued)
Graphic Organizer for Organizational Development and Systems Theory

System-Level Services: SWPPL

Organizational Development and Systems Theory

1. Problem Identification	2. Problem Analysis Stage	3. Intervention Stage	4. Evaluation Stage
Involve actions that help to: • operationally define the referred problem (individual or organizational) • specify the goals of the consultation, problem solving, and/or planning process • begin to verify the existence and extent of the problem and to generate hypotheses to explain why the problem is occurring	Involves actions such as: • a full investigation of the referred and operationalized problem in all of its ecological, organizational, situational, and behavioral contexts • the generation of hypotheses to explain the problem; hypotheses are assessed and confirmed or rejected • identification and development of interventions related to the confirmed hypotheses; concurrent evaluation of potential acceptability, social validity, treatment integrity, and generalizability of intervention	Includes: • the development of the organization and its members' capacity to implement the intervention plan • the identification of criteria to determine whether the intervention has been successful • the methods to evaluate this success and an estimate of the amount of time needed to begin to see success • the implementation of the intervention is necessary to increase its effectiveness or to respond to unexpected outcomes	Includes evaluation of: • formative and summative factors to determine if goals of the problem-solving process and the intervention have been met • how the implementation process was qualitatively perceived • how long the intervention should be continued and if there needs to be changes • the degree to which the organization and its members should independently continue the interventions and whether ongoing consultation is needed

TABLE 7.2
Graphic Organizer for Educational Policies

System-Level Services: SWPPL

Educational Policies

Social Promotion	High-Stakes Testing	High-Stakes Testing (continued)	High-Stakes Testing (continued)
• The promotion of students to higher grades based on age rather than demonstrated academic accomplishment • Opposed by President George Bush (1988) and Gov. Bill Clinton due to their concerns with promoting students who did not demonstrate adequate proficiency • Preceded a *Nation at Risk,* which addressed issues related to equal educational opportunity and placed accountability for student achievement in schools	Low stakes - consequences not directly tied to individuals involved in assessment Medium stakes - consequences directly tied to assessment stakeholders, but effects delayed or nonspecific High stakes - consequences directly tied to stakeholders and have major significance for their lives	Testing common themes: • low-scoring schools lose autonomy, gain or maintain funding • high-scoring schools gain praise, autonomy, and sometimes funding • schools always the unit of state analysis • more consequences for students then adults Intended outcomes: • Monitoring makes students, educators, parents accountable for student learning, thus provokes stronger efforts	Unintended outcomes: • curricular narrowing • scholastic demoralization • student discouragement • corruption • cheating, providing answers

TABLE 7.2 (Continued)
Graphic Organizer for Educational Policies

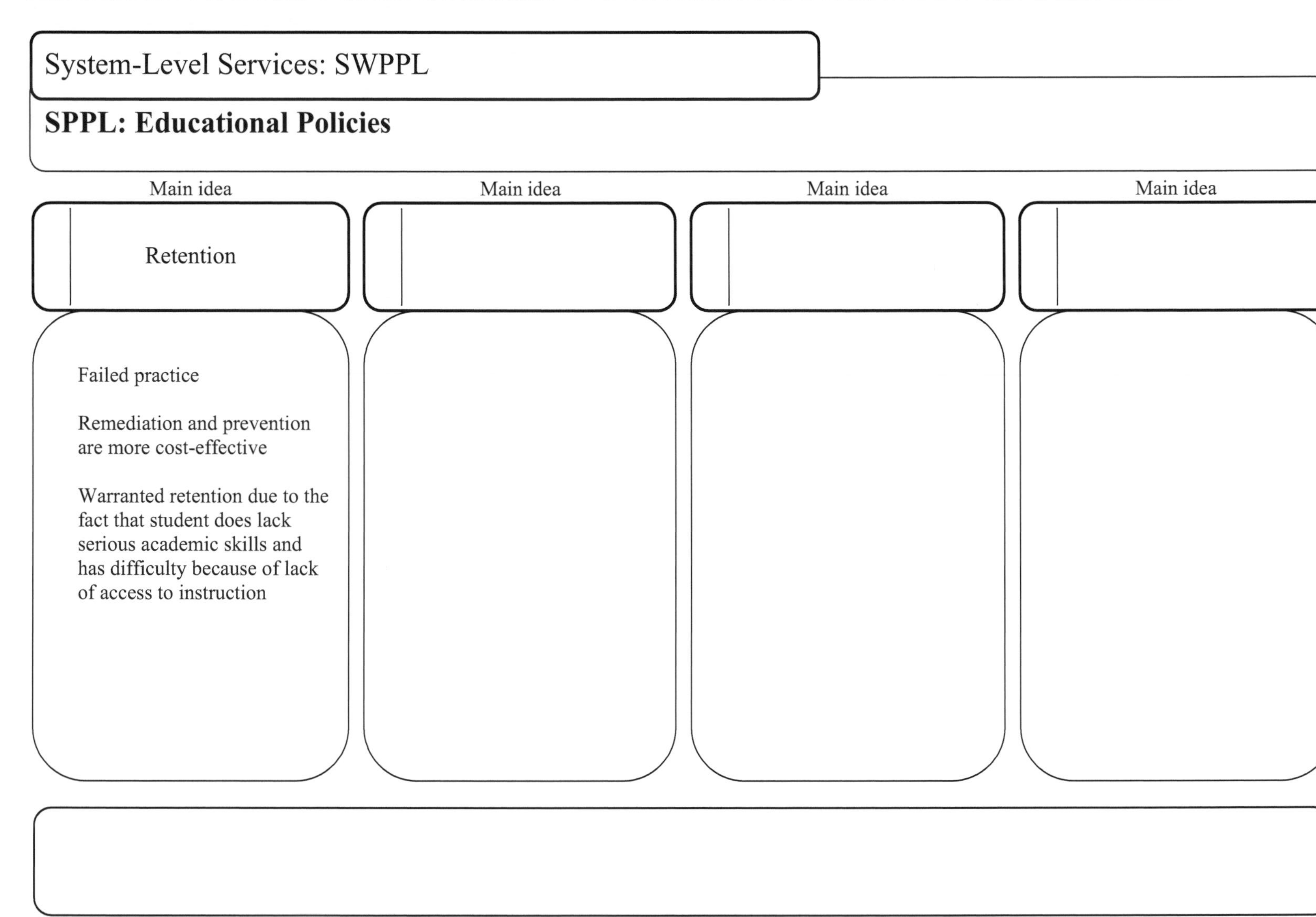

TABLE 7.3
Graphic Organizer for Research for School Intervention Plans

System-Level Services: SWPPL

Research for School Intervention Plans

Designing and Implementing Interventions	Monitoring Interventions	Evaluating Learning Outcomes	Treatment Integrity and Fidelity
• Identify and define problem • Collect baseline data o what are current levels o measure in natural setting • Generate hypothesis • Develop/carry out an intervention plan to resolve the problem • Goal setting o intended outcome of intervention, extent to which behavior is to be changed • Intervention plan development o described procedures to be used during intervention • Decision-making plan o how decisions will be made throughout intervention	• Must determine if intervention is working and any changes that need to be made • Need frequent and repeated progress monitoring • Data collected over time can be used to create an illustration of trends in performance • Progress-monitoring process must be put into place to evaluate the plan's effectiveness • If no improvement, make adjustments to intervention	• Summarize information about performance providing continuous feedback on progress toward goals • Provide a measure of professional accountability demonstrating how change is functionally related to intervention being implemented Formative evaluation - occurs throughout implementation of intervention to determine success so it can be modified/changed to increase achievement of goals Summative evaluation - occurs after intervention is completed to determine if intervention was successful and produced positive student outcomes	Integrity: Intervention needs to be implemented as planned in order to determine its effectiveness o observation of teacher to ensure steps are being carried out o write a step-by-step plan as a checklist Fidelity: How accurately or faithfully a program (or intervention) is reproduced from a manual, protocol, or model

TABLE 7.4
Graphic Organizers for Research for School Improvement Plans

System-Level Services: SWPPL

Research for School Improvement Plans

Components of School Improvement Plan	Components of School Improvement Plan (continued)	Phases of Strategic Planning	Other
Layer One: Identifies critical components of the effective school and schooling process Sections include: • Student academic achievement supported by curriculum • Student social, emotional, and behavioral development supported by classroom management • Multitiered academic and behavioral supports for at-risk students • School-wide professional development • School and administrative initiatives and supports • Parent and community training and support	Layer Two: Reflects a planning and execution template Sections include: • Goals or targets • Evidence-based methods • Sequence of activities needed to implement the support • Personnel needed to implement initiative • Resources needed • How implementation will be evaluated	Phase 1: Assessing organizational readiness/needs assessments and audits Phase 2: Writing the school improvement plan Phase 3: Establishing the infrastructure to implement the school improvement plan Phase 4: Implementing, monitoring, and evaluating the school improvement plan Phase 5: Reviewing, retooling, and renewing the school improvement plan	

TABLE 7.5
Graphic Organizers for System-Level Resource Mapping

System-Level Services: SWPPL

System-Level Resource Mapping

Purpose	Steps	Personnel	Programs/Services
Visual representation of resources and gaps Process for collecting and analyzing Mode of information sharing Starting point for comprehensive and effective partnerships Identify school and community resources and barriers	Identify resources available in school How well are resources coordinated and integrated? Which programs and activities could be enhanced? What is missing and where is the capacity to fill these gaps?	Who is at your school and in the community? What do they do? • Title? • Function? • Projects? • Hidden assets? Ways of communicating? When and to whom are they available?	What are the existing programs and services? What do they do? • Title? • Function? • Population served? What resources does this service utilize? How effective is this program/service at addressing needs? What are the gaps in programming/services?

Preventive and Responsive Services

Preventive and Responsive Services in general refer to what we formerly considered to be crisis prevention, intervention, and response. Now from a broader perspective, this area encompasses school psychologists' knowledge of research related to wellness (i.e., resilience and risk factors in learning and mental health), the services within the school and community to support multitiered prevention and intervention, and evidence-based strategies for effective crisis response.

Graphic Organizers for Preventive and Responsive Services

TABLE 7.6
Graphic Organizer for School System-Wide Prevention

System-Level Services: P and RS

School System-Wide Prevention

Positive School Climate	Positive Behavior Support (PBS)	Bullying Prevention	Program and School Reform
• Uses cooperative learning strategies • Has programs addressing violence or bullying • Takes a problem-solving approach • Establishes cross-grade-level partnerships • Holds weekly school meetings • Seeks student feedback	• Enhances the capacity of schools to teach students positive behaviors • Teaches pro-social behaviors • Tertiary interventions: specific and highly specialized support (e.g., FBA or BIP) • Secondary interventions: targeted or specialized for students who require more intensive supports (e.g., mentoring or tutoring) • Primary interventions: universal interventions and supports that will establish a vision for the entire school environment	• Intensive individual interventions provide bullies and victims with individual support through meetings with students and parents, counseling, and support • Early interventions target specific risk factors and teach positive behavior and critical thinking skills at the classroom level, including lessons and discussions • School-wide value systems based on caring, respect, and personal responsibility; positive discipline and supports; clearly defined expectations and consequences reduce the incidences of bullying	• New staff must receive training and become participants • New parents must be involved and encouraged • Veteran staff/parents must be continually encouraged to maintain the focus on sustaining healthy psychological development and high levels of academic performance

TABLE 7.7
Graphic Organizers for Risk and Protective Factors

System-Level Services: P and RS

Risk and Protective Factors

School Failure, Truancy, and Dropout	School Failure, Truancy, and Dropout (continued)	Suicide	Suicide (continued)
Risk factors Student: High rates of absences Behavior problems Poor academic performance Grade retention Employed Family: Low educational expectations Frequent changes in schools due to family moves Permissive parenting styles School: Weak adult authority Large school size High pupil-teacher ratios Few caring relationships with staff Poor or uninteresting curricula Low expectations and high rates of truancy	Protective factors Student: Completes homework Comes to class prepared High locus of control Good self-concept Expectations for school completion Family: Academic support Motivational support Parental monitoring School: Orderly school environment Committed, caring teachers Fair discipline policies	Risk factors Gender Involvement in bullying Previous suicide attempts Psychological disorder Substance abuse disorder Family history of suicide Family violence Sexual orientation Socially isolated	Protective factors High self-esteem Peer and family support Resilience Trustworthy relationships with adults Positive attitude about seeking help from staff Actively engaged in school

TABLE 7.8
Graphic Organizer for Crisis Prevention and Intervention

System-Level Services: Preventive and Responsive Services

Crisis Prevention and Intervention

Role of School Psychologist	Crisis Prevention Techniques	Before the Crisis: Violence Prevention	Other
• Participate with the entire school staff in developing and implementing positive behavioral interventions that increase social skills and reduce aggressive behaviors • Help communities prepare for responses to crisis spawned by violence • Provide group process and consultation to help schools form effective safety and crisis planning teams • Counsel victims of violence of all forms	• Positive school environments typically have lower levels of violence • Factors linked to reduced violence in schools: o educational environments that promote positive academic and social success o positive relationships among students and teachers o community support and involvement o involving students in conflict resolution, social problem solving, and anger management programs	• Develop and implement mentoring programs • Teach social and adaptive skills • Improve environmental factors • Intervene with at-risk students • Maintain an active level of involvement with staff, students, and parents	

TABLE 7.9
Graphic Organizer for District- and School-Wide Crisis Management

System-Level Services: P and RS

District- and School-Wide Crisis Management

Planning System-Wide Crisis Management Programs	During the Crisis	Crisis Counseling	NOVA Model
• Form building and district teams • Select and train team members • Prepare materials and "ready" files; prepare an emergency box • Develop emergency signals • Evacuation plans should include teachers taking their class rolls and being able to account for each student in their class • Hold crisis drills	• During the crisis: o organize a supervised area for students o share information as it becomes available o hold faculty meetings to share information o develop plans and provide guidance as needed • After the crisis: o provide opportunities for students/faculty to talk o do not underestimate the impact of the incident	• Everyone needs time to process the experience within 24–36 hours after the event • It is beneficial for traumatized individuals to know what to expect and to know how to best confront them • Psychological first aid o make contact with the victim and give him/her permission to express thoughts and emotions o explore problems in terms of the past, present, and future o identify possible solutions to assist the victim o take definite actions to assist the victim o provide follow-up assistance	• Victims are asked to remember where they were when they first became aware of the tragedy • What were the accompanying thoughts and feelings? • What are they worried about in the near future? • What previously helped them when bad things occurred in their lives and what or who has provided some comfort now?

Family-School Collaboration Services

School psychologists have knowledge regarding the beneficial outcomes of family-school collaboration, including research related to family systems, strengths, needs, and culture. Included in this area are practices and methods that foster communication between home, school, and community agencies with sensitivity and appreciation for diverse characteristics.

Graphic Organizers for Family-School Collaboration Services

TABLE 7.10
Graphic Organizers for Involvement of Family

System Level Services: FSC

Involvement of Families

Promoting Family Engagement	Creating Connections Between Home and School	Understanding Barriers	Other
Convey genuineness/sincerity Build trust Convey respect Engage in effective, bidirectional communication Collaborate and partner Help parents and families recognize themselves as resources and use them as resources	Provide context for parents to feel empowered Negotiate roles and responsibilities Create spirit of cooperation Take parents' perspectives Make school welcoming and family-friendly	• Common to families of various cultures and socioeconomic status is an innate desire to support their children's learning and success at school • Parents engage in multiple forms of involvement spanning home, school, and community contexts • Parents are faced with personal stressors that can impede their involvement, yet often parents are resilient in maintaining involvement • Barriers that are likely to restrict involvement pertain to the demands and relevance of the opportunity as well as the parents' relationship with school personnel	

TABLE 7.11
Graphic Organizers for Interagency Collaboration

System-Level Services: FSC

Interagency Collaboration

School-Community Partnerships	Benefits of School-Community Partnerships	Barriers to School-Community Partnerships	Other
• Business corporations • Universities • Educational institutions • Government organizations • Military organizations • Healthcare organizations • Faith-based organizations • Volunteer groups • National service groups • Senior citizens' organizations • Cultural institutions • Recreational institutions	• Gains in academic achievement • Better access to mental health and health services • Greater parental involvement • Increased student attendance • Decreased number of suspensions • Increased teacher satisfaction • Reductions in rates of substance abuse, teen pregnancy, and disruptive behavior • Upgraded facilities, new resources, and new funding for new programs and family supports	• Participation • Time commitment • Identification of community partners • Leadership • Funding • Communication • Focus	

Sample Questions for Direct and Indirect Services for Children, Families, and Schools (System-Level Services)

1. The school psychologist is conducting a functional behavioral assessment. Which of the following is an example of direct assessment?
   a. Systematic observations of the individual within natural settings
   b. Record review
   c. Behavior analytic rating scales
   d. Behavior analytic interviews
   e. None of the above

2. Kareem, a second grader, has learned how to initiate play through watching and modeling other children in his classroom. Kareem is learning social skills through what model?
   a. Psychosocial development theory
   b. Social learning theory
   c. Behaviorist theory
   d. Systems theory
   e. Psychosexual development theory

3. The following are all components of positive behavior support (PBS) EXCEPT:
   a. Grouping students into enrichment clusters to increase academic interest
   b. Meeting with staff to review specific behavior referrals
   c. Developing a unified system to rank behaviors by means of severity
   d. Incorporating academic and behavior instruction into classroom lessons
   e. Strengthening behavior using tangible and nontangible reinforcers

4. Maurice is a school psychologist who used to be optimistic and very proactive at work. Recently he has become cynical toward his clients and "blames the victims" for their own difficulties. Maurice is most likely experiencing which form of the developmental model of burnout?
   a. Interpersonal struggle
   b. Emotional exhaustion
   c. Chronic stomach pains
   d. Depersonalization
   e. Reduced ambiguity

5. A school administration may develop an organizational chart representing a school district for all of the following reasons EXCEPT:
   a. To demonstrate direct relationships between superior and subordinate staff members
   b. To demonstrate relationships between specialist positions and other areas
   c. To provide a visual map of leadership to parents and community members
   d. To demonstrate the pattern of social relationships developed within the district
   e. To provide a visual of departmental interaction within the district

6. A school committee is in the process of identifying and adopting a new school-wide intervention program. Evaluating the quality of the evidence related to this intervention, the committee finds that the research studies consistently present a difference between the control and trial groups, but the size of this difference is not reported. The committee's finding represents a concern with:
   a. Internal validity
   b. External validity

c. Construct validity
d. Conclusion validity
e. Face validity

7. Which of the following statements is NOT true regarding an implementer's acceptability of a proposed intervention?
   a. Acceptability is higher when the description of the intervention presented to potential implementers is plain.
   b. Acceptability is higher when interventions address more severe behaviors rather than milder behavior issues.
   c. Acceptability is higher when potential implementers are not required to take part in the planning of intervention.
   d. Acceptability is higher when effectiveness of intervention is presented to potential implementers.
   e. All of the above.

8. In family-school collaboration the ______________ is the person who has the most empowerment in the decision-making process.
   a. Parent
   b. School psychologist
   c. Student
   d. Teacher
   e. All of the above

9. When collaborating with families, the foundation of working together efficiently is to:
   a. Allow the parent/guardian to make the final decision
   b. Meet with the parents/guardians without the student
   c. Avoid conflict
   d. Build a trustworthy relationship between the school and family
   e. All the above

10. All of the following are appropriate to say when delivering negative information EXCEPT:
   a. Johnny's behaviors are unacceptable for his age; he is out of control.
   b. I know this might be a lot to take in, Mrs. B. What are your reactions so far?
   c. Johnny received detention because his teacher, Ms. Smith, saw him open his textbook during the exam and when he was asked to put the textbook away, he placed it in the trash can and walked out of the classroom.
   d. We believe that we can resolve this problem together and help Johnny succeed.
   e. All of the above.

11. According to NASP's *Model for School Psychologists' Services* Domain 6, school psychologists have knowledge of principles and research related to resilience and risk factors in learning and mental health, services in schools and communities to support ______________, and ______________ strategies for effective crisis response.
   a. Multitiered prevention and evidence-based
   b. Families and evidence-based
   c. Counseling and evidence-based
   d. Collaboration and evidence-based
   e. None of the above

12. According to the NASP's *PREPaRE* model, which of the following characterize a crisis:
   a. Is unexpected and often unpredictable
   b. Overwhelms ordinary resources for coping
   c. Comes in all shapes and sizes
   d. Requires advance preparation to respond to effectively
   e. All of the above

13. The roles of the school psychologist in crisis prevention and intervention include all of the following EXCEPT:
    a. Participating with the entire school staff in developing and implementing positive behavioral interventions
    b. Helping communities respond to a crisis spawned by violence
    c. Providing group process and consultation to help schools form effective safety and crisis planning teams
    d. Becoming the rescuer
    e. Counseling victims of violence of all types

14. A second-grade student, Matthew, is referred to the problem-solving team at the beginning of the third marking period due to difficulties in reading. As a result, an intervention is implemented to address these concerns. A progress monitoring tool is utilized to assess the effectiveness of the intervention. The teacher, collaborating with the school psychologist, also conducts periodic functional assessments to monitor his progress. At the end of the school year the teacher discusses the techniques used, analyzes the data collected, and determines the overall effectiveness of the intervention. This is an example of:
    a. Formative evaluation
    b. Consumer-oriented evaluation
    c. Treatment integrity evaluation
    d. Summative evaluation
    e. Participant-oriented evaluation

15. The philosophy that states that students should be promoted to higher grades based on age rather than academic accomplishment is known as what?
    a. Accountability
    b. Social production
    c. Tracking
    d. Social attainment
    e. Social promotion

Answers With Rationale

1. The best answer is ***a***. It is the only choice that is an example of a direct climate measure. Climate surveys, questionnaires, interviews, and focus groups are all direct measures. The other choices are examples of indirect measures.

    Reference: Steege, M. W., & Scheib, M. A. (2014). Best practices in conducting functional behavioral assessments. In P. Harrison & A. Thomas (Eds.), *Best practices in school psychology VI: Data-based and collaborative decision making* (pp. 273–286). Bethesda, MD: National Association of School Psychologists.

2. The best answer is ***b***. Social learning theory explains that behavior change is influenced by observing another person's behavior.

    Reference: Forman, S. G., Lubin, A. R., & Tripptree, A. L. (2014). Best practices in implementing evidence-based school interventions. In P. Harrison & A. Thomas (Eds.), *Best practices in school psychology VI: Systems-level services* (pp. 43–55). Bethesda, MD: National Association of School Psychologists.

3. The best answer is ***a***. It is a strategy that could be used by schools, but it is not part of the positive behavior support model. The other choices are components of PBS that should be implemented if a school is following the PBS model.

    Reference: Reschly, A. L., Appleton, J. J., & Pohl, A. (2014). Best practices in fostering student engagement. In P. Harrison & A. Thomas (Eds.), *Best practices in school psychology VI: Student-level services* (pp. 37–50). Bethesda, MD: National Association of School Psychologists.

4. The best answer is ***d***. Depersonalization is experienced through negative, detached responses to clients. Interpersonal struggle is a part of burnout, but not a developmental model. Emotional exhaustion is when one feels emotionally depleted and often reduces one's involvement with coworkers or clients. Chronic stomach pains relate to physical problems that could stem from burnout, but they are not part of the developmental model of burnout. Reduced ambiguity is an organizational risk factor, but not in the developmental model of burnout. It refers to a lack of clarity of job role and responsibility, privileges, status, objectives, and so forth.

   Reference: Codding, R. S., Hagermoser Sanetti, L. M., & DiGennaro Reed, F. D. (2014). Best practices in facilitating consultation and collaboration with teachers and administrators. In P. Harrison & A. Thomas (Eds.), *Best practices in school psychology VI: Data-based and collaborative decision making* (pp. 525–539). Bethesda, MD: National Association of School Psychologists.

5. The correct answer is ***d***. Organizational charts display only formal relationships and cannot speak to the social relationships that have informally developed within a district. Also, organizational charts can be used to convey information to many different interested parties. While staff members may be interested in the chain of command as it directly relates to them, community members and parents may be interested in how these "checks and balances" are used to protect their community and their children. A parent can use this chart to determine the appropriate contact for a concern at hand.

   Reference: Cordeiro, P. A., & Cunningham, W. G. (2013). *Educational leadership: A bridge to improved practice* (5th ed.). New York, NY: Pearson Education.

6. The correct answer is ***d***. Conclusion validity refers to the degree to which reported results are true findings or chance findings. In contrast, internal validity refers to whether a reported outcome of a study was the result of the intervention or an alternative factor. External validity refers to whether a study occurred in a setting that is similar to the proposed practice context. Construct validity refers to the extent to which the measure used actually measures the target behaviors of interest. Face validity refers to the degree to which an assessment or test subjectively appears to measure the variable or construct that it is supposed to measure.

   Reference: Forman, S. G., & Burke, C. R. (2008). Best practices in selecting and implementing evidence-based school interventions. In A. Thomas & J. Grimes (Eds.), *Best practices in school psychology V* (pp. 799–811). Bethesda, MD: National Association of School Psychologists.

7. The correct answer is ***c***. Potential implementers are more likely to accept an intervention and be supportive of its proceedings if they are involved in the selection and planning process.

   Reference: Forman, S. G., & Burke, C. R. (2008). Best practices in selecting and implementing evidence-based school interventions. In A. Thomas & J. Grimes (Eds.), *Best practices in school psychology V* (pp. 799–811). Bethesda, MD: National Association of School Psychologists.

8. The correct answer is ***e***, all of the above. In family-school collaboration, all participants are equals and share power and decision making.

   Reference: Esler, A. N., Godber, Y., & Christenson, S. L. (2008). Best practices in supporting school-family partnerships. In A. Thomas & J. Grimes (Eds.), *Best practices in school psychology V* (pp. 917–936). Bethesda, MD: National Association of School Psychologists.

9. The correct answer is ***d***, build a trustworthy relationship between the school and family. Relationships with families should help make them feel welcomed and motivated to work as partners in education. Option *a* is incorrect because all members should be equals and share decision making. Option *b* is incorrect because it is encouraged for the student to participate, and the student will gain benefits from the experience. Option *c* is incorrect because conflict should not be ignored. Conflict helps with group cohesion, and prevents the issue from "building up" and potentially becoming a larger issue in the future. Therefore, the answer could not be *e* (all of the above).

   Reference: Esler, A. N., Godber, Y., & Christenson, S. L. (2008). Best practices in supporting school-family partnerships. In A. Thomas & J. Grimes (Eds.), *Best practices in school psychology V* (pp. 917–936). Bethesda, MD: National Association of School Psychologists.

10. The correct answer is ***a***, because it includes negative judgment. Option *b* is appropriate because you should ask for a reaction. Option ***c*** is appropriate because it is clear and specific. Option *d* is appropriate because it conveys confidence that the problem can be solved. Option *e* is wrong because the correct answer is *a*.

    Reference: Eckert, T. L., Russo, N., & Hier, B. O. (2014). Best practices in school psychologists' promotion of effective collaboration and communication among school professionals. In P. Harrison & A. Thomas (Eds.), *Best practices in school psychology VI: Data-based and collaborative decision making* (pp. 541–551). Bethesda, MD: National Association of School Psychologists.

11. The correct answer is ***a***. According to NASP's *Model for School Psychologists' Services* Domain 6, school psychologist have knowledge of principles and research related to resilience and risk factors in learning and mental health, services in schools and communities to support multitiered prevention, and evidence-based strategies for effective crisis response.

    Reference: Brock, S. E., Louvar Reeves, M. A., & Nickerson, A. B. (2014). Best practices in school crisis intervention. In P. Harrison & A. Thomas (Eds.), *Best practices in school psychology VI: Systems-level services* (pp. 211–230). Bethesda, MD: National Association of School Psychologists.

12. Option ***e***, all of the above, is the correct answer. A crisis is unexpected and often unpredictable, and it comes in all shapes and sizes. A crisis often overwhelms ordinary resources for coping. This is why advanced preparation is essential.

    Reference: Brock, S. E., Louvar Reeves, M. A., & Nickerson, A. B. (2014). Best practices in school crisis intervention. In P. Harrison & A. Thomas (Eds.), *Best practices in school psychology VI: Systems-level services* (pp. 211–230). Bethesda, MD: National Association of School Psychologists.

13. Option ***d*** is the correct answer. According to the PREPaRE Model, crisis responders are trained to respond to the need to nurture but be wary of becoming a rescuer on whom victims become dependent.

    Reference: Brock, S. E., Louvar Reeves, M. A., & Nickerson, A. B. (2014). Best practices in school crisis intervention. In P. Harrison & A. Thomas (Eds.), *Best practices in school psychology VI: Systems-level services* (pp. 211–230). Bethesda, MD: National Association of School Psychologists.

14. The best answer is ***d***. Summative evaluation occurs after an intervention is completed to determine if the intervention was successful and produced positive student outcomes.

    Reference: Gibbons, K., & Brown, S. (2014). Best practices in evaluating psychoeducational services based on student outcome data. In P. Harrison & A. Thomas (Eds.), *Best practices in school psychology VI: Foundations* (pp. 355–369). Bethesda, MD: National Association of School Psychologists.

15. The best answer is ***e***. Social promotion was a philosophy that was opposed by Presidents George Bush (1988) and Bill Clinton, which led to *A Nation at Risk*, which made schools accountable for student achievement and allowed for equal educational opportunities.

    Reference: Rafoth, M. A., & Parker, S. W. (2014). Preventing academic failure and promoting alternatives to retention. In P. Harrison & A. Thomas (Eds.), *Best practices in school psychology VI: Student-level services* (pp. 143–155). Bethesda, MD: National Association of School Psychologists.

Chapter 8

Foundations of School Psychological Service Delivery

Chapter 8 covers the areas considered within the broad category of *Foundations of School Psychological Service Delivery*. This area includes core underpinnings of the practice of school psychology: *Diversity in Development and Learning*; *Research and Program Evaluation*; and *Legal, Ethical, and Professional Practice*. As in the preceding chapters, you will encounter an explanation of the category, *Foundations of School Psychological Services*, and a graphic organizer that will provide an overview of the content, followed by a series of graphic organizers that outline the content knowledge covered on the Praxis Exam in School Psychology. Fifteen sample questions with answers and rationale are also included. While you are reviewing the key information outlined and answering the sample questions, you may want to add your own information to supplement what is provided.

Diversity in Development and Learning

The area of *Diversity in Development and Learning* focuses primarily on the child as a learner viewed from multiple perspectives. For example, cultural background (i.e., language, religion, ethnicity, race, sexual and gender orientation) is most often the first perspective many school psychologists consider. However, this area also addresses individual learning characteristics—for example, disabilities and abilities. An understanding of all of these components of diversity promotes the school psychologist's ability to develop interventions to support optimum learning and behavioral well-being of students. Assisting school psychologists in this process includes collaborating with cultural brokers and community liaisons to better understand the diverse characteristics of children. School psychologists first should become aware of their own personal biases and the biases of others in order to promote fairness and social justice for all programs and services provided to students.

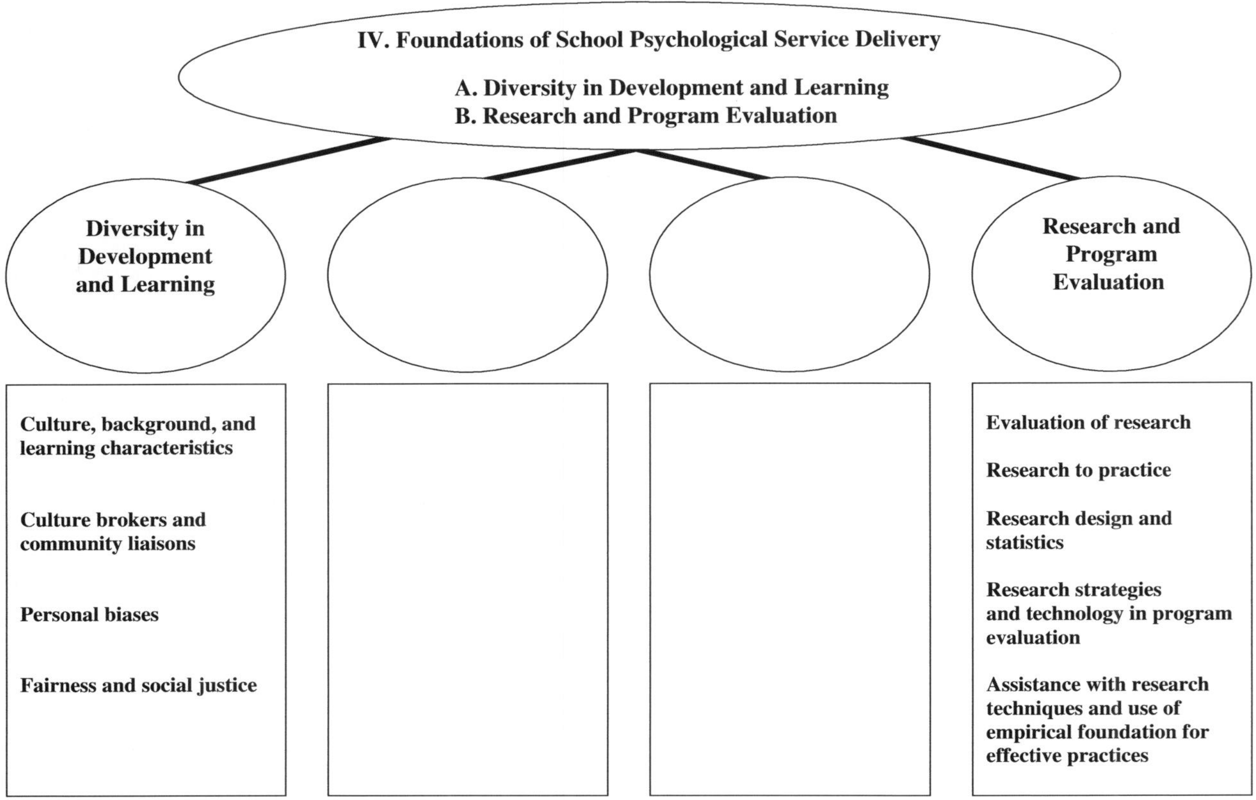

Figure 8.1
Foundations of School Psychological Service Delivery: Diversity in Development and Learning and Research and Program Evaluation

Graphic Organizers for Diversity in Development and Learning

TABLE 8.1
Graphic Organizer for Culture, Background, and Learning Characteristics

FSPSD: Diversity in Development and Learning

Culture, Background, and Learning Characteristics

Providing Culturally Responsive Interventions	Providing Culturally Responsive Interventions (continued)	Providing Culturally Responsive Interventions (continued)	Other
• Explore one's own culture, beliefs, and values • Strengthen cultural literacy through dialogue and learning • Believe in serving individuals of different race or ethnicity • Practice with multicultural intentionality • Develop knowledge of student culture through interaction with student and family • Apply microskills based on cultural norms and behaviors of student and family	• Develop resource list of professionals for consultation on multicultural issues • Work systematically • Believe that heterogeneity within an ethnic group exists but the foundation of cultural values may be homogenous • Be aware of culture-bound syndromes, behaviors, and symptoms and their meaning in relation to the culture of the student and family • Assess acculturation • Focus intervention around student acculturation style	• Involve the family in intervention planning, progress monitoring, and evaluation • Maintain a strengths-based perspective • Maintain cultural exploration throughout the intervention planning, implementing, and evaluating process	

TABLE 8.2
Graphic Organizer for Culture Brokers and Community Liaisons

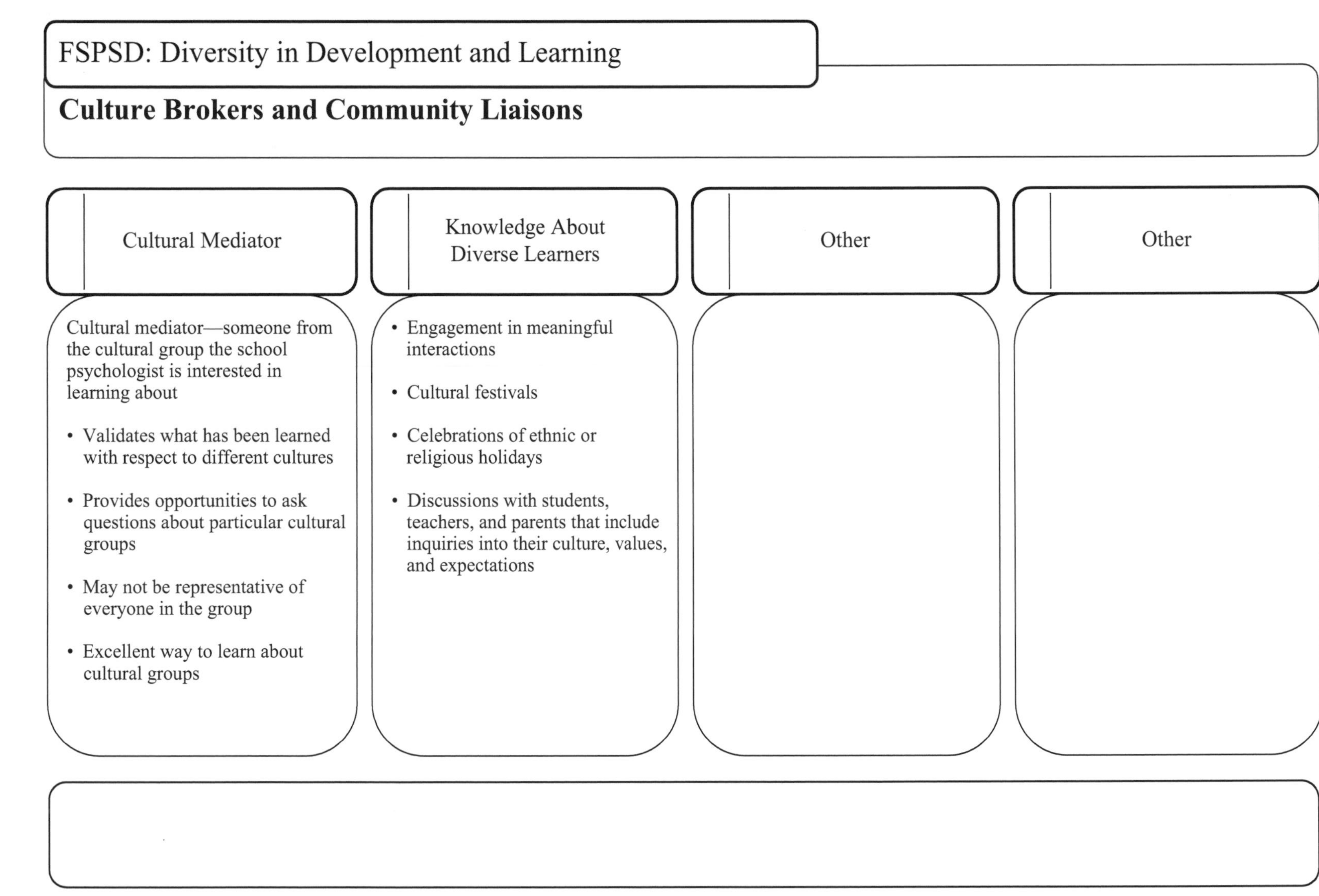

TABLE 8.3
Graphic Organizer for Personal Biases

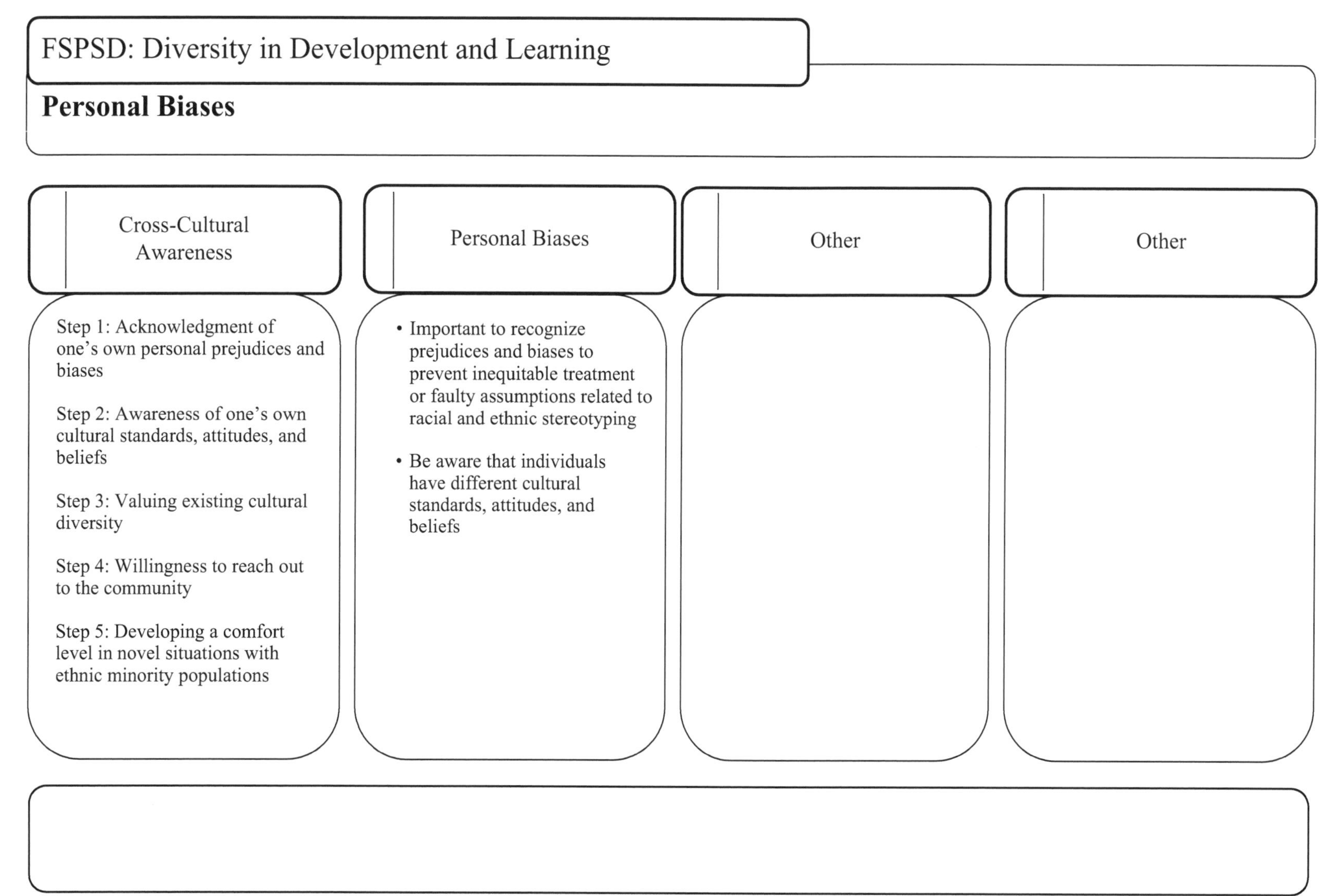

TABLE 8.4
Graphic Organizer for Fairness and Social Justice

FSPSD: Diversity in Development and Learning

Fairness and Social Justice

Promoting Fairness and Social Justice	Collaboration and Advocacy	Social Justice	Other
• Reflects right to be treated with respect and dignity • Equitable sharing of wealth and power • Strong grounding in ethics and the law • Cultivate school climate that is safe and welcoming to all regardless of actual or perceived characteristics	• Challenge institutional power structures • Advocacy is key activity for school psychologist to support social justice • Related to knowledge of best practices and the law • Advocacy to support children and families	• Are resources distributed equitably? • Do all students have a fair opportunity to learn and grow? • Are students being treated respectfully and in a nondiscriminatory manner?	

Research and Program Evaluation

Research and Program Evaluation emphasizes the importance of translating research into practice. In order to be able to accomplish this, you must be knowledgeable in the areas of research design, statistics, and assisting schools in using empirical foundations to develop programs at an individual, group, or systems level.

Graphic Organizers for Research and Program Evaluation

TABLE 8.5
Graphic Organizer for Evaluation of Research

FSPSD: Research and Program Evaluation

Evaluation of Research

Definition of Research	Steps to Evaluate Research	Understanding Research Design	Quality of Research
• Research is defined as activities to produce new scientific knowledge and to apply knowledge to improve school psychological practice • School psychologists' role in research: o Consumers: be competent consumers of research o Distributors: summarize research in order to draw conclusions from it for other interested groups o Conductors: perform research	1. Conceptual understanding of research methods 2. Ability to read carefully and skeptically 3. Knowledge and understanding of research design 4. Understanding of internal and external validity: o Are the internal features of research conducted well enough to have confidence in results? o Can the results be generalized or applied? o Is the article written well enough so reader can understand results?	• Purpose of representative sample • Random assignment of groups • Experimental design (manipulating independent variable; studying cause and effect relationship) • Non-experimental design (correlational; looks at associations between variables and not causality) • Statistical significance (probability that the results occurred by chance)	• Peer-reviewed journals (primary source of research) accept only a limited amount of research • Some research may not be up to par because: o Research problems are poorly conceived or trivial o Sample size is small or poorly selected o Use of inappropriate statistics o Mistakes made in calculating and reporting statistics o Weak research designs that do not rule out plausible alternative hypotheses o Research design does not fit the purpose of study or test the hypothesis o Conclusions are extended beyond what research can reasonably conclude o Discussions address different issues than study was designed for

TABLE 8.6
Graphic Organizer for Research to Practice

FSPSD: Research and Program Evaluation

Research to Practice

Evidence-Based Practice

"The term 'evidence-based practice' (EBP) refers to a body of scientific knowledge, defined usually by reference to research methods or designs, about a range of service practices (e.g., referral, assessment, case management, therapies, or support services)…The knowledge base is usually generated through application of particular inclusions criteria (e.g., type of design, types of outcome assessments) and it generally describes the impact of particular service practices on child, adolescent, or family outcomes. 'Evidence-based practice' or EBP is a shorthand term denoting the quality, robustness, or validity of scientific evidence as it is brought to bear on these issues."
~Hoagwood and Johnson, 2003

Interventions Backed by "Strong" Evidence

Studies that produce a high quality of evidence should:

- Clearly describe the intervention
- Provide information on how groups were assigned
- Provide information about whether there were any systematic differences between intervention and control groups prior to intervention
- Use "valid" outcome measures
- Report effect size, statistical tests to show significance of findings
- Report all findings, not just positive outcomes
- Utilize more than one site of implementation (sites should be typical school or community settings)

Applying Research to Practice

- Applied research is more easily translated into practice than highly theoretical research
- Both types can be translated into practice if there is an understanding of how and under what conditions a treatment would be useful
- NASP's *School Psychology Forum: Research in Practice* is a good resource to communicate and translate scholarly research into practical applications

Professional Development

- School psychologists should read research and attend research presentations in order to remain up-to-date
- School psychologists should read and evaluate research on their area of interest and several related topics

TABLE 8.7
Graphic Organizer for Research Design and Statistics

FSPSD: Research and Program Evaluation

Research Design and Statistics

Research Designs – Collecting Information	Quantitative Research	Descriptive Statistics	Statistical Comparison of Data
• Data can be collected from a variety of sources: direct observation, surveys, interviews, tests • Tests include scores from: 1) Standardized norm-referenced tests 2) Criterion-referenced tests 3) Curriculum performance standards competency tests • Quantitative research is characterized by use of statistical analysis. It has 3 basic purposes: 1) To describe 2) To compare 3) To attribute causality	• Quantitative research is considered to be objective; "scientific method" • Types of quantitative research: 1. Quantitative descriptive research—answers questions about variables' status through numerical descriptions 2. Comparative research—examines numerical descriptions of two or more variables and makes decisions about their differences or relationships 3. Experimental research—draws conclusions about influence of one or more variables on another	• Measures of central tendency: o **Mean**: arithmetic average o **Median**: middle score of group • Measure of variability: o **Standard deviation**: shows how alike or varied the group is	• Statistical procedures are used to determine whether a difference exists between or among groups • Statistical procedure used in comparative research is **correlation**: shows whether two or more variables have systematic relationships • **Significance** - Is the difference between variables significant or could it have occurred by chance?

TABLE 8.7 (Continued)
Graphic Organizer for Research Design and Statistics

FSPSD: Research and Program Evaluation

Research Design and Statistics

Experimental Research	Experimental Research (continued)	Analysis of Experimental Statistical Data	Qualitative Research
• Researchers set out to answer questions about causation • **Independent variable**: o Influencing variable o measurable human and nonhuman characteristics—e.g., age, intelligence, frequency of occurrence o Also called experimental variable or treatment variable	• **Dependent variable**: o Acted-upon variable o Variable being studied for possible change • **Control**: use of procedures by researchers to limit or account for possible influence of variables not being studied • **Randomization**: unbiased systematic selection or assignment of subjects	• After data are collected, means and standard deviations are calculated • Submit to statistical procedures: o One-variable studies often use ***t* test** to determine whether the difference between the means of the two groups on a dependent variable is significant o Multiple-variable research often uses **analysis of variance (ANOVA)** to determine if difference can be attributed to one or a combination of independent variables	• **Qualitative research** has roots in social sciences, especially anthropology and sociology • Terms: ethnographic and ethnologic research • Qualitative research is characterized by use of text (written words) to document variables and inductive analysis of the collected information

TABLE 8.8
Graphic Organizer for Research Strategies and Technology in Program Evaluation

FSPSD: Research and Program Evaluation

Research Strategies and Technology in Program Evaluation

Program Evaluation	Program Evaluation Logic	Progress Monitoring	Technology
Program evaluation is defined as the systematic collection of information about outcomes of programs in order to: • Determine the program's effectiveness • Improve the program's effectiveness • Inform decisions about future programming	Steps: 1. Establish criteria 2. Construct standards 3. Measure performance and compare with standards 4. Synthesize and integrate evidence into a judgment of worth 5. Make recommendations	• Use empirical foundations for effective practices at individual, group, and systems levels • Incorporate: o Data collection repeatedly over time o Valid, reliable, and accurate measurement o Analysis with emphasis on careful inspection of overlap of data points between conditions o Accountability o Systematic replication and control of independent variables	• Facilitate and guide data-driven decision-making process • Making data available • Powerful reporting can be accomplished using: o Spreadsheet software o Relational database software o Single-function software o Data warehouse technology

TABLE 8.9
Graphic Organizers for Assistance With Research Techniques and Use of Empirical Foundations for Effective Practice

FSPSD: Research and Program Evaluation

Assistance With Research Techniques and Use of Empirical Foundations for Effective Practice

Research Techniques	Steps for Program Evaluation	Empirical Foundations	Other
Program evaluation efforts should result in data that allow opportunities for both formative and summative decision making The accuracy of decisions can be improved when multiple data sources and multiple informants are included in program evaluation designs Needs assessment involves collecting data to identify both strengths and targets for improvement	1. Identify implementation targets 2. Identify and develop strategic plan 3. Develop an evaluation plan o Use evaluation questions to drive data collection o Identify data sources to answer evaluation questions o Specify data collection, management, and reporting procedures o Report data to key stakeholders	Use empirical foundations for effective practices at individual, group, and systems levels Incorporate: • Data collection repeatedly over time • Valid, reliable, and accurate measurement • Analysis with emphasis on careful inspection of overlap of data points between conditions • Accountability • Systematic replication and control of independent variables	

Legal, Ethical, and Professional Practice

Included in this area are ethical principles and standards for practices, laws, and regulations that apply to schools and professional practice, professional foundations (e.g., history of the profession, advocacy and mentoring), and responsibility for engaging in continued professional development.

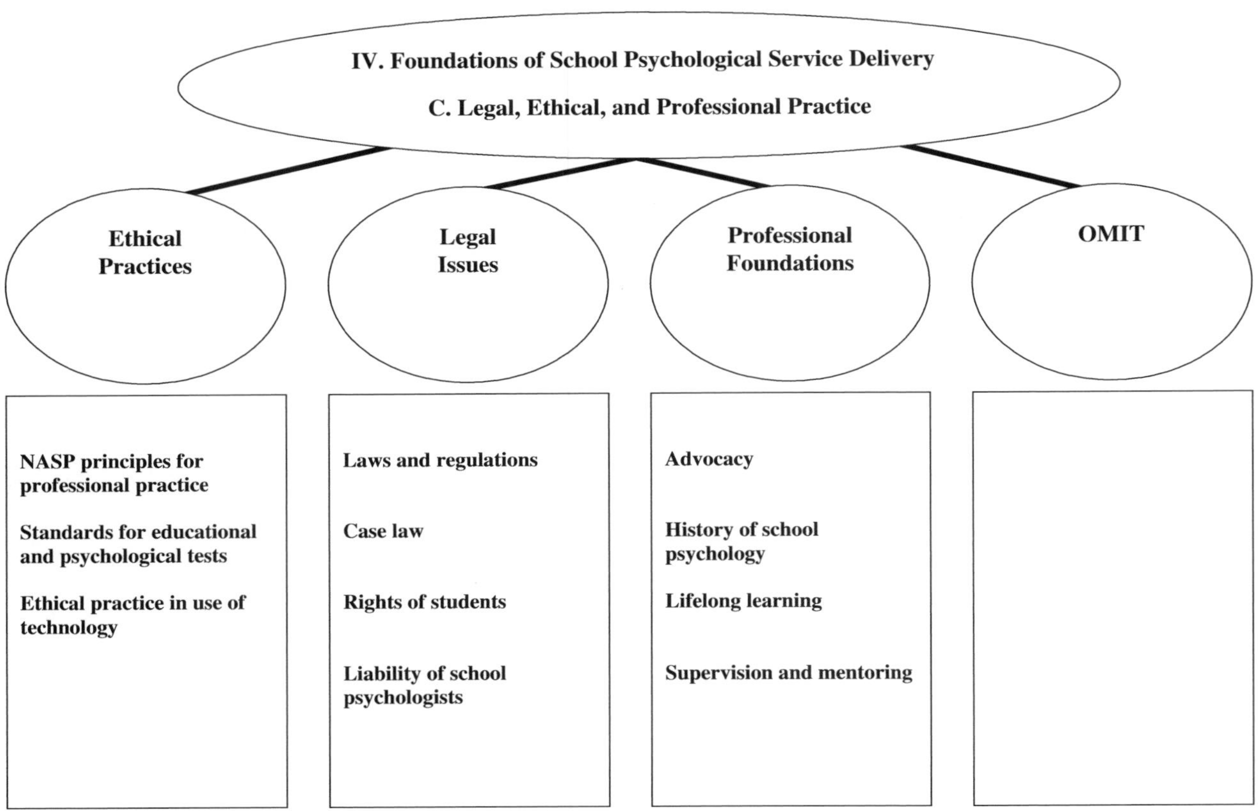

Figure 8.2
Foundations of School Psychological Service Delivery: Legal, Ethical, and Professional Practice

Graphic Organizers for Ethical Practices

TABLE 8.10
Graphic Organizer for NASP Principles for Professional Practice

FSPSD: Ethical Practices

NASP Principles for Professional Practice

Ethical Principles in School Psychology	Professional Standards and Conduct	Standards for Educational and Psychological Tests	Considerations in the Use of Technology
Respecting the dignity and rights of all persons Professional competence and responsibility Honesty and integrity in professional relationships Responsibility to schools, families, communities, the profession, and society NASP Principles for Professional Ethics serve to protect public by educating professionals and providing a foundation for ethically sound decision making	Advocacy • The child is the primary client Service delivery • Promote changes in employing agencies and community service systems that will benefit the client Assessment and intervention • Maintain standards	• Maintain highest standard for psychological assessments • Maintain knowledge about reliability and validity of instruments • Use multiple assessment methods • Use research-based interventions • Use interventions that are appropriate to the presenting problems and collect data • Use current assessment and interventions • Prepare written reports so that others will be able to assist the child • Review written reports for accuracy	Responsible use of technology requires practitioners to: • Ensure that information about children/clients reaches only authorized persons • Comply with laws, regulations, and policies pertaining to the adequate storage and disposal of records • Maintain test security • Maintain full responsibility for any technological services used • Ensure confidentiality; student records are not transmitted electronically without the guarantee of privacy • Email messages must be encrypted or else stripped of all identifying information

TABLE 8.11
Graphic Organizer for Educational and Psychological Tests

FSPSD: Ethical Practices

Standards for Educational and Psychological Tests

Family Educational Rights and Privacy Act of 1974 (FERPA)	Educational Records Defined	Health Insurance Portability and Accountability Act (1996)	Test Protocols
• Under FERPA, federal funds will be withheld from schools unless pupil record-keeping procedures are followed as outlined in the law • FERPA ensures confidentiality of records and parent access to school records that concern their children • Under FERPA, parents have access to all official school records of their children and the right to challenge the accuracy of the records • Pupil records are available only to those in the school setting who have a legitimate educational need to see the records	• Educational records are defined as any records maintained by the school that are directly related to the student • Parental consent must be given before records are released to any outside agencies • Sole possession records are excluded under law, are defined as records that are kept in the sole possession of the maker, and are used only as a memory aid • When records are disclosed to specific persons or agencies at the request of the parent or the eligible student, the school must obtain signed written consent	• HIPAA is a federal law created to protect the privacy and security of patient physical and mental health information and to ensure the efficient electronic exchange of patient information and health care claims • 3 components of HIPAA: 1. Privacy Rules 2. Security Rules 3. Transmission Rules • School psychologists who receive federal funds are required to comply only with FERPA regulations (not HIPAA regulations)	Parents have legal right to inspect and review their child's test protocols NASP code of ethics requires practitioners to maintain test security but also comply with all laws and regulations When choosing between the legal and ethical obligations, legal is paramount Under FERPA, school is not legally required to provide copies of test protocols but parents can view them

TABLE 8.12
Graphic Organizers for Ethical Practice in Use of Technology

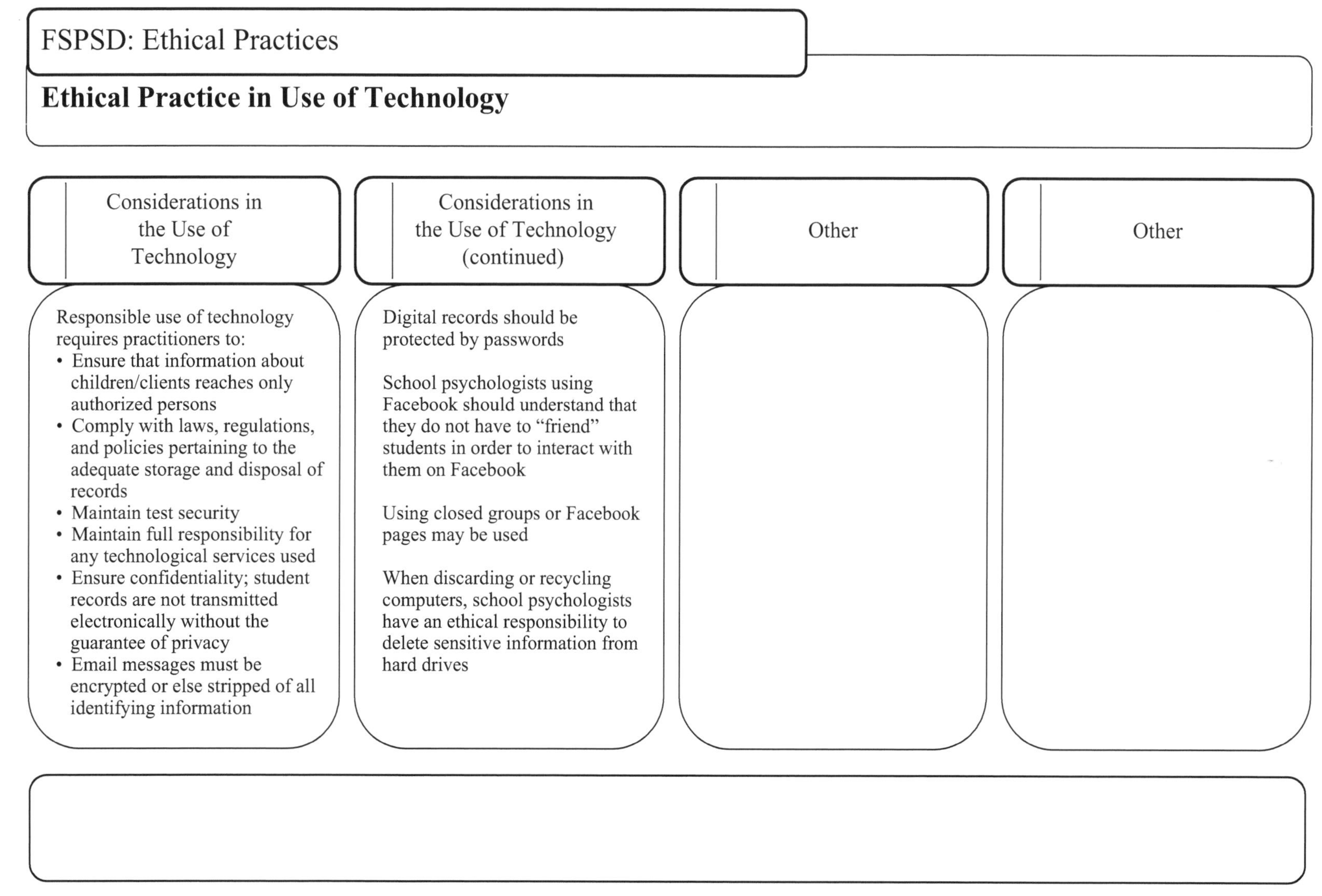

FSPSD: Ethical Practices

Ethical Practice in Use of Technology

Considerations in the Use of Technology	Considerations in the Use of Technology (continued)	Other	Other
Responsible use of technology requires practitioners to: • Ensure that information about children/clients reaches only authorized persons • Comply with laws, regulations, and policies pertaining to the adequate storage and disposal of records • Maintain test security • Maintain full responsibility for any technological services used • Ensure confidentiality; student records are not transmitted electronically without the guarantee of privacy • Email messages must be encrypted or else stripped of all identifying information	Digital records should be protected by passwords School psychologists using Facebook should understand that they do not have to "friend" students in order to interact with them on Facebook Using closed groups or Facebook pages may be used When discarding or recycling computers, school psychologists have an ethical responsibility to delete sensitive information from hard drives		

Graphic Organizers for Legal Issues

TABLE 8.13
Graphic Organizer for Laws and Regulations

FSPSD: Legal Issues

Laws and Regulations

Civil Rights Law (Section 504 and ADA)

Section 504 of the Rehabilitation Act of 1973
- Prohibits discrimination on the basis of a disability in those institutions receiving federal funds
- Disability is defined as a condition that inhibits one or more major life activities
- Requires a district to provide FAPE
- Districts are required to provide a range of accommodations and modifications

American With Disabilities Act (1990)
- Law that prohibits discrimination of people with disabilities in programs and activities, public and private, and ensures the civil rights of all those with disabilities
- Unlike 504, is not limited to those receiving funds
- Does not distinguish between public and private institutions and extends to education, employment, and state and local government

Federal Law (IDEA and IDIEA)

Individuals With Disabilities Education Act (1974)
- Congress passed a funding bill that requires states to adopt goals to ensure equal educational opportunities for all handicapped children
- In 1997 and 2004, Congress amended IDEA through reauthorization

IDIEA (2004)
- Zero reject: all children are to be afforded an equal educational opportunity, and states may not deny any education on the basis of a disability
- Child Find: States must actively seek those who are disabled
- Individuals are eligible for services from birth through age 21
- Students may not be denied or excluded from school only on the basis of a disability
- Schools are required to provide students with disabilities a free appropriate public education (FAPE)

Federal Law (FERPA and Buckley Amendment to FERPA)

Family Educational Rights and Privacy Act of 1974 (FERPA)
- Pupil record-keeping procedures must be followed as outlined in the law or funds withheld
- FERPA ensures confidentiality of records and parent access to school records that concern their children
- Under FERPA, parents have access to all official school records of their children, the right to challenge the accuracy of the records
- Pupil records are available only to those in the school setting who have a legitimate educational need to see the records

Buckley Amendment to FERPA
- Senator James Buckley of New York was principal sponsor of the amendment, which was effective on November 19, 1974, and intended to address concerns identified by the educational community

Federal Law (NCLB)

No Child Left Behind Act (2002)
- Signed by President Bush in 2002
- Developed school accountability for results, provided freedom to states and communities, encouraged proven educational methods, and provided more choices for parents
- Reauthorization of Elementary and Secondary Education Act of 1965
- Looked at adequate yearly progress on accountability goals for all students, including economically disadvantaged children with disabilities, children of different race and ethnicity, and children with limited English proficiency
- NCLB required schools to produce annual report cards regarding school progress in core subjects
- In 2012, President Obama's administration began offering flexibility to states regarding specific requirements of NCLB in exchange for state-developed plans designed to close achievement gaps

TABLE 8.13 (Continued)
Graphic Organizer for Laws and Regulations

FSPSD: Legal Issues

Laws and Regulations

Consent and Notice	Procedural Safeguards Notice	Individualized Education Program (IEP)	Least Restrictive Environment (LRE)
• Consent: o Parental consent must be obtained prior to conducting any evaluations and prior to the initial placement of a child in special education o If parent refuses to consent to the initial placement in special education, the school may not use procedural safeguards to override parent consent • Prior written notice: o Must be provided in a mode of communication parents can understand o Must include a description of proposed action o Must include a description of each evaluation procedure	• Includes information on protections available to the parents of a child with a disability • Must include a full explanation of procedural safeguards written in an understandable manner and sources to contact to obtain assistance and other options in the IEP • Provided at least one time per year; also at initial referral and at parent request for evaluation • Copy may be on school's website	• **Must include:** o How child's disability affects the child's involvement and progress in general education curriculum o Statement of measurable annual goals and benchmarks that relate to how the child will be involved in the general education curriculum o Statement of special education and related services and supplementary aids as well as accommodations and modifications o Individual modifications for district and state assessments	• Requires that "to the maximum extent appropriate, handicapped children are educated with children who are not handicapped" • Congress intended that LEA make available a continuum of alternative placements to meet the needs of children with disabilities • Decisions should be made on basis of the child's individual needs and capabilities

TABLE 8.14
Graphic Organizer for Case Law

FSPSD: Legal Issues

Case Law

Due Process

No person may be deprived of life, liberty, or property without due process of law

Goss v. Lopez, 1975
- Education is a property right and may not be taken away without due process of law
- Schools may not suspend or expel children from school without fair hearings

Newport-Mesa School Unified School District v. Parents on behalf of student, 2011
- After due process, placement of student at Estancia High School Special Day Class for Moderate to Severely Handicapped offered student free appropriate public education in the least restrictive environment

Equal Protection Clause

Guarantees a person the same rights and benefits all other citizens receive; equal education for all children

Brown v. Bd. of Ed, 1954
- Was overturned

Plessy v. Ferguson, 1896
- Educating minority children in separate but equal facilities violates equal protection clause of 14th Amendment and denies them equal education opportunity

Larry P. v. Riles, 1979
- Federal District Court enjoined California from using any standardized intelligence test to assess Black children for eligibility for classes of educable mentally retarded

Program Availability

- **PARC v. Commonwealth of Pennsylvania, 1972**
  - Challenged the exclusion of mentally retarded children (who were deemed “uneducable”) from school on the basis that it violated the equal protection clause and due process rights
- **Mills v. BOE of District of Columbia, 1972**
  - Denied students equal education opportunity because of their handicapping conditions by utilizing procedures such as suspensions, exclusion, and class reassignment
  - Court dismissed limited financial resources as basis for exclusion

Constitutional Foundations

- **10th Amendment**
  - Establishes education as a state function
- **14th Amendment**
  - No state shall make or enforce any law that shall abridge the privileges, nor shall any state deprive the person of life, liberty, or property without due process of law or deny to any person within its jurisdiction the equal protection of laws

TABLE 8.14 (Continued)
Graphic Organizer for Case Law

FSPSD: Legal Issues

Case Law

FAPE	LRE and Inclusion	Inclusion Cases	Other Court Cases
• **Board of Ed. of Hendrick Hudson v. Rowley (1982)** o School districts must grant access to educational opportunity and provide a reasonable opportunity for students to learn by providing comparable treatment not necessarily providing the maximum opportunity to learn • **Irving Independent School District v. Taro (1984)** o Determined scope of health services required under IDEA; schools must provide health services as a related service that the child needs to benefit from special education	• **Tokarcik v. Forest Hill School District (1982)** o Denying access to a regular public school classroom without compelling education justification constitutes discrimination • **Ronecker v. Walter (1983) and Oberti v. Clementon BOE (1993)** o Schools cannot refuse to place special educational services in regular education settings o IDEA requires school systems to supplement and realign their resources	• **Greer v. Rome City BOE (1991)** o Preference for educating disabled and nondisabled children together • **BOE v. Holland (1992)** o Placement decisions must begin with the assumption that the child can be educated in a regular classroom and must consider supplemental aids and services	• **Lau v. Nicholas (1974)** o Schools must provide assistance to ensure that children with limited English proficiency have access to meaningful education • **Tarasoff v. Regents of California (1976)** o School personnel have the legal duty to protect pupils from reasonably foreseeable harm • **Pesce v. J. Sterling Morton HS (1987)** o The duty to protect school children by reporting child abuse outweighs any right to confidentiality

TABLE 8.15
Graphic Organizer for Rights of Students

FSPSD: Legal Issues

Rights of Students

Consent, Notice, and Confidentiality

Consent:
- Parental consent must be obtained prior to conducting any evaluations and prior to the initial placement of a child in special education
- If parent refuses to consent to the initial placement in special education, the school may not use procedural safeguards to override parent consent

Prior written notice:
- Must be provided in a mode of communication parents can understand
- Must include a description of proposed action
- Must include a description of each evaluation procedure

Confidentiality
- Explicit promise or contract to reveal nothing about an individual except under conditions agreed to by the source or subject

Procedural Safeguards Notice and Manifest Determination

Includes information on protections available to the parents of a child with a disability

It must include a full explanation of procedural safeguards written in an understandable manner and must include sources to contact to obtain assistance and other options in the IEP

Provided at least one time per year; also at initial referral and at parent request for evaluation

Copy may be on school's website

Manifest determination
- Determining whether a student's misbehavior is a manifestation of disability
- Unfair to punish student for engaging in misbehavior that is part of disability

Seclusion, Restraint, and Individualized Education Program (IEP)

Seclusion – involuntary confinement

Restraint – physical method used to restrict movement
- Use alternatives whenever possible
- Use as last resort when student poses danger to self or others

IEP must include:
- How child's disability affects the child's involvement and progress in general education curriculum
- Statement of measurable annual goals and benchmarks that relate to how the child will be involved in the general education curriculum
- Statement of special education and related services and supplementary aids as well as accommodations and modifications
- Individual modifications for district and state assessments

Least Restrictive Environment (LRE)

Requires that "to the maximum extent appropriate, handicapped children are educated with children who are not handicapped"

Congress intended that LEA make available a continuum of alternative placements to meet the needs of children with disabilities

Decisions should be made on basis of the child's individual needs and capabilities

TABLE 8.16
Graphic Organizer for Liability of School Psychologists

FSPSD: Legal Issues

Liability of School Psychologists

Legal Liability	Negligence	ESEA (2001)	Supervision
• Malpractice occurs when harm is caused to a client in psychologist-client professional relationship, and it is determined that harm was caused by departure from acceptable standards of care • School psychologists who disclose privileged information to others without obtaining consent put themselves at risk for a malpractice lawsuit under privileged communication law	• Lawsuits generally allege schools have a duty to protect students from foreseeable harm (i.e., are held negligent if school had knowledge of a specific danger, negligently failed to take reasonable precautions to protect students, and caused injuries by allowing an incident to occur) • Schools must perform in the scope of their authority for the betterment of those they serve; if schools act outside of their authority and violate students' rights, they may be held accountable	• **Paul D. Coverdell Teacher Protection Act** o Provides limitations on liability for teachers, principals, and other school professionals when they take reasonable actions to maintain order, discipline, and appropriate educational environment	• Supervisors must be state certified or NCSP, must have 3+ years of working experience • Interns receive 2 hours of supervision per week • Supervisors review and cosign psychological reports • Supervisors offer and provide supervision only within the areas of their own expertise

Graphic Organizers for Professional Foundations

TABLE 8.17
Graphic Organizer for Advocacy

FSPSD: Professional Foundations

Advocacy

Advocating for Children and Their Families	Continued Professional Development (CPD)	Individualized CPD Plan	Disproportionality, Poverty, and Equity
The effects of low SES on the development of students and families have led to the term "culture of poverty." It can even affect the quality of schools, buildings, and teachers. *Loving justice* - vision for social justice practice • Outwardness – focus on students who do not represent majority group and environmental factors • Transformation – meet needs of students in short term as well as long term	NASP established the ethical obligation of school psychologists to engage in continuing professional development Professional development is also a requirement for state and national certification For NCSP, 75 hours of continuing professional development activities are required within a 3-year renewal period	The construction of an individualized CPD plan is based on a 4-step model that includes: • Setting context and identifying needs • Prioritizing needs • Selecting and implementing developmental activities • Evaluation and documenting activities	Disproportionality • Racial disproportionality is evident in the type of discipline students receive as well as the intensity of the punishment with African American and Latino students in comparison to their Caucasian classmates Students in poverty • Disproportionately affected by developmental, mental health, and academic problems • Can be helped with protective factors Equity • Non-discriminatory assessment • Evaluate validity of data • Interpret data fairly • Make non-discriminatory decisions • Engender equitable outcomes

TABLE 8.18
Graphic Organizer for History of School Psychology

FSPSD: Professional Foundations

History of School Psychology

Hybrid Years 1890 to 1969	Hybrid Years 1890 to 1969 (continued)	Thoroughbred Years 1970 to Present	Thoroughbred Years 1970 to Present (continued)
• Blend of many educational and psychological practitioners loosely mobilized around the dominant role of assessment for special class placement • Lightner Witmer: father of clinical and school psychology • G. Stanley Hall: founded APA in 1892; father of child study movement • Arnold Gesell: thought to have held first position as "school psychologist" from 1915 to 1919	• Development of group and individual ability and achievement tests in the early 20th century became the primary role of the school psychologist • Therapeutic activities were often thwarted by the psychiatric community • 1945: Division 16 was formed under APA • 1969: NASP was formed as a rival to APA-Division 16	• Signified growth of training programs, practitioners, state and national associations, and the expansion of literature and regulations • Marked by regulations, association growth, and professional division and reorganization • Passage of Education for all Handicapped Children Act in 1975, which required every school district to provide special education services	• Dominance of the assessment role has persisted • Since the late 1980s, inclusion and pre-referral assessment and intervention models have rapidly gained attention • In the 1990s, school violence captured public attention

TABLE 8.19
Graphic Organizer for Lifelong Learning

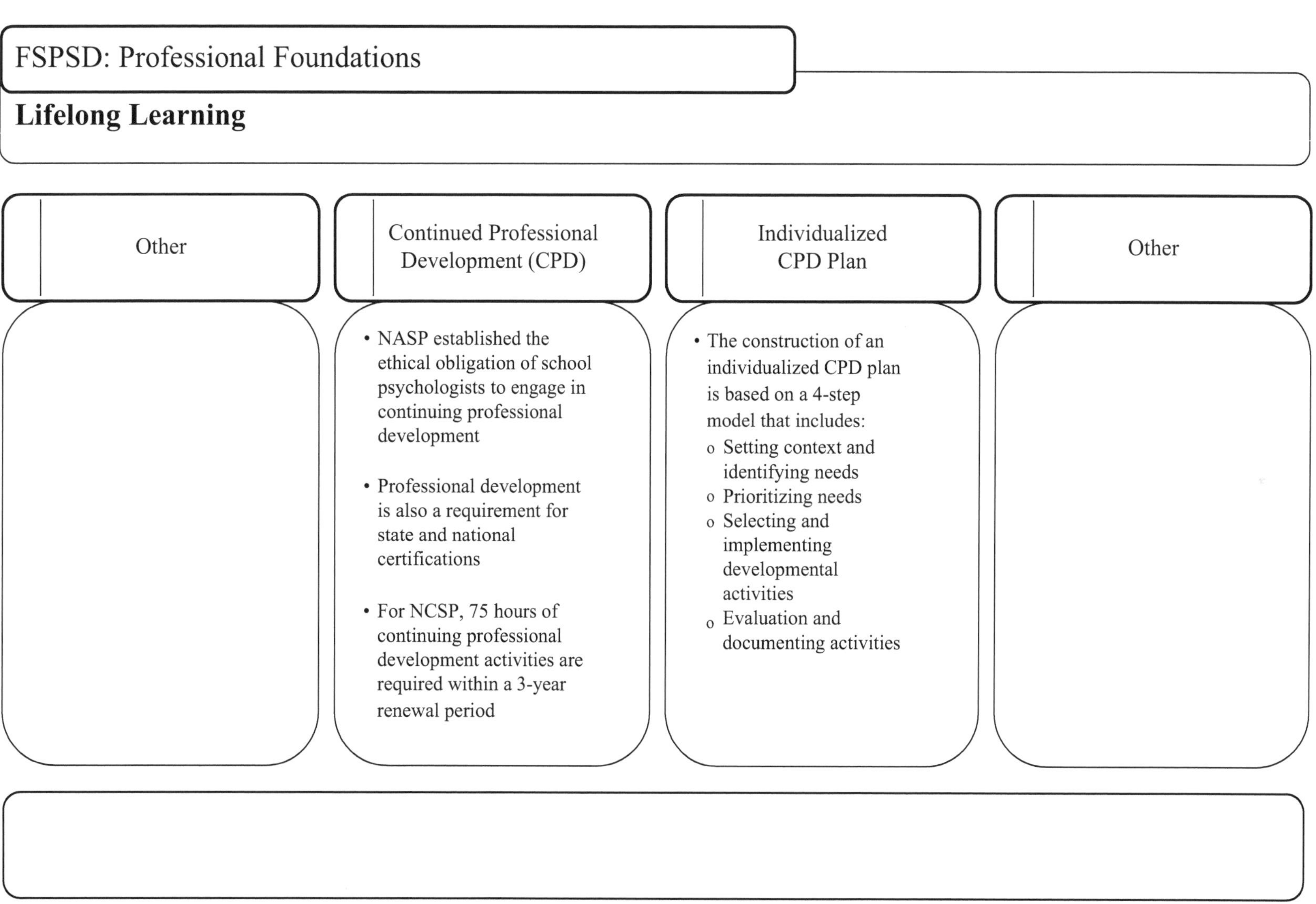

TABLE 8.20
Graphic Organizer for Supervision and Mentoring

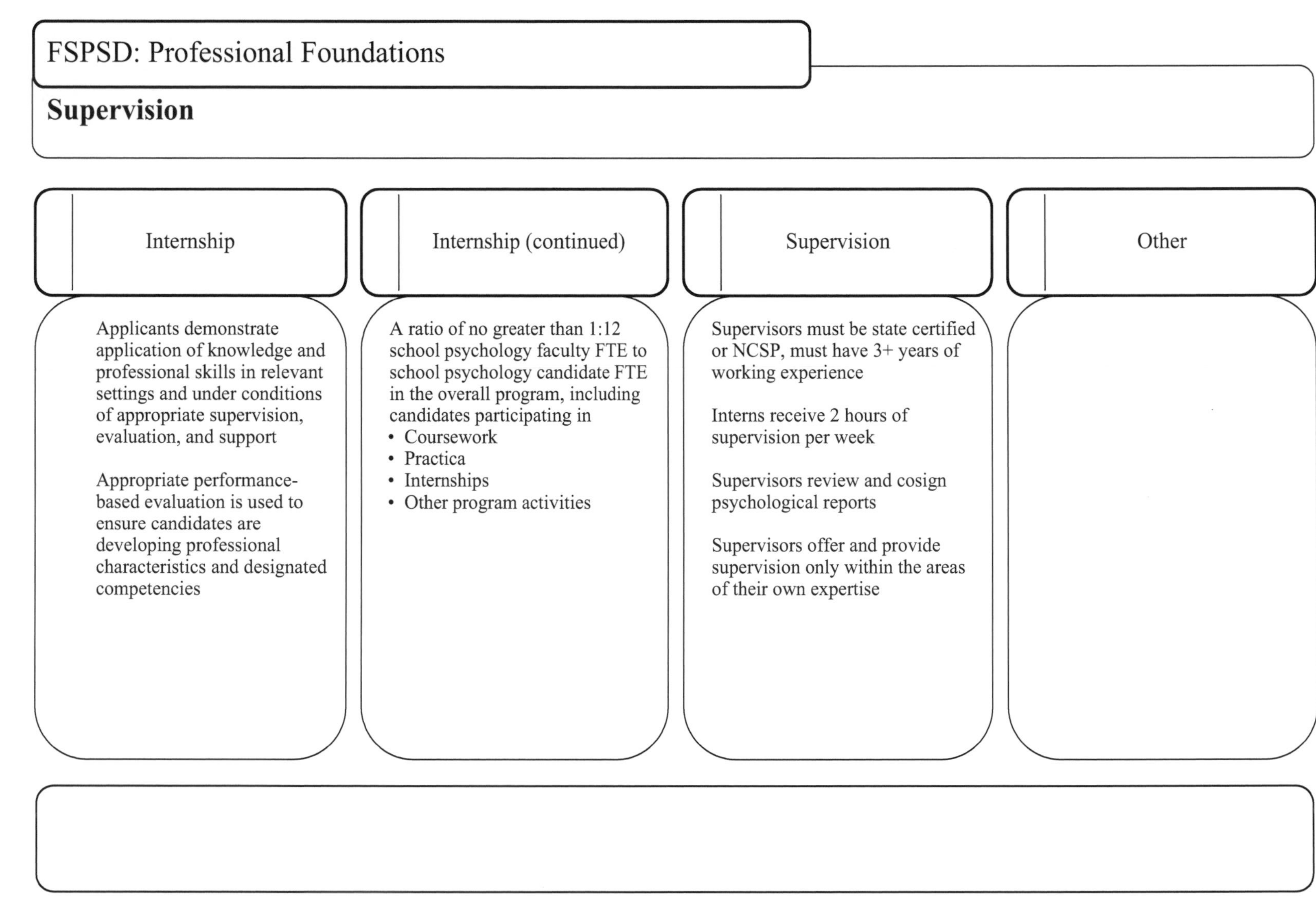

FSPSD: Professional Foundations

Supervision

Internship	Internship (continued)	Supervision	Other
Applicants demonstrate application of knowledge and professional skills in relevant settings and under conditions of appropriate supervision, evaluation, and support Appropriate performance-based evaluation is used to ensure candidates are developing professional characteristics and designated competencies	A ratio of no greater than 1:12 school psychology faculty FTE to school psychology candidate FTE in the overall program, including candidates participating in • Coursework • Practica • Internships • Other program activities	Supervisors must be state certified or NCSP, must have 3+ years of working experience Interns receive 2 hours of supervision per week Supervisors review and cosign psychological reports Supervisors offer and provide supervision only within the areas of their own expertise	

Sample Questions for Foundations of School Psychological Service Delivery

1. Ms. Miller is currently working on developing a new preschool curriculum for the district to adopt because of problems and complaints about the current curriculum. Along with her district problem-solving and planning teams, Ms. Miller is currently investigating the strengths and weaknesses of the curriculum in all of its contexts, hypothesizing possible reasons for the problem, and creating interventions. She is currently at which stage of the planning and problem-solving model?
   a. Evaluation stage
   b. Problem analysis stage
   c. Intervention stage
   d. Problem identification
   e. Post hoc analysis

2. Utilizing a whole-system perspective for adopting a response to intervention (RTI) approach by the district, Ms. South attempted to consider all of the pervasive system variables that can affect morale, motivation, and satisfaction with program implementation. A fellow team member rejected the model adopted. Which factor sums up this team member's attitude?
   a. Arational factors
   b. Cultural factors
   c. Needs of clients
   d. Environmental factors
   e. None of the above

3. Which of the following is NOT an advantage of curriculum-based measurement (CBM)?
   a. CBMs are acceptable evidence-based practices under IDEA and NCLB.
   b. The results of CBMs will indicate why a problem is occurring.
   c. CBMs are short and take only 1–5 minutes to complete.
   d. CBMs can provide data regarding reading, math, and writing achievement.
   e. CBMs can be used in conjunction with the 80–15–5 problem-solving model.

4. When it comes to the roles of a school psychologist in applying research, in what order does the hierarchy of roles fall from least specialized to most specialized?
   a. Distributor of research -> consumer of research -> conductor of research
   b. Consumer of research -> distributor of research -> conductor of research
   c. Consumer of research -> distributor of research -> conductor of research
   d. Conductor of research -> consumer of research -> distributor of research
   e. None of the above

5. Which of the following is the type of evaluation that occurs while a program is in progress?
   a. Formative evaluation
   b. Final evaluation
   c. Collaborative evaluation
   d. Summative evaluation
   e. None of the above

6. Which of the following can be a reason that research is considered "not up to par"?
   a. Small sample size
   b. Mistakes made in calculating and reporting statistics
   c. Weak research designs

d. Conclusions are extended beyond what research can reasonably conclude
e. All of the above

7. Which of the following describes QUALITATIVE research?
   a. Answers questions about variables' status through numerical descriptions.
   b. Has roots in social science, especially anthropology and sociology.
   c. Draws conclusions about the influence of one or more variables on another.
   d. Examines numerical descriptions of two or more variables and makes decisions about their differences or relationships.
   e. None of the above.

8. Which of the following is the second step in the culturally and linguistically diverse (CLD) problem-solving model?
   a. Plan evaluation
   b. Problem analysis
   c. Establishing relationships
   d. Intervention
   e. Problem identification

9. Which is generally the best way to address a parent regarding concern about his/her child's academic performance when the family is from a Latino culture?
   a. Send a letter to the parent explaining current concerns.
   b. Conduct a conference call with the parent and the student's teachers.
   c. Request a time to meet with the parent in person.
   d. Email the parent and arrange for ongoing correspondence to occur in this manner.
   e. Inform the student that he/she needs to inform his/her parent that the school psychologist is concerned.

10. To avoid making incorrect/inappropriate generalizations about a group, the school psychologist must be aware of all of the following, EXCEPT:
    a. Culture is dynamic and ever-changing.
    b. Culture, language, and ethnicity are not the only determinants of groups having shared beliefs, values, and behaviors.
    c. Difference within a culture may be as significant as difference between cultures.
    d. Everyone has a culture.
    e. School is the only context in which students are free of cultural influence/pressure.

11. The school psychologist requests that a teacher complete a behavior rating scale as part of a student's functional behavioral assessment (FBA). Upon receiving the completed behavior rating scale, the school psychologist realizes that the age-range of the form was inappropriate for the particular student who is being assessed. Which of the following actions should the school psychologist pursue?
    a. Transfer the responses to the appropriate form
    b. Score the completed form
    c. Request the teacher complete the age-appropriate form
    d. Blame the teacher
    e. Eliminate the behavior rating scale from the FBA

12. A teacher requests that the school psychologist share information discussed in counseling sessions with her student. How should the school psychologist respond to the teacher's request?
    a. Provide the requested information using electronic mail.
    b. Explain how ethical principles of confidentially prohibit the sharing of this information.
    c. Provide a written report.
    d. Invite the teacher to listen in on the next counseling session.
    e. Schedule a conference with the teacher to discuss the information shared during the student's counseling session.

13. During a counseling session, the school psychologist becomes concerned that the counselee may intend to inflict harm upon him-/herself. How should the school psychologist respond in this situation?
    a. The school psychologist is unable to act due to client confidentiality.
    b. Continue to discuss the situation at the next counseling session.
    c. Address the situation and alert the appropriate personnel to ensure the child's safety.
    d. Send a letter to the child's parents expressing concern for the child's intention to harm him- or herself.
    e. Ignore the issue.

14. Court case decisions have supported the inclusion of disabled students in general education classrooms. School districts must meet the burden of showing that a student cannot be educated satisfactorily in a general education classroom with supplementary aids and services. Schools must make reasonable attempts to include disabled children, including cognitively impaired children, in regular education classes. Which court case was influential in supporting the inclusion of disabled students?
    a. Brown v. Topeka Board of Education
    b. Lau v. Nichols
    c. Tarasoff v. Regents of California
    d. Oberti v. Clementon
    e. Riles v. Larry P.

15. Section 504 of the Rehabilitation Act of 1973 and the Americans With Disabilities Act both prohibit discrimination against people with disabilities. The prohibitions of both laws apply directly to public school districts and require schools to make reasonable accommodations for students with disabilities. What type of law is this and who handles violations?
    a. Program law, federal department of education
    b. Funding law, department of state education
    c. Civil rights law, Office of Civil Rights
    d. Special education law, state department of special education
    e. LEA policies and procedures, local board of education

Answers With Rationale

1. The best answer is ***b***. The problem analysis stage involves actions whereby (1) the referred and operationalized problem is fully investigated in all of its ecological, organizational, situational, and behavioral contexts; (2) the hypotheses generated to explain the problem are assessed and confirmed or rejected; and (3) interventions related to the confirmed hypotheses are identified and developed while their potential acceptability, social validity, treatment integrity, and generalizability are concurrently evaluated. Choice *a* is incorrect because the evaluation step must come last, after the problem has been analyzed and an intervention has been implemented (choice *c*). Choice *d* is also incorrect because the problem identification stage must be the first step in the process.

    Reference: Pluymert, K. (2014). Problem-solving foundations for school psychological services. In P. Harrison & A. Thomas (Eds.), *Best practices in school psychology VI: Data-based and collaborative decision making* (pp. 25–39). Bethesda, MD: National Association of School Psychologists.

2. The best answer is ***a***. Arational factors translate as dysfunctional, skewed, and unchangeable characteristics that interfere with the system's progress if allowed. These characteristics include system resistance, inertia, self-interest, unpredictability, emotionality, rejection of data, hidden agendas, and many more. Response *c* is at the core of the model. Response *d* refers to communication and roles of the people within the model. Lastly, response *b* relates to the opposite of arational factors, regarding the cultural factors that may influence the outcome.

    Reference: Knoff, H. (2002). Best practices in facilitating school reform, organizational change, and strategic planning. In A. Thomas & J. Grimes (Eds.), *Best practices in school psychology IV* (pp. 235–252). Bethesda, MD: National Association of School Psychologists.

3. Option ***b*** is the best answer. The results of the CBM will not provide information as to why the problem is occurring. The data provided may indicate the skill level of the child or can be used to establish a baseline. Further investigation is necessary to discover the source of problems.

   Reference: Shinn, M. R. (2008). Best practices in using curriculum-based measurement in a problem-solving model. In J. Grimes & A. Thomas (Eds.), Best practices in school psychology V (Vol. 2, pp. 243–261). Bethesda, MD: National Association of School Psychologists.

4. Option ***c*** is the best answer. The consumer of research includes all school psychologists, while the distributor includes fewer and requires competent skills in consuming research. Finally, the conductor of research requires competence in both areas as well as the largest skill set.

   Reference: Keith, T. Z. (2008). Best practice in using and conducting research in applied settings. In J. Grimes & A. Thomas (Eds.), *Best practices in school psychology V* (Vol. 6, pp. 2165–2175). Bethesda, MD: National Association of School Psychologists.

5. Option ***a*** is the best answer. Summative evaluations occur after a program is completed. Collaboration is recommended on all evaluations so the input of all stakeholders can be incorporated. Formative evaluations occur while the program is in progress and allow the evaluator to take part in the program and make adjustments along the way.

   Reference: Godber, Y. (2008). Best practice in program evaluation. In J. Grimes & A. Thomas (Eds.), *Best practices in school psychology V* (Vol. 6, pp. 2193–2205). Bethesda, MD: National Association of School Psychologists.

6. Option ***e*** is the best answer. Some research may not be up to par for the following reasons: research problems are poorly conceived or trivial, sample size is small or poorly selected (makes it hard to generalize), inappropriate statistics are used, mistakes were made in calculating and reporting statistics, weak research designs do not rule out plausible alternative hypotheses, the research design does not fit the purpose of the study or test the hypothesis, conclusions are extended beyond what the research can reasonably conclude, and the discussion addressed different issues than what the study was designed for.

   Reference: Cozby, P. C., & Bates, S. C. (2012). *Methods in behavioral research* (11th ed.). New York, NY: McGraw-Hill.

7. Option ***b*** is the best answer. Qualitative research has roots in social science, especially anthropology and sociology. It is characterized by the use of text (written words) to document variables and inductive analysis of the collected information.

   Reference: Cozby, P. C., & Bates, S. C. (2012). *Methods in behavioral research* (11th ed.). New York, NY: McGraw-Hill.

8. Option ***e*** is the correct answer. Problem identification is the second step in this model, after establishing the necessary relationships to be able to do so.

   Reference: Lineman, J. M., & Miller, G. E. (2012). Strengthening competence in working with culturally and linguistically diverse students. *NASP Communiqué, 40*(8), 20–21.

9. Option ***c*** is the correct answer. High-context cultures, such as Latinos, value nonverbal communication and interpretation when getting new information. Therefore, a meeting would allow them to use the skills with which they are most comfortable and your communication can be most effective.

   Reference: Ortiz, S. O., Flanagan, D. P., & Dynda, A. M. (2008). Best practices in working with culturally diverse children and families. In A. Thomas & J. Grimes (Eds.), Best practices in school psychology V (Vol. 5, pp. 1730). Bethesda, MD: National Association of School Psychologists.

10. Option ***e*** is the correct answer. Each school has been shown to have a culture, which often has significant influence on learning and development. Research shows that the cultures in schools often mirror those of the U.S. mainstream.

    Reference: Ortiz, S. O., Flanagan, D. P., & Dynda, A. M. (2008). Best practices in working with culturally diverse children and families. In A. Thomas & J. Grimes (Eds.), *Best practices in school psychology V* (Vol. 5, pp. 1723). Bethesda, MD: National Association of School Psychologists.

11. The best answer is ***c***. NASP PPE (2010b), Standard II.3.2, states that school psychologists use assessment techniques and practices that the profession considers to be responsible, research-based practice. Further, if using norm-referenced measures, school psychologists choose instruments with up-to-date normative data.

    Reference: National Association of School Psychologists. (2010b). *Principles for professional ethics.* Retrieved from http://www.nasponline.org/standards/2010standards/1_%20Ethical%20Principles.pdf.

12. The best answer is ***b***. NASP PPE (2010b), Standard 1.2.5, states that school psychologists discuss and/or release confidential information only for professional purposes and only with persons who have a legitimate need to know. They do so within the strict boundaries of relevant privacy statuses.

    Reference: National Association of School Psychologists. (2010b). *Principles for professional ethics.* Retrieved from http://www.nasponline.org/standards/2010standards/1_%20Ethical%20Principles.pdf.

13. The best answer is ***c***. NASP PPE Standard I.2.3 states that school psychologists inform students and other clients of the boundaries of confidentiality at the outset of establishing a professional relationship. The boundary in this particular situation is that the school psychologist must release information when the client intends to harm him- or herself and/or other individuals.

    Reference: National Association of School Psychologists. (2010b). *Principles for professional ethics.* Retrieved from http://www.nasponline.org/standards/2010standards/1_%20Ethical%20Principles.pdf.

14. The best answer is ***d***. In Oberti v. Clementon, the court ruled that if services could be provided in the general education classroom, then the school cannot refuse to do so. The Obertis wanted their cognitively impaired son to attend the local public school, but the district wanted a more restrictive placement. The Oberti case opened the doors for providing special services in the regular classroom. In short, schools cannot refuse to place special services in general education classrooms if services can be provided within the general education setting with the use of supplementary aids and services.

    Reference: Oberti v. Board of Education of Borough of Clementon School District (1992). 995 F. 2d 1204.

15. The best answer is ***c***. The Office of Civil Rights is responsible to ensure compliance with these laws, not the Department of Education. They are civil rights laws with implications that extend to educational settings.

    Reference: McBride, G. M., Willis, J. O., & Dumont, R. (2014). Best practices in applying legal standards for students with disabilities. In P. Harrison & A. Thomas (Eds.), *Best practices in school psychology VI: Foundations* (pp. 421–436). Bethesda, MD: National Association of School Psychologists.

Chapter 

General Knowledge of Psychological Principles and Theories

Chapter 9 covers the areas considered within the broad category of *General Knowledge of Psychological Principles and Theories*. As in the preceding chapters, you will encounter an explanation of the category, a graphic representation that will provide an overview of the content, and a series of graphic organizers that outline the content knowledge covered on the Praxis® Subject Assessment School Psychologist exam. (You may notice that this category is no longer included on the *TAAG*. However, in the judgment of the authors, these topics are important to review in order to help you recall these basic psychological principles that may be included in application questions.) Fifteen sample questions with answers and rationale are also included. You may want to supplement the sections with your own information as you move through the chapter.

Knowledge of Psychological Principles and Theories

Psychological principles and theory include knowledge of scientific theories and research findings that form the basis for school psychological practice. Included in this category are biological basis of behavior, developmental milestones from birth through adolescence, and motivation/cognition. In addition, psychological theory includes human learning and development, personality theory, intelligence, and language development.

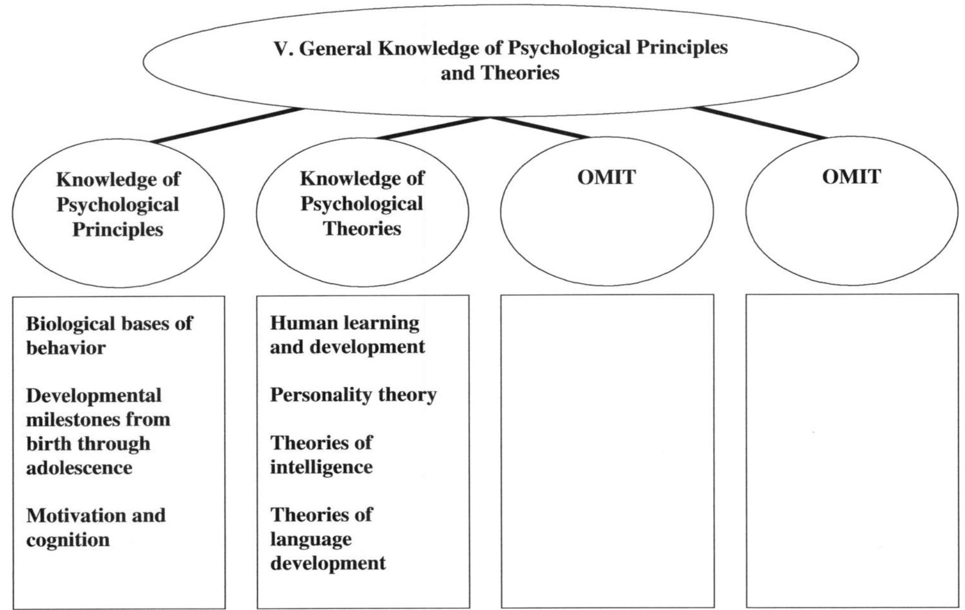

Figure 9.1
Overview of General Knowledge of Psychological Principles and Theories

Graphic Organizers for Knowledge of Psychological Principles

TABLE 9.1
Graphic Organizer for Biological Bases of Behavior

GKPPT: Knowledge of Psychological Principles

Biological Bases of Behavior

Biological Bases of Behavior	Neurotransmitters	Endocrine and Limbic Systems	Parts of the Brain
• Psychologists study relationship between genes and behaviors using: o Family studies: look for patterns/influences within nuclear and extended family structures o Twin studies: seek to identify genetic and environmental influences on development of psychological traits o Adoption studies: seek to identify genetic and environmental influences on development of psychological traits	• Acetylocholine (Ach): o Excitatory o Involved with affect arousal, attention, memory, motivation, and movement • Dopamine (Da): o Inhibits many behaviors and emotions o Implicated in schizophrenia and Parkinson's disease • Serotonin: o Inhibits all activities including sleep onset, mood, and eating • Norepinephrine: o Excitatory o Affects arousal, wakefulness, learning, memory, and mood	• Endocrine System: o Endocrine glands produce hormones; hormones guide process for: ▪ Metabolism ▪ Growth ▪ Sexual development ▪ Regulating emotional life • Limbic System: o "Emotional brain"; governs motivation, emotion o Parts include: ▪ Hippocampus ▪ Amygdala ▪ Hypthothalamus ▪ Thalamus (major message relay center; regulates higher brain centers and peripheral nervous system	• Hindbrain: o Medulla o Pons o Cerebellum • Midbrain: o Hearing o Vision relay point o Pain is registered here • Forebrain: o Thalamus o Hypothalamus

TABLE 9.1 (Continued)
Graphic Organizer for Biological Bases of Behavior

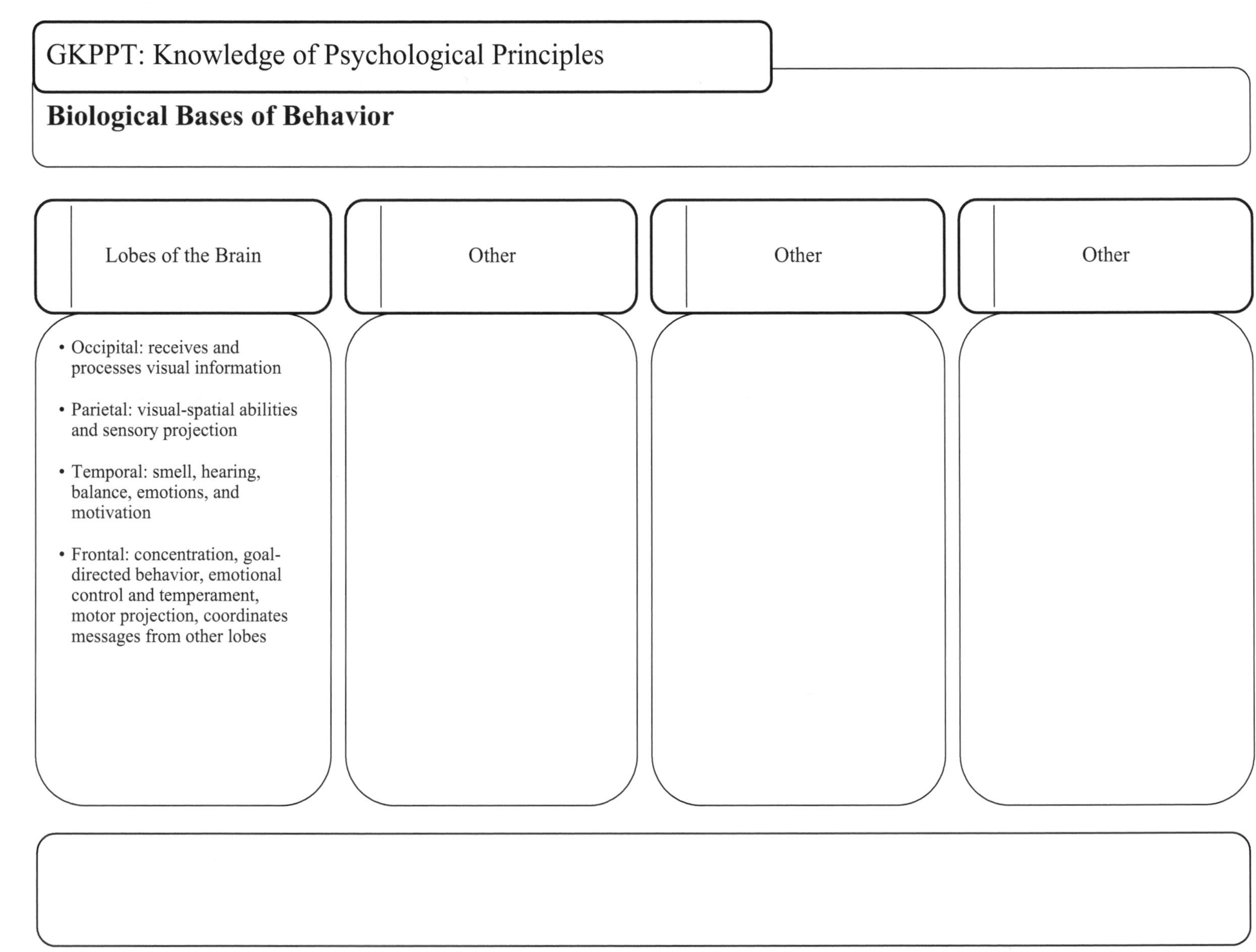

TABLE 9.2
Graphic Organizer for Developmental Milestones From Birth Through Adolescence

GKPPT: Knowledge of Psychological Principles

Developmental Milestones From Birth Through Adolescence

Developmental Milestones in Infancy and Toddlerhood	Development in Early Childhood	Milestones of Middle Childhood	Milestones During Adolescence
• Birth–6 months: o Expresses basic emotions o Demonstrates rapid height and weight growth o Uses imitation • 7–12 months: o Sits, crawls, walks o Uses intentional behaviors o Uses nonverbal gestures • 13–18 months: o Speaks first words o Shows empathy o Joins in play • 19–24 months: o Jumps, runs, climbs o Solves sensorimotor problems o Begins emotional vocabulary uses name for self	• 2 years: o Demonstrates improved balance and walking skills o Sees perspective of others in simple situations o Self-concept and self-esteem emerge • 3–4 years: o Uses scissors, draws pictures of more concrete items, counts objects o Demonstrates self-conscious emotions o Hostile aggression increases • 5–6 years: o Gross motor skills increase o Attention is more sustained o Average vocabulary is 10,000 words o Develop morally relevant rules and behaviors	• 6–8 years: o Fine motor skills increase o Understanding of spatial concepts develops o Vocabulary rapidly increases o Self-esteem becomes more realistic o Engages in more positive peer interactions • 9–11 years: o Gross motor skills are executed more quickly o Logical thought is still tied to concrete situations o More refined conversational skills emerge o Personality traits are usually gender-stereotyped	• 11–14 years: o Girls: menstruation begins, peak of growth spurt o Boys: begin growth spurt o Become more idealistic and critical o Grasp irony and sarcasm o Abstract words added to vocabulary • 14–18 years: o Girls: complete growth spurt o Boys: peak and completion of growth spurt o Develop more complex rules for problem solving o Decision and plan making improves o Search for identity

TABLE 9.3
Graphic Organizer for Motivation and Cognition

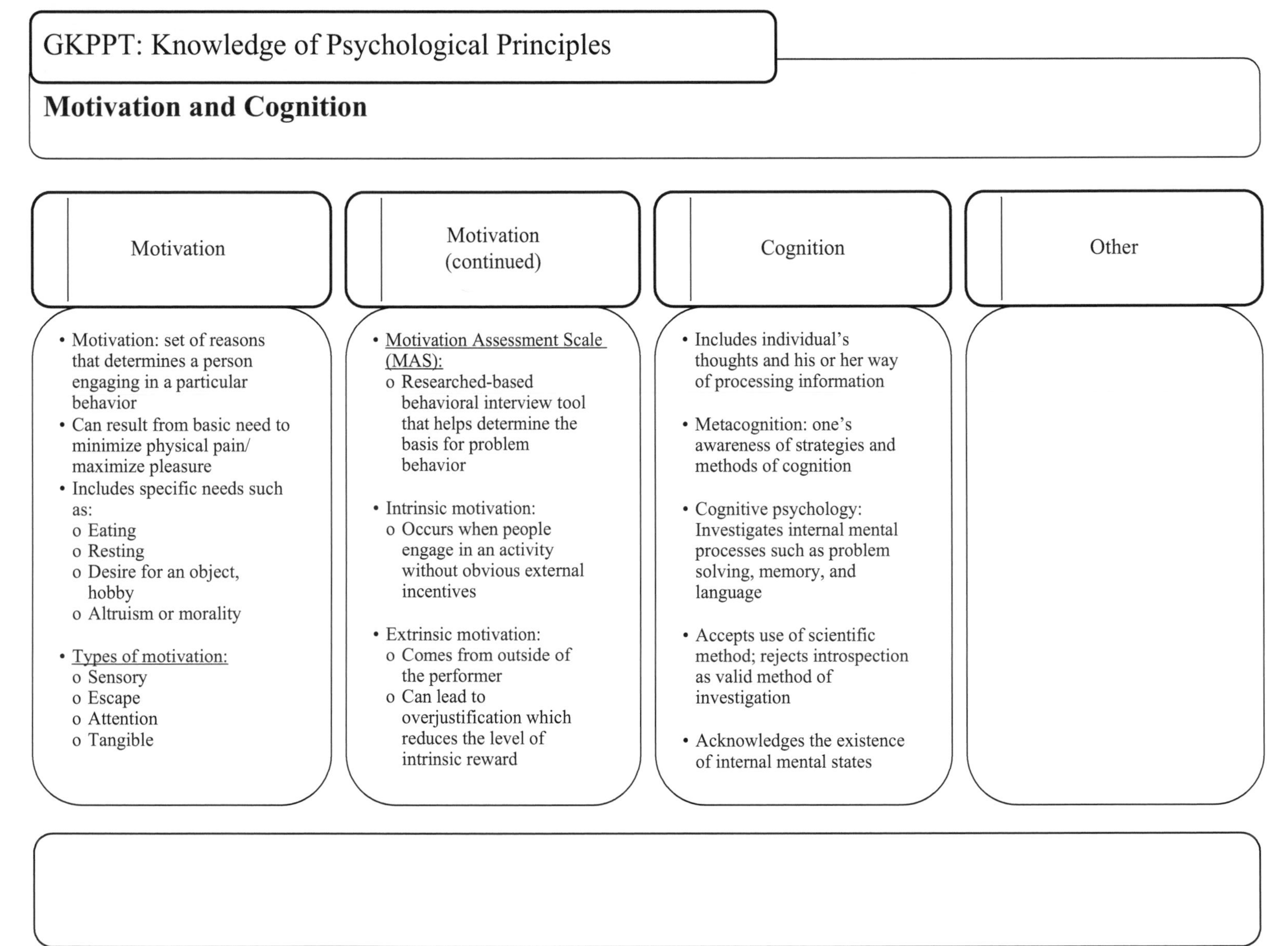

GKPPT: Knowledge of Psychological Principles

Motivation and Cognition

Motivation	Motivation (continued)	Cognition	Other
• Motivation: set of reasons that determines a person engaging in a particular behavior • Can result from basic need to minimize physical pain/ maximize pleasure • Includes specific needs such as: o Eating o Resting o Desire for an object, hobby o Altruism or morality • <u>Types of motivation:</u> o Sensory o Escape o Attention o Tangible	• <u>Motivation Assessment Scale (MAS):</u> o Researched-based behavioral interview tool that helps determine the basis for problem behavior • Intrinsic motivation: o Occurs when people engage in an activity without obvious external incentives • Extrinsic motivation: o Comes from outside of the performer o Can lead to overjustification which reduces the level of intrinsic reward	• Includes individual's thoughts and his or her way of processing information • Metacognition: one's awareness of strategies and methods of cognition • Cognitive psychology: Investigates internal mental processes such as problem solving, memory, and language • Accepts use of scientific method; rejects introspection as valid method of investigation • Acknowledges the existence of internal mental states	

Graphic Organizers for Knowledge of Psychological Theories

TABLE 9.4
Graphic Organizer for Human Learning and Development

GKPPT: Knowledge of Psychological Theories

Human Learning and Development

Piaget's Cognitive Development Theory	Freud's Psychosexual Stages of Development	Erikson's Psychosocial Stages	Kohlberg's Stages of Moral Development
• Sensorimotor (birth–2): o Act on world using senses o Here and now • Preoperational (2–7): o Reason dominated by perception o Intuitive reasoning • Concrete operational (7–11): o Logical sequencing o Concrete problem solving • Formal operational (11–adult): o Abstract thinking	• Oral (0–18 months): o Sucking, mouth and lips o Dependent • Anal (18 months–3 years): o Self-control and obedience • Phallic (3–6 years): o Morality o Identity with gender • Latency (6–puberty): o Period of calm • Genital stage (post puberty): o Maturity o Reproduction o Intellectual and artistic creativity	• Trust vs. mistrust (birth–1 year): o Needs comfort with minimal uncertainty • Autonomy vs. shame and doubt (1–3 years): o Works to master physical environment • Initiative vs. guilt (3–6 years): o Initiates activity o Needs to develop a sense of responsibility • Industry vs. inferiority (6–11 years): o Developing sense of self-worth • Intimacy vs. isolation (young adulthood): o Establish intimate relationships • Generativity vs. stagnation (middle adulthood): o Giving to next generation • Ego integrity vs. despair (maturity): o Review life's accomplishments	• Preconventional level: o Morality is externally controlled o Behavior is motivated by avoidance of punishment ▪ Punishment and obedience ▪ Instrumental purpose of orientation • Conventional level: o Conform to social norms and avoid disapproval of others ▪ Morality of interpersonal cooperation ▪ Maintaining social order • Postconventional level: o Focuses on high ethics and personal principles, as opposed to just laws of society ▪ Social contract orientation ▪ Universal ethical principles

TABLE 9.4 (Continued)
Graphic Organizer for Human Learning and Development

GKPPT: Knowledge of Psychological Theory

Human Learning and Development

Freud's Defense Mechanisms	Social-Cognitive Theory	Sociocultural Theory	Halo and Hawthorne Effect
• Denial: claim that what is actually true is false • Displacement: redirecting emotions onto another target • Projection: attributing one's own uncomfortable feelings to others • Sublimination: redirecting urges one considers wrong into acceptable actions • Rationalization: creating credible justification that is false • Reaction formation: showing the opposite emotions of one's true feelings • Regression: returning to a former state • Repression: pushing uncomfortable thoughts out of consciousness • Intellectualization: utilizing an objective viewpoint	Albert Bandura: • Modeling o Bases for many behaviors o Children learn both desirable and undesirable behaviors by watching and imitating others • With time, children become more selective in the behaviors they model • Set up personal standards by watching others give praise or blame • **Self-efficacy** o Belief about own abilities and characteristics	Lev Vygotsky: • Focuses on how culture is transmitted to the next generation • Social interaction is pertinent for children to acquire the customs of a community's culture • Cognitive development is a socially mediated process; it is dependent on the support of adults and more mature peers	Halo Effect: • E. L. Thorndike • Suggests that if a person has one outstanding positive trait, it will affect others' total judgment of that person Hawthorne Effect: • Elton Mayo • Suggests that performance improves if a person if made to feel important or singled out • Pertains to being observed

TABLE 9.5
Graphic Organizer for Personality Theory

GKPPT: Knowledge of Psychological Theory

Personality Theory

Sigmund Freud's Psychoanalytic Theory

- Personality is composed of three elements:
  1. Id:
     - Present from birth
     - Unconscious aspect of personality
     - Driven by *pleasure principle*
  2. Ego:
     - Deals with reality
     - Develops from the Id
     - Functions in the conscious, preconscious, and unconscious mind
     - Operates by the *reality principle*

Sigmund Freud's Psychoanalytic Theory (continued)

3. Superego:
   - Emerges around age 5
   - Provides guidelines for making judgments

- <u>Ego ideal:</u> rules for good behaviors
- <u>Conscience:</u> includes information about things that are viewed as bad by society

Alfred Adler Birth Order

- Birth order influences personality
- First-born: the leader, somewhat spoiled before the second child, feeling of being "dethroned" when second child comes along, bossy
- Second child: also referred to as the neglected middle child, strives to be different and stand out for attention
- Third child: usually the youngest, is babied and spoiled
- Only child: sometimes socially inept, finds it difficult to get along with others

Kohlberg's Stages of Moral Development

- Evaluated moral reasoning of children and adults by assessing moral decision making
- 3 levels:
  - o Preconventional
  - o Conventional
  - o Postconventional
- 6 stages—two at each level

TABLE 9.6
Graphic Organizer for Theories of Intelligence

GKPPT: Knowledge of Psychological Theory

Theories of Intelligence

Cattell and Horn	Information-Processing Approaches to Intelligence	Piaget's Theory	Thorndike
• Developed a theory of two different types of intelligence: fluid and crystallized • **Fluid** intelligence refers to nonverbal, culture-free mental efficiency • **Crystallized** intelligence refers to acquired skills and knowledge strongly dependent on exposure to culture	• Information-processing conceptions of intelligence deal with ways individuals mentally represent and process information • Emphasis on different operations performed on information • Human cognition occurs in discrete stages with information being acted on at each stage and passed along to next stage for further processing • Assumes all behavior results from combination of various processing stages • Analogy of computer processing often used	• Intelligence viewed as form of biological adaptation of individual to environment • Cognitive processes emerge through developmental process • Psychological structures reorganize as a result of interaction between organism and environment • Adaptation, accommodation, and assimilation are three important processes	• Believed intelligence to be the product of large number of interconnected but distinct intellectual abilities

TABLE 9.6 (Continued)
Graphic Organizer for Theories of Intelligence

GKPPT: Knowledge of Psychological Theory

Theories of Intelligence

Charles Spearman "General Intelligence"	Louis L. Thurston Primary Mental Abilities	Howard Gardner Theory of Multiple Intelligences	Robert Sternberg Triarchic Theory of Intelligence
• Described a concept he referred to as general intelligence, or the *g factor* • Used factor analysis to examine a number of mental aptitude tests • Concluded that scores on these tests were remarkably similar and that people who performed well on one cognitive test tended to perform well on others • Believed that intelligence is general cognitive ability that could be measured and numerically expressed	• Instead of viewing intelligence as a single, general ability, he focused on several different theories: 1. Verbal comprehension 2. Reasoning 3. Perceptual speed 4. Numerical ability 5. Word fluency 6. Associative memory 7. Spatial visualization	• Linguistic: ability to use words effectively through gesture and writing • Logical-mathematical: ability to analyze problems logically • Spatial: ability to represent the spatial world in their mind • Musical: ability to compose and perform music • Body-kinesthetic: ability to use mental abilities to coordinate bodily movements • Interpersonal: ability to understand the intentions, motivations, and desires of others • Intrapersonal: capacity to understand oneself • Naturalist: recognize features of environment • Spiritual: explore nature of existence • Existential: concern with "ultimate issues" • Moral: concern with rules and behaviors	• Defined intelligence as "mental activity directed towards purposive adaptation to, selection and shaping of, real-world environments relevant to one's life" • "Successful intelligence" is composed of 3 factors: 1. Analytical-problem solving abilities 2. Creative-ability to deal with new situations using past experiences and current skills 3. Practical-ability to adapt to a changing environment

TABLE 9.7
Graphic Organizer for Theories of Language Development

GKPPT: Knowledge of Psychological Theory

Theories of Language Development

Language Development	Behaviorist Theory of Language Development B. F. Skinner	Nativist Theory of Language Development Noam Chomsky	Interactionist Perspective of Language Development
• Individual acquires language by learning it as it is spoken and through mimicry • Oral language development is foundation of literacy skills • There is an interrelatedness between language, thinking, values, and culture that is fostered by effective language development	• Says that language is learned through operant conditioning (reinforcement and imitation) • Goes along with nature-nuture debate	• Says that language is a unique human accomplishment • All children have an language acquisition device (LAD) that allows them to produce consistent sentences once vocabulary is learned • Believes grammar is universal	• Combination of both nativist and behaviorist theories 1. <u>Information-processing:</u> o Brain is excellent at detecting patterns 2. <u>Social-interactionist:</u> o There is a native desire to understand others and to be understood by others

Sample Questions for General Knowledge of Psychological Principles and Theories

1. Which theorist believed that children imitate the behavior of significant people in their lives as a result of observational learning?
   a. Thorndike
   b. Bandura
   c. Skinner
   d. Pavlov
   e. Watson

2. A student was referred to the school psychologist for difficulty with attention and focus in the classroom. The school psychologist considered many factors that could be impacting this student's ability to maintain focus during class time. Neurologically, the school psychologist understands that most attention difficulties stem from dysfunction in the orbital circuit of the frontal lobe. What is another area of the brain that could be the alternate cause of the student's attention difficulties?
   a. Left hemisphere
   b. Right-hemisphere parietal lobe dysfunction
   c. Left hemisphere temporal lobe dysfunction
   d. Left posterior temporal lobe dysfunction
   e. Right-hemisphere supplementary motor cortex

3. Which brain chemical is largely implicated in depression?
   a. Melatonin
   b. Serotonin
   c. Neuropeptides
   d. Endorphins
   e. Dopamine

4. According to Erikson, a 14-year-old adolescent is negotiating which stage of development?
   a. Industry vs. inferiority
   b. Intimacy vs. isolation
   c. Initiation vs. dependency
   d. Identity vs. role confusion
   e. Initiative vs. guilt

5. Timmy does not want to get into trouble at school because he does not want the disapproval of his authoritarian parents. Which stage of moral development would this child fall under according to Kohlberg?
   a. Assimilation
   b. Preconventional
   c. Conventional
   d. Postconventional
   e. Concrete operational

6. According to Freud, the component of personality responsible for dealing with reality is which of the following?
   a. Superego
   b. Id
   c. Reality principle
   d. Ego
   e. Superlative ego

7. Shakira enjoys playing the piano. She comes home nearly every day after school and plays for about an hour. This is an example of which of the following?
   a. Extrinsic motivation
   b. Extrinsic reward
   c. Intrinsic motivation
   d. Metacognition
   e. Premack principle

8. The theory of multiple intelligences involves the idea that all humans have core abilities in various areas of intelligence. Which of the following psychologists is best known for this theory?
   a. Howard Gardner
   b. Abraham Maslow
   c. Louis L. Thurstone
   d. Erik Erikson
   e. Daniel Goleman

9. Which of the following terms describes the process the brain goes through when attempting to reach an equilibrium that optimizes beneficial pathways, and minimizes dysfunctional ones?
   a. Myelination
   b. Dendritic branching
   c. Neuronal pruning
   d. Agenesis of the corpus collosum
   e. Resting potential

10. Which theory of intelligence is a recent informational processing theory that emphasizes three aspects of intelligent behavior not normally tapped by IQ tests?
    a. Sternberg's triarchic theory of intelligence
    b. Carroll's three-stratum theory of intelligence
    c. Guilford's theory of intelligence
    d. Thurstone's theory of intelligence
    e. Thorndike's theory of intelligence

11. According to Freud, the component of personality responsible for housing sexual and aggressive drives, physical needs, and simple psychological needs is which of the following?
    a. Superego
    b. Id
    c. Reality principle
    d. Ego
    e. Superlative ego

12. Attributing threatening thoughts to others is which common defense mechanism?
    a. Denial
    b. Intellectualization
    c. Projection
    d. Rationalization
    e. Reaction formation

13. According to Erikson, a five-year-old child is negotiating which stage of development?
    a. Basic trust vs. mistrust
    b. Identity vs. role confusion
    c. Industry vs. inferiority
    d. Initiative vs. guilt
    e. Autonomy vs. doubt

14. Which theorist believes that language is learned through reinforcement and imitation?
    a. Skinner
    b. Chomsky
    c. Freud
    d. Erikson
    e. Kohlberg

15. Unconsciously changing an unacceptable feeling into its opposite is which common defense mechanism?
    a. Reaction formation
    b. Sublimation
    c. Undoing
    d. Repression
    e. Denial

Answers With Rationale

1. The best answer is ***b***. Bandura's theory is called social cognitive theory. His theory was based on previous behaviorist theories of learning; however, he did not believe that a person needed to do the action to learn it.

   Reference: Forman, S.G., Lubin, A.R., & Tripptree, A.L. (2014). Best practices in implementing evidence-based school interventions. In P. Harrison & A. Thomas (Eds.), *Best practices in school psychology VI: Systems-level services* (pp. 43–55). Bethesda, MD: National Association of School Psychologists.

2. The best answer is ***b***. Right-hemisphere parietal lobe dysfunction can also cause attention difficulties. Dysfunction in this area can cause neglect of oneself and the environment, which manifests in poor attention and self-awareness.

   Reference: Semrud-Clikeman, M., & Ellison, P.A.T. (2009). *Child neuropsychology* (2nd ed.). New York, NY: Springer Science and Business Media.

3. The best answer is ***b***. Those suffering with depression often do not have enough serotonin traveling in and out of their frontal lobes. Therefore, SSRIs are the class of antidepressants prescribed in most cases.

   Reference: Semrud-Clikeman, M., & Ellison, P.A.T. (2009). *Child neuropsychology* (2nd ed.). New York, NY: Springer Science and Business Media.

4. The best answer is ***d***. According to Erickson, adolescents are considered to be in the stage of identity vs. role confusion. They are attempting to integrate many different roles and create a self-image.

   Reference: Santrock, J.W. (2013). *Life-span development* (14th ed.). New York, NY: McGraw-Hill.

5. The best answer is ***c***. During the conventional stage, people are seeking good interpersonal relationships and want to maintain social order. They believe that they should live up to the expectations of their family and community.

   Reference: Santrock, J. W. (2013). *Life-span development* (14th ed.). New York, NY: McGraw-Hill.

6. The best answer is ***d***. The ego is the component of personality responsible for dealing with reality. According to Freud, the ego develops from the id and ensures that the impulses of the id can be expressed in a manner acceptable in the real world. The ego functions in the conscious, preconscious, and unconscious mind.

   Reference: Whitbourne, S. K., & Halgin, R. P. (2013). *Abnormal psychology: Clinical perspectives on psychological disorders* (7th ed.). New York, NY: McGraw-Hill.

7. The best answer is ***c***. Intrinsic motivation occurs when people engage in an activity without obvious external incentives (i.e., a hobby).

   Reference: Ormrod, J. E. (2012). *Human learning* (6th ed.). New York, NY: Pearson.

8. The best answer is ***a***. Howard Gardner is an American psychologist best known for his theory of multiple intelligences.

   Reference: Sternberg, R. J., & Sternberg, K. (2012). *Cognitive psychology* (6th ed.). Belmont, CA: Wadsworth.

9. The best answer is ***c***. Neuronal pruning occurs during brain development after birth, primarily for the first five years of life. Its purpose is to assist in creating useful connections between neurons.

   Reference: Semrud-Clikeman, M., & Ellison, P.A.T. (2009). *Child neuropsychology* (2nd ed.). New York, NY: Springer Science and Business Media.

10. The best answer is ***a***. Sternberg's triarchic theory of intelligence is composed of three factors: analytical, creative, and practical.

    Reference: Sternberg, R. J., & Sternberg, K. (2012). *Cognitive psychology* (6th ed.). Belmont, CA: Wadsworth.

11. The best answer is ***b***. The id is the component of personality that houses sexual and aggressive drives. It also houses physical needs, such as needing to sleep and eat, and psychological needs, such as needing comfort. The id wants immediate gratification of its needs.

    Reference: Kosslyn, S. M., & Rosenberg, R. S. (2007). *Fundamentals of psychology in context* (3rd ed.). New York, NY: Pearson Education.

12. The best answer is ***c***. Projection is when threatening thoughts are projected onto others. It is a common defense mechanism used by the ego to prevent threatening thoughts from entering awareness.

    Reference: Kosslyn, S. M., & Rosenberg, R. S. (2007). *Fundamentals of psychology in context* (3rd ed.). New York, NY: Pearson Education.

13. The best answer is ***d***. According to Erikson, children ages three through six are considered to be in the stage of initiative vs. guilt, where they either develop a sense of purpose and direction or are overly controlled by their parents and made to feel guilty.

    Reference: Kosslyn, S. M., & Rosenberg, R. S. (2007). *Fundamentals of psychology in context* (3rd ed.). New York, NY: Pearson Education.

14. The best answer is ***a***. According to Skinner, learning is acquired through association and reinforcement. He believed that parents are expert teachers and babies repeat sounds through operant conditioning when babbling is reinforced.

    Reference: Berger, K. S. (2009). *The developing person through childhood* (5th ed.). New York, NY: Worth.

15. The best answer is ***a***. Reaction formation is the process of unconsciously changing an unacceptable feeling into its opposite. It is a common defense mechanism used by the ego to prevent threatening thoughts from entering awareness.

    Reference: Kosslyn, S.M., & Rosenberg, R.S. (2007). *Fundamentals of psychology in context* (3rd ed.). New York, NY: Pearson Education.

Part III

Succeeding

Chapter 10

Obtaining and Maintaining the NCSP

As we discussed in Chapter 1, the Nationally Certified School Psychologist (NCSP) credential had its origin in 1989. Since then, the NCSP has become the hallmark of a well-trained school psychologist who has demonstrated both knowledge and skills consistent with the Standards of the National Association of School Psychologists (NASP). At this writing, more than 14,000 school psychologists in the country hold the NCSP.

In July 2015, NASP (NASP, 2015) announced the formal recognition of the Nationally Certified School Psychologist (NCSP) credential by the National Register of Health Service Psychologists. With this recognition came an acknowledgment that those school psychologists holding the NCSP meet the rigorous criteria for providers of mental and behavioral health services as identified by the National Register of Health Service Psychologists. Moreover, the recognition attested to the NCSP being a highly credible credential for identifying qualified school psychologists to consumers.

Earning the credential of NCSP is required by some states to meet certification requirements for state licensure as a school psychologist. However, regardless of state requirements, adding the NCSP after your name on a resume may assist you in your quest to find a job as a school psychologist. Much like national teacher certification, employers look for applicants for school psychologist positions who have earned their NCSP. The credential provides evidence that the person holding the NCSP has met the highest professional standards of graduate preparation, certification, and ethics, as determined by NASP.

Applicants for the NCSP must meet the established standards of NASP according to the *Standards for Graduate Preparation of School Psychologists* (formerly Training and Field Placement Program in School Psychologists), *Standards for the Credentialing of School Psychologists*, and the *Principles for Professional Ethics*. (Copies of all of these documents are available through the NASP website at http://www.nasponline.org/certification/becomeNCSP.aspx.)

Applicants for the NCSP may be graduates of either a NASP-approved program or a non-NASP-approved program. However, the application requirements differ for these two groups of candidates (as outlined on the NASP website at http://www.nasponline.org/certification/becomeNCSP.aspx). Readers are strongly urged to refer to the detailed information available on the NASP website to learn the specific requirements for applying for the NCSP.

Whether you are a graduate of a NASP-approved or non-NASP-approved program, you will be required to take the Praxis School Psychologist exam and earn a score at or above the determined "cut score." As of September 2014, the cut score is 147.

Once you earn the NCSP, your credential is active for three years and then must be renewed. Requirements for renewal include documentation of at least 75 Continuing Professional Development units. You do not need to retake the Praxis Exam in School Psychology. Please refer to the specifics of renewal requirements (available on the NASP website at http://www.nasponline.org/certification/renew_overview.aspx).

Chapter

Personal Reflections

Introduction

This chapter captures the thoughts, feelings, and reflections of school psychology graduate students as they prepared for the Praxis exam using the PASS (Prepare, Assist, Survive, and Succeed) model. In their own words, they describe their personal experiences and the strategies that helped them during the process of preparing for and taking the exam. These reflections are organized by topic, beginning with preparing for the exam, the actual experience of taking the exam, and some of the challenges they faced and how they coped with them. We've also included some of the helpful hints that may be beneficial to others, like you, who are preparing for this new endeavor.

Preparing for the Praxis

There are a variety of ways to approach the task of studying for the Praxis. In the section that follows, students reflect upon the strategies that they found helpful. It is our hope that some of these strategies will be helpful for you to consider when you are preparing for the Praxis.

First, students described methods they used to gather information. As an alternative to becoming bogged down with an overwhelming amount of information, the PASS model suggests that students work together by dividing into groups, with each group taking responsibility for a section of the material. Each group's assignment was to develop comprehensive study guides—that is, guides that included key points and relevant information and avoided minutia. In preparing these study guides, the group was able to divide and conquer the vast amount of information. Each member of the group shared his or her study guide with others, and thus every member wound up with a set of comprehensive review materials, as described by the students:

> We split into pairs/groups and divided up the major sections of the test. Each group then studied that area in depth and shared the key points of that topic with the whole group. We provided an outline of information to each student that was extremely helpful when studying. These information sheets were a vital piece of my preparation for taking and passing the Praxis.
>
> Delegating material to individuals was less stressful than trying to tackle all of the material on my own. Rather than requesting an easy topic to get through the assignment quickly, I chose an area that I knew I needed to thoroughly research. Once I had all the handouts, I added them to a binder as a study reference. The handouts that were clear and organized were extremely helpful while those who gave pages of technical information were much harder to learn from. My tip to a cohort is to develop handouts that are easy to read and to try to keep in the back of your mind that your classmates are depending on you to learn this information.
>
> (Personal communication, 2009)

Once the material is organized, we recommend that you develop an approach to reviewing and learning the important information. Developing a study plan, including a schedule, might be the next step. Then we suggest that you determine the strategies that will help you learn and that are congruent with your learning style. Here are some examples of methods that students found helpful.

> My experience preparing for the Praxis was not as difficult as I had suspected it would be. It was, however, time-consuming. The best advice I could give would be to allow yourself enough time to review prior to the test date. I began studying the semester prior to taking the test. For me, it was important to begin reviewing slowly and in chronological order the way I had first learned the information. For example, I started with the Psychological Foundations sections because I was most familiar with that information. I also suggest taking a practice test prior to the exam. I took a practice test prior to studying to see how much I knew and then took a different practice test after I had thoroughly studied all the material. The practice tests were very helpful for me to see what types of questions would be asked.
>
> To begin my preparation, I created a study schedule. One and a half to two hours per night for five nights a week seemed like a reasonable goal. Once settled, I started the process by reading the study guides my group and I had prepared. For my first round, I resisted the urge to take notes. I simply used the time to once again familiarize myself with the material. When I went over the material a second time, I created flashcards for the facts, strategies and ideas I found most pertinent. From that point forward I spent most of my study time reviewing the flashcards, with occasional glances back in the book or notes to remind me of something or to explore a new idea.
>
> (Personal communication, 2009)

> I created an organized and detailed study plan at the very beginning of the study season. Be sensible regarding your time, availability, and the amount of content needed to be covered. Also, be careful not to fall into the trap of setting aside time that you realistically do not have and hold yourself accountable for the reasonable goals that you set. It helped me to take advantage of small chunks of downtime for quick review.
>
> It was helpful for me to make note cards in my own words based on my notes and reading rather than simply scanning over materials. I would bring the study material with me while on the go to glance over during those free minutes spent waiting before my next activity or appointment.
>
> (Personal communication, 2015)

> The first thing I did to help myself prepare for the Praxis was develop a study plan based on the exam content. After I registered for the test, I prepared an organized and realistic study plan with scheduled sessions to avoid cramming. Cramming makes me more nervous. I decided that I was only going to study for 40 minutes a day and only on weekdays; if I studied longer, "great." I also organized my materials and prioritized. I looked at the materials and focused first on my weakest area: the areas in which I had the least knowledge and confidence. The materials that I studied were the ones given in class. I also made my own study sheet that was made from the list of content remembered and suggestions given from previous test takers, which was extremely helpful. I also studied from internet resources and the ETS website, particularly the *Test at a Glance* section. I also reflected on what kind of test taker I was. I am not a good test taker, and I often read quickly just to finish and avoid the task. I made sure to remind myself to read the questions and answers carefully and to take my time. In addition, underlining key words was helpful because sometimes it can help you in obtaining the correct answer or narrowing the answer to two.
>
> (Personal communication, 2009)

> In preparing for the Praxis, I had to work hard to keep my anxiety in check. This meant starting to study early and budgeting my time wisely. There is a lot of information and looking at it all piled together can be overwhelming. However, once I began going through my massive pile of study material, I realized how much had already sunk in. I read everything in the PASS book as well as the PowerPoints the class had made and weeded out the information I needed to spend extra time on. This allowed me to refresh information I already understood without taking time away from the areas that needed more attention. I prepared flashcards for the information that could be memorized (such as court cases, definitions, and cognitive testing information) and focused on understanding the application of other theories (i.e., consultation models and when/why each

would be used and psychopathology related to education, etc.). I used the PASS book as a starting point, referred to classmates' presentations, class notes/handouts, and researched online any information I wasn't sure of/wanted to know more about. All of this was very time-consuming and stressful, but in the end I knew that I had done everything I could to walk into the test center prepared for the exam.

(Personal communication, 2015)

In an attempt to minimize the length of time I stressed over this seemingly giant task, I decided to begin studying exactly one month before the date of the exam. This kept me focused for that one month and forced me to buckle down and do some disciplined studying.

(Personal communication, 2009)

I began studying approximately six months before taking the exam. However, it was in the last month that my studying was the most intensive. I consistently dedicated almost all of my free time to studying during that month, and it was this preparation that helped me to feel calm during the exam.

As far as preparing for the test, I feel what helped me the most was creating note cards from my three-inch binder of data organized and collected through my internship class. I carried these cards with me everywhere and pulled them out whenever I had a lull in my day. Whether I was on the treadmill, waiting for a perpetually late parent for an out-of-district IEP meeting, in the car (as a passenger, that is), on a plane, or in the waiting room of my doctor's office, you could find me flipping through my trusty note cards. While my studying technically began six months prior to the exam with the start of my internship course, I didn't truly get down and dirty with the data until about a month prior.

(Personal communication, 2009)

I began preparing for the exam approximately six weeks before the testing date. After completing the exam, I would recommend the same amount of study time for other students. However, students preparing to take the exam should also consider their own personal study habits when making this decision.

Organization was also a key to my success while preparing. I kept a folder with handouts, notes, and questions. I divided my folder into sections, corresponding with the sections that would be on the exam. As I collected information pertaining to each topic, I put it into its proper place in the folder. This helped me from getting overwhelmed with the amount of information that I was collecting.

My friends and I then set aside a scheduled day each week to study each portion of our outlines and to prepare for the exam. Two weeks before the exam we each took the practice exam from ETS. We then reviewed our answers and used our performance on the practice exam to determine which areas we needed to spend extra time reviewing before taking the exam. Our approach was successful; we all passed the School Psychology Praxis Exam.

(Personal communication, 2009)

I began by reading and taping the class study guides and PowerPoint presentations, then listening to them on my drive to and from work.

(Personal communication, 2009)

There was no need to memorize a large amount of material verbatim. Rather, I reviewed all of my notes briefly and focused on basic psychological concepts and theories. I also found it helpful to study and review concepts with a partner rather than simply review the information on my own. Developing mnemonic devices for the more difficult information with a fellow student helped me to retrieve these important concepts during the actual test. Another traditional study method that I used was creating flashcards for the more difficult concepts, which was helpful.

Practice answering questions in a timed fashion, e.g., take 25 to 30 questions at a time, and practice answering each question within a 60 to 90 second time frame. It helped me to answer the questions I found easy, and leave myself time for more "thought-provoking questions."

(Personal communication, 2009)

> After studying the information independently, I spent the last week before the exam meeting with other students and discussing the topics. This was by far the most helpful strategy for me because it allowed me to discuss and reinforce learned information and pointed out the areas that I needed to review more. I would then review on my own and prepare questions for the other group members.
>
> (Personal communication, 2009)

> Regarding preparation, the only materials I used were study guides compiled by my classmates and the PASS book. Many of the questions involved scenarios in which the examinee must apply the knowledge that has been learned in both class and in the field. I felt as though my classes and practicum/internship experience fully prepared me for this assessment. These tools combined with the PASS book were the keys to my success!
>
> (Personal communication, 2015)

> Once I had a study binder and the book to utilize, I organized a few of my friends from the program for some study sessions. By merely sitting around the table and throwing out questions to one another, we were able to make sense of the material. We explained different concepts to each other, and we gave ourselves memory aids for the test. We even made up fun mnemonic devices to help us memorize some of the information. Sure, we would talk and laugh in between, but when test time came, remembering our jokes helped me to remember some of the answers. Working in a group to study definitely helped me get through the material, and it allowed me to study in a positive way rather than torturing myself by sitting alone in my bedroom.
>
> (Personal communication, 2009)

> Review the practice questions a few times. They provide you with explanations of the questions and their answers. Use the questions with which you have trouble to help develop your study plan.
>
> I found flashcards very helpful. Simply writing them and researching the information was useful, but it also helped to have the ability to take them out to study for a few minutes whenever I had free time.
>
> Start studying early in the school year. You will only get busier with your internship as the year goes on.
>
> (Personal communication, 2015)

Taking the Praxis

In this section, students describe a variety of test-taking strategies they found helpful while they took the Praxis. Reading through these reflections may give you some food for thought on what might help you while you are actually taking the exam.

> My strategy for answering these questions was simple. I didn't let myself overthink the question. I read each question 2–3 times to make sure I understood what was being asked. I then went to the options to eliminate choices I knew were not possible. This usually left me with two possible answers, and I made my best guess between them. Though I never was fully convinced I chose the right answer, I knew my decision was not made without an educated strategy behind it.
>
> As for my fear of not having enough time, it was unfounded. I had plenty of time. I was very glad that I did not feel rushed and that I had plenty of time to put forth my best effort. In the end I did pass the test on my first attempt. It was a relief to receive the score.
>
> (Personal communication, 2009)

> I feel that I have high test anxiety, especially on standardized tests. Learning that we would be the first group to take the Praxis as a computer-based test brought about many different emotions. I'm the kind of test taker that marks an unknown question and returns to it after answering others. I was unsure how that would work on a computer-based test and I began to worry about the pressure of answering the test questions as they were presented. However, once I learned more about test formatting, I realized that there would be an option that

TABLE 11.1
Do's and Don'ts of Taking the Praxis

Do's	Don'ts
Come prepared for the test	Don't second-guess yourself
Begin by taking a deep breath	Don't be anxious
Do your best	Don't panic if you don't know an answer
Trust your first answer	Don't be fearful of having enough time; rather, implement strategies for self-pacing
Thoroughly understand the question before reading the answer choices	Don't rely on memorization
Make educated guesses	Don't doom yourself to failure—wait for the results
Know the passing scores for your university, state, and NASP	Don't make yourself crazy—a passing score is not 100%

> allowed me to mark questions I would like to go back to. This tool was very beneficial to me and I used it (more than I thought I would, which also made me nervous) even on some questions where I already answered but wanted to double-check it later. I had plenty of time to go back and review the questions I had marked. This allowed me to focus on the particular question and not worry about other questions and the clock.
>
> (Personal communication, 2015)

> I recently took and passed the Praxis in the computer-delivered format. I am a former teacher, so I have taken several Praxis exams in the past, but they were all paper-based assessments. Now that I have experienced this type of assessment in both formats, I can say that I definitely prefer the computer test. I found that it allowed me to concentrate on one question at a time. When the questions are on paper, I tend to look ahead at upcoming questions, which can be distracting. On the computer you are given one question at a time and you can flag a question if you want to return to it later.
>
> (Personal communication, 2015)

> In February, I sat for the Praxis II School Psychology Exam. I was terrified. Despite countless hours of studying our PASS book, countless hours of prepping, countless hours of presenting with classmates, I was terrified. If I didn't pass, it could derail my future plans to become a school psychologist. I would possibly have to take it again, and other agonizing thoughts popped into my head. After about 10 questions in, I began to relax. My mind was no longer drawing a blank. Things were coming back to me and I was starting to feel better. Yes, I remember this from practicum, or from internship. I remember giving this presentation. I remember discussing this topic in class, were my thoughts. I no longer felt that panic or dread. By the end of the Praxis, I received my score. I had passed! I do not have to retake this exam! I am on my way to becoming a school psychologist.
>
> (Personal communication, 2015)

Words of Wisdom

In this section, students write about the tidbits of information that they thought would be helpful for you to know. Advice is offered, and it's up to you to sift through and select what has meaning to you.

> Some general tips for making the Praxis experience as painless as possible are below. Knowing facts, terms, interventions, etc. is obviously helpful, but knowing the appropriate application of these is even more important. About 75% of the test I took asked questions regarding practical application of theories, definitions, consultation models, etc. If you can't choose between two answers, ask yourself, "What is the best practice? What would NASP endorse?" This helps keep your ultimate goal in mind and narrow your choices.
>
> (Personal communication, 2009)

In preparing for the exam, my best advice to you is RELAX. You've been well trained and you are prepared. Think about your areas of strength. Think about topics that you need to review more thoroughly. Intentionally do things to keep your anxiety under control.

The night before the big day, I made sure that I did something that I loved and that would make me feel relaxed. When going into the test the next day, I was not nervous and felt calm. I knew that if I didn't do well on the test, the worst that would happen would be to take it again. When taking the test, there was some information that I was unfamiliar with, but most of it I either knew or was able to make a reasonable guess. I really believe that my on-the-job experience helped me to excel on the test. Most of the information dealt with what I was doing on a daily basis as a school psychologist.

(Personal communication, 2009)

Don't wait until the last minute to study!! Even simply refreshing information is time-consuming. Adding that to the time it takes to fully understand something that may have gotten by you in class can add extra stress. Starting to study early also helps with breaking material into smaller, manageable chunks.

The day/night before the test, put everything down. Do something that you find relaxing or makes you happy to put you in a good mood and positive mind-set. Cramming the night before the test isn't helpful.

During the test, stop and breathe every now and then. It's easy to get wrapped up in the test. Take a quick moment to refocus your energy and tell yourself "I can do this" to help keep away negative thinking and anxiety.

(Personal communication, 2015)

When I signed up to take the Praxis in February there was only one date left available, which was only one week away; otherwise I would have had to wait until April for the next available date. If you are someone who does not study well under time pressure, I suggest signing up for the exam well in advance. I had one week to study for the Praxis. At first I was overwhelmed and didn't know where to begin. I studied about three hours a day for the first three days by reading articles from the NASP website and taking practice tests online. The last three days before the test I spent the entire day reading and highlighting the PASS book and reviewing a few additional court cases. The most helpful source for studying, and reason for passing the Praxis on my first try, was definitely the PASS book. If I could go back and study again I would focus all of my study time on the PASS book, court cases, and one practice round of the ETS practice test. I am not a person who does well on standardized tests, and I was able to pass the Praxis on my first try. If you put in the study time, you can pass the exam, so relax and try not to stress too much.

(Personal communication, 2015)

As I sat in my internship class, listening to the daunting task of taking this 140-question exam in 140 minutes, I began to worry. "That's a question a minute," I thought. "What if I get stuck on a question and run out of time?" I pondered. Then, my nervousness began to subside as I began to formulate a plan. The discussion turned to the content of the Praxis Exam in School Psychology. "Four sections broken down into topics. . ." The professors handed out a lot of information. "Okay, I can do this," I said to myself. The night before the exam my nervousness returned. But, I thought, "I had a plan, I followed my plan, and I am ready for this!"

The questions on the Praxis are based on the material we have been taught since day one of our school psychology training program. Nothing is new or unexpected on the test. It is information that has passed in front of your eyes many, many times and has been discussed thoroughly. I found it most beneficial to rely on the fact that I have at some point learned the required information, and that I learned it well enough to apply it.

(Personal communication, 2009)

As the ETS website explicitly says, there is no way to predict how many questions you need to answer correctly to pass the test. Each edition of the test contains different questions at varying difficulty levels, so that raw scores are adjusted accordingly.

(Personal communication, 2015)

Don't procrastinate studying any more than you already have. The thought of studying for yet another strenuous assessment is daunting. In my experience, I procrastinated because I felt as though I didn't have time to absorb an abundance of new information, to worry, or to prepare. At the time, I was not confident in my abilities to balance school, work, studying, and internship requirements. What I learned throughout the process of preparing for the Praxis was that I was wrong for three main reasons.

First, I thought the information I needed to study was going to be mostly new and overwhelming. That couldn't be further from the truth. You need to trust that some pretty amazing and well-rounded school psychologists have prepared you. They have helped you develop broad knowledge and the ability to think rationally in many difficult scenarios, which will help you pass this assessment. The first thing I realized when I started studying was that most of the information was easy to recall or remember since none of it was completely new information. You know a lot more than you think you do but the only way to find out is to start studying.

The second reason I put off studying was because I thought I was going to have to memorize facts or learn random, maybe even irrelevant, information. Wrong again. All of the information I learned while studying for the Praxis has helped me during my internship and professional endeavors. My newly acquired knowledge was not only relevant but, at times, crucial during my field experience. Learning additional details about my field of study, in preparation for the Praxis, also helped build my confidence in working with students and other professionals. Remember, we are all lifelong learners, so try to take advantage of this opportunity to build upon your knowledge base.

Lastly, I thought studying was going to be a tedious task that would take up what was left of my time. Although studying and preparing do take a considerable amount of time, it is what you make it. Studying doesn't have to be boring; meet up with a friend or go to your favorite café shop for a few hours a week. For me, reviewing with a friend and studying outside on nice days helped turned preparing for the practice into an enjoyable experience.

(Personal communication, 2015)

Tips for Studying for the Praxis

- **Plan out your study schedule!** Open the PASS book as soon as you get it, look at the topics/chapters, and plan accordingly.
- **Read the PASS book student reflections.** I found it really helpful to read the reflections in this book before jumping into the chapters. Reading advice, helpful tips, and regrets from students who have already taken the Praxis may help ease your nerves too.
- **Review class materials relevant to Praxis topics.** Reviewing PowerPoints and materials developed by internship classmates was helpful since they were easy to read and materials that I had already reviewed. It's a good place to start and to figure out which topics are your strengths and which are your weaknesses.
- **Read each chapter in the PASS book thoroughly.** Personally, I found the PASS book to be the most important part of my preparation. I read comprehensively through each chapter while simultaneously developing a list of any terms or fragments of information that I wasn't confident with.
- **Review, review, review.** If you're studying over the span of several weeks, don't forget to review previously read materials and chapters. The worst feeling is when you are stuck on a question that you knew the answer to but you forgot because you failed to review it prior to the test.
- **Take the practice Praxis test.** With your purchase, offered to you when you schedule and purchase your ticket to take the Praxis, you are provided a number of opportunities to take the same practice test over and over again. Since this was an extra cost, I paired up with a friend to take the practice test. We took it once together and a few times on our own until we felt comfortable with the testing software, our pacing, and our responses. We also reviewed, researched, and discussed each question we got wrong. After taking the practice test I felt like I knew what to expect going into the Praxis.

Tips for Taking the Praxis

- **Be prepared.** You need to print out a testing ticket, so make sure you print that out prior to the day you take the test; maybe print out two just in case. If you get lost easily, like I do, make sure you know where you're going and plan for traffic or accidents. Eat and drink enough before you go. It's a long test—the last thing you want to do is worry about your stomach. Wear layers. For me the waiting room was uncomfortably warm and the testing room was freezing.

- **Get there early.** As you wait to be brought into the testing room, everyone waits in a crowded room, feeling anxious, impatient, and awkward. In my experience, I sat in the hallway to calmly review my notes until they were ready to take my picture and send me into the testing room. I was able to lock my notes and other belongings in a convenient locker.
- **Confidence is key.** My biggest regret is changing my answers with five minutes left. After I left the test, I checked my notes and realized that every single answer that I changed was changed to the wrong choice.
- **Don't focus on the time.** Since you can see the time as you take the test, it's hard not to obsess over it. This was a challenge for me. I constantly looked at the time and tried to calculate my speed. I wanted to make sure I had time left over to review questions I flagged. I would recommend answering each question, as they come, to the best of your ability. If you need to, write down questions that you were stuck on so that you can review when you're finished, if you have time. Definitely take your time and answer all of the questions the best you can. Don't count on having time left at the end of the test to go back to, read, think about, and answer questions that you were unsure of the first time.
- **Scrap paper.** During the exam I found it odd that the proctor attempted to collect my scrap paper and provide me with a new blank piece of paper. After a moment of panic, because I was keeping a list of questions I wanted to return to, I asked if I could keep my original scrap paper and she apologetically returned it.
- **Give your BEST answer.** Many of the questions on the Praxis and the practice test threw me off because they asked for the "best" answer. On most of these types of questions I had a difficult time choosing between two similar answers that I felt could be "best" depending on factors that were not presented in the question itself. These types of questions would still trap me regardless of how much studying I did. The only thing that I found useful for preparing for these types of questions was going over these questions with a friend. By reviewing these questions with a friend you can practice choosing and arguing for a one "best" answer choice over another.

(Personal communication, 2015)

TABLE 11.2
Helpful Tips for Students by Students

- Go in relaxed and confident.
- Realize that you can't know everything, but begin somewhere.
- In the event that you do not pass on the first try, remember you can take it again, and having taken it once will prepare you even better for taking it again. It's not a failure, but a rehearsal.
- If distance from home to the test center is a concern, consider staying in a hotel close to the place where the test will be given.
- Get a good night's sleep.
- Eat a good breakfast.
- Plan ahead.
- Do not take the Praxis test without some preparation.
- Preparing enables you to feel confident and to genuinely expect to pass.
- Study in such a way as to get a global view. However, if a specific detail jumps out as important, it probably is just that.
- Take the practice tests and read every explanation.
- If your anxiety level is high, bring yourself down—anxiety is your number one enemy.
- Do not focus on time; just get a good pace going—hopefully, you will have a "quiet" time keeper.
- Try to totally understand the question before you attempt to look at the answer choices.
- Many times, there are clues to the answer in the question. Take time to look for them.
- To ease my building worries, I reminded myself that I could retake the test if necessary.
- Overall, the test was less intimidating than anticipated due to the familiar multiple-choice format.
- Get there early—it is helpful in terms of getting a seat in a location that is comfortable.
- Bring plenty of pencils and a bottle of water.
- Dress in layers.
- Bring tissues even if you don't have a cold.
- Trust your instincts.
- Remember to remain focused during the day of the test and think positively.
- After testing, do something special for you. You deserve it!

References

Anderson, J. (2000). *Learning and memory: An integrated approach.* New York, NY: Wiley.

August, D., McCardle, P., & Shanahan, T. (2014). Developing literacy in English language learners: Findings from a review of the experimental research. *School Psychology Review*, *43*(4), 490–498.

Bahrick, H., & Phelps, E. (1987). Retention of Spanish vocabulary over eight years. *Journal of Experimental Psychology: Learning, Memory and Cognition*, *13*, 344–349.

Batsche, G. M., & Curtis, M. J. (2003, December). The creation of the National School Psychology Certification System. *NASP Communiqué*, *32*, 6.

Bear, G. G., & Manning, M. A. (2014). Best practices in classroom discipline. In P. Harrison & A. Thomas (Eds.), *Best practices in school psychology VI: Student-level services* (pp. 251–267). Bethesda, MD: National Association of School Psychologists.

Berger, K. S. (2009). *The developing person through childhood* (5th ed.). New York, NY: Worth.

Bloom, B. S., & Krathwohl, D. R. (1956). *Taxonomy of educational objectives: The classification of educational goals by a committee of college and university examiners. Handbook 1: Cognitive domain.* New York, NY: Longmans.

Bradley-Johnson, S., & Cook, A. (2014). Best practices in school-based services for students with visual impairments. In P. Harrison & A. Thomas (Eds.), *Best practices in school psychology VI: Foundations* (pp. 243–256). Bethesda, MD: National Association of School Psychologists.

Brock, S. E., Louvar Reeves, M. A., & Nickerson, A. B. (2014). Best practices in school crisis intervention. In P. Harrison & A. Thomas (Eds.), *Best practices in school psychology VI: Systems-level services* (pp. 211–230). Bethesda, MD: National Association of School Psychologists.

Chi, M., Glaser, R., & Rees, E. (1988). *The nature of expertise.* Hillsdale, NJ: Lawrence Erlbaum.

Christ, T. J., & Arañas, Y. A. (2014). Best practices in problem analysis. In P. Harrison & A. Thomas (Eds.), *Best practices in school psychology VI: Data-based and collaborative decision making* (pp. 87–98). Bethesda, MD: National Association of School Psychologists.

Codding, R. S., Hagermoser Sanetti, L. M., & DiGennaro Reed, F. D. (2014). Best practices in facilitating consultation and collaboration with teachers and administrators. In P. Harrison & A. Thomas (Eds.), *Best practices in school psychology VI: Data-based and collaborative decision making* (pp. 525–539). Bethesda, MD: National Association of School Psychologists.

Cordeiro, P. A., & Cunningham, W. G. (2013). *Educational leadership: A bridge to improved practice* (5th ed.). New York, NY: Pearson Education.

Cozby, P. C., & Bates, S. C. (2012). *Methods in behavioral research* (11th ed.). New York, NY: McGraw-Hill.

Dawson, P. (2014). Best practices in assessing and improving executive skills. In P. Harrison & A. Thomas (Eds.), *Best practices in school psychology VI: Student-level services* (pp. 269–285). Bethesda, MD: National Association of School Psychologists.

Diet, exercise and sleep. (n.d.). National Sleep Foundation. Retrieved from http://www.sleepfoundation.org/site/c.huIXKjM0IxF/b.2421185/k.7198/Let-Sleep-Work-for-You

Eckert, T. L., Russo, N., & Hier, B. O. (2014). Best practices in school psychologists' promotion of effective collaboration and communication among school professionals. In P. Harrison & A. Thomas (Eds.), *Best practices in school psychology VI: Data-based and collaborative decision making* (pp. 541–552). Bethesda, MD: National Association of School Psychologists.

Educational Testing Service. (2005). *Reducing test anxiety: A guide for Praxis test takers.* Retrieved July 26, 2015, from https://www.ets.org/s/praxis/pdf/reducing_test_anxiety.pdf

Educational Testing Service. (2015). *Bulletin supplement for test takers with disabilities*. Retrieved July 26, 2015, from http://www.ets.org/s/disabilities/pdf/bulletin_supplement_test_takers_with_disabilities_health_needs.pdf

Educational Testing Service. (n.d.). *2015–16 Praxis series information bulletin*. Retrieved July 26, 2015, from http://www.ets.org/s/praxis/pdf/praxis_information_bulletin.pdf

Esler, A. N., Godber, Y., & Christenson, S. L. (2008). Best practices in supporting school-family partnerships. In A. Thomas & J. Grimes (Eds.), *Best practices in school psychology V* (pp. 917–936). Bethesda, MD: National Association of School Psychologists.

Forman, S. G., & Burke, C. R. (2008). Best practices in selecting and implementing evidence-based school interventions. In A. Thomas & J. Grimes (Eds.), *Best practices in school psychology V* (pp. 799–811). Bethesda, MD: National Association of School Psychologists.

Forman, S. G., Lubin, A. R., & Tripptree, A. L. (2014). Best practices in implementing evidence-based school interventions. In P. Harrison & A. Thomas (Eds.), *Best practices in school psychology VI: Systems-level services* (pp. 43–55). Bethesda, MD: National Association of School Psychologists.

Fredrickson, B., & Branigan, C. (2005). Positive emotions broaden the scope of attention and thought-action repertoires. *Cognition and Emotion*, *19*(3), 313–332.

Fredrickson, B., & Losada, M. (2005). Positive affect and the complex dynamics of human flourishing. *American Psychologist, 60,* 678–686.

Frey, J. R., Elliott, S. N., & Miller, C. F. (2014). Best practices in social skills training. In P. Harrison & A. Thomas (Eds.), *Best practices in school psychology VI: Student-level services* (pp. 213–224). Bethesda, MD: National Association of School Psychologists.

Gettinger, M., & Miller, K. (2014). Best practices in increasing academic engaged time. In P. Harrison & A. Thomas (Eds.), *Best practices in school psychology VI: Student-level services* (pp. 19–35). Bethesda, MD: National Association of School Psychologists.

Gibbons, K., & Brown, S. (2014). Best practices in evaluating psychoeducational services based on student outcome data. In P. Harrison & A. Thomas (Eds.), *Best practices in school psychology VI: Foundations* (pp. 357–358). Bethesda, MD: National Association of School Psychologists.

Godber, Y. (2008). Best practice in program evaluation. In J. Grimes & A. Thomas (Eds.), *Best practices in school psychology V* (Vol. 6, pp. 2193–2205). Bethesda, MD: National Association of School Psychologists.

Hale, J. B., Semrud-Clikeman, M., & Kubas, H. A. (2014). Best practices in medication treatment for children with emotional and behavioral disorders: A primer for school psychologists. In P. Harrison & A. Thomas (Eds.), *Best practices in school psychology VI: Systems-level services* (pp. 347–360). Bethesda, MD: National Association of School Psychologists.

Hallahan, D. P., Kauffman, J. M., & Pullen, P. C. (2012). *Exceptional learners: An introduction to special education.* Upper Saddle River, NJ: Pearson Education.

Hoagwood, K., & Johnson, J. (2003). School psychology: A public health framework I. From evidence-based practices to evidence-based policies. *Journal of School Psychology*, *41*, 3–21.

Huberty, T. J. (2014). Best practices in school-based interventions for anxiety and depression. In P. Harrison & A. Thomas (Eds.), *Best practices in school psychology VI: Student-level services* (pp. 349–363). Bethesda, MD: National Association of School Psychologists.

Hughes, T. L., Kolbert, J. B., & Crothers, L. M. (2014). Best practices in behavioral/ecological consultation. In P. Harrison & A. Thomas (Eds.), *Best practices in school psychology VI: Data-based and collaborative decision making* (pp. 483–492). Bethesda, MD: National Association of School Psychologists.

Individuals with Disabilities Education Act, 20 U.S.C. § 1400 (2004).

Isen, A. (2005). A role for neuropsychology in understanding the facilitating influence of positive affect on social behavior and cognitive processes. In C. R. Snyder & S. J. Lopez (Eds.), *The handbook of positive psychology* (pp. 528–540). New York, NY: Oxford Press.

Isen, A., Daubman, K., & Nowicki, G. (1987). Positive affect facilitates creative problem solving. *Journal of Personality and Social Psychology, 52,* 1122–1131.

Jacob, S. (2014). Best practices in ethical school psychological practice. In P. Harrison & A. Thomas (Eds.), *Best practices in school psychology VI: Foundations* (pp. 437–448). Bethesda, MD: National Association of School Psychologists.

Keith, T. Z. (2008). Best practice in using and conducting research in applied settings. In J. Grimes & A. Thomas (Eds.), *Best practices in school psychology V* (Vol. 6, pp. 2165–2175). Bethesda, MD: National Association of School Psychologists.

Knoff, H. (2002). Best practices in facilitating school reform, organizational change, and strategic planning. In A. Thomas & J. Grimes (Eds.), *Best practices in school psychology IV* (pp. 235–252). Bethesda, MD: National Association of School Psychologists.

Kosslyn, S. M., & Rosenberg, R. S. (2007). *Fundamentals of psychology in context* (3rd ed.). New York, NY: Pearson Education.

Kratochwill, T. R., Altschaefl, M. R., & Bice-Urbach, B. (2014). Best practices in school-based problem-solving consultation: Applications in prevention and intervention systems. In P. Harrison & A. Thomas (Eds.), *Best practices in school psychology VI: Data-based and collaborative decision making* (pp. 461–482). Bethesda, MD: National Association of School Psychologists.

Lichtenstein, R. (2014). Best practices in identification of learning disabilities. In P. Harrison & A. Thomas (Eds.), *Best practices in school psychology VI: Data-based and collaborative decision making* (pp. 331–354). Bethesda, MD: National Association of School Psychologists.

Lineman, J. M., & Miller, G. E. (2012). Strengthening competence in working with culturally and linguistically diverse students. *NASP Communiqué, 40*(8), 20–21.

Maccow, G. (2011). *Overview of WASI-II.* Retrieved from http://images.pearsonclinical.com/images/PDF/Webinar/WASI-IIHandoutOct2011.pdf

McBride, G. M., Willis, J. O., & Dumont, R. (2014). Best practices in applying legal standards for students with disabilities. In P. Harrison & A. Thomas (Eds.), *Best practices in school psychology VI: Foundations* (pp. 421–436). Bethesda, MD: National Association of School Psychologists.

McCloskey, G., Perkins, L., & Van Divner, B. (2009). *Assessment and intervention for executive function difficulties.* New York, NY: Routledge.

McConaughy, S. H., & Ritter, D. R. (2014). Best practices in multimethod assessment of emotional and behavioral disorder. In P. Harrison & A. Thomas (Eds.), *Best practices in school psychology VI: Data-based and collaborative decision making* (pp. 367–390). Bethesda, MD: National Association of School Psychologists.

National Association of School Psychologists (NASP). (2000). *Standards for training and field placement programs in school psychology.* Bethesda, MD: Author.

National Association of School Psychologists (NASP). (2010a). *Model for comprehensive and integrated school psychological services.* Bethesda, MD: Author. Retrieved from http://www.nasponline.org/standards/2010standards/2_PracticeModel.pdf

National Association of School Psychologists (NASP). (2010b). *Principles for professional ethics.* Bethesda, MD: Author. Retrieved from http://www.nasponline.org/Documents/Standards%20and%20Certification/Standards/1_%20Ethical%20Principles.pdf

National Association of School Psychologists (NASP). (2010c). *Standards for graduate preparation of school psychologists.* Bethesda, MD: Author. Retrieved from http://www.nasponline.org/standards/2010standards/1_Graduate_Preparation.pdf

Oberti v. Board of Education of Borough of Clementon School District (1992). 995 F. 2d 1204.

Ormrod, J. E. (2012). *Human learning* (6th ed.). New York, NY: Pearson.

Ortiz, S. O. (2004). *Comprehensive assessment of culturally and linguistically diverse students: A systematic, practical approach for nondiscriminatory assessment* [PDF file]. Retrieved from www.nasponline.org/resources/culturalcompetence/ortiz.pdf

Ortiz, S. O., Flanagan, D. P., & Dynda, A. M. (2008). Best practices in working with culturally diverse children and families. In A. Thomas & J. Grimes (Eds.), *Best practices in school psychology V* (Vol. 5, pp. 1730). Bethesda, MD: National Association of School Psychologists.

Pluymert, K. (2014). Problem-solving foundations for school psychological services. In P. Harrison & A. Thomas (Eds.), *Best practices in school psychology VI: Data-based and collaborative decision making* (pp. 25–40). Bethesda, MD: National Association of School Psychologists.

Rafoth, M. A., & Parker, S. W. (2014). Preventing academic failure and promoting alternatives to retention. In P. Harrison & A. Thomas (Eds.), *Best practices in school psychology VI: Student-level services* (pp. 143–155). Bethesda, MD: National Association of School Psychologists.

Raiford, S. E., & Coalson, D. L. (2014). *Essentials of WPPSI-IV assessment.* Hoboken, NJ: Wiley.

Reschly, A. L., Appleton, J. J., & Pohl, A. (2014). Best practices in fostering student engagement. In P. Harrison & A. Thomas (Eds.), *Best practices in school psychology VI: Student-level services* (pp. 37–50). Bethesda, MD: National Association of School Psychologists.

Richardson, J., & Morgan, R. (1997). *Reading to learn in the content areas*. Belmont, CA: Wadsworth.

Rossen, E. (2015). NCSP earns formal recognition from national register. NASP *Communique*, *44* (1), 32.

Sandoval, J. (2014). Best practices in school-based mental health/consultee-centered consultation by school psychologists. In P. Harrison & A. Thomas (Eds.), *Best practices in school psychology VI: Data-based and collaborative decision making* (pp. 493–507). Bethesda, MD: National Association of School Psychologists.

Santrock, J. W. (2013). *Life-span development* (14th ed.). New York, NY: McGraw-Hill.

Sattler, J. M., & Hoge, R. D. (2001). *Assessment of children: Behavioral, social, and clinical foundations*. San Diego, CA: Author.

Semrud-Clikeman, M., & Ellison, P.A.T. (2009). *Child neuropsychology* (2nd ed.). New York, NY: Springer Science and Business Media.

Sheridan, S. M., Clarke, B. L., & Christenson, S. L. (2014). Best practices in promoting family engagement in education. In P. Harrison & A. Thomas (Eds.), *Best practices in school psychology VI: Systems-level services* (pp. 439–453). Bethesda, MD: National Association of School Psychologists.

Shinn, M. R. (2008). Best practices in using curriculum-based measurement in a problem-solving model. In J. Grimes & A. Thomas (Eds.), *Best practices in school psychology V* (Vol. 2, pp. 243–261). Bethesda, MD: National Association of School Psychologists.

Steege, M. W., & Scheib, M. A. (2014). Best practices in conducting functional behavioral assessments. In P. Harrison & A. Thomas (Eds.), *Best practices in school psychology VI: Data-based and collaborative decision making* (pp. 273–286). Bethesda, MD: National Association of School Psychologists.

Sternberg, R. (2003). *Cognitive psychology.* Belmont, CA: Wadsworth/Thomson Learning.

Sternberg, R. J., & Sternberg, K. (2012). *Cognitive psychology* (6th ed.). Belmont, CA: Wadsworth.

Upah, K. (2008). Best practices in designing, implementing, and evaluating quality interventions. In A. Thomas & J. Grimes (Eds.), *Best practices in school psychology V* (pp. 209–203). Bethesda, MD: National Association of School Psychologist.

Van Dongen, H. P., Maislin, G., Mullington, J. M., & Dinges, D. F. (2003). The cumulative cost of additional wakefulness: Dose-response effects on neurobehavioral functions and sleep physiology from chronic sleep restriction and total sleep deprivation. *Sleep*, *15*, 117–126.

Vroom, V. H. (1995). *Work and motivation*. San Francisco, CA: Jossey-Bass.

Watson, D. (2005). Positive affectivity. In C. R. Snyder & S. J. Lopez (Eds.), *Handbook of positive psychology* (pp. 106–119). New York, NY: Oxford Press.

Whitbourne, S. K., & Halgin, R. P. (2013). *Abnormal psychology: Clinical perspectives on psychological disorders* (7th ed.). New York, NY: McGraw-Hill.

Wicks-Nelson, R., & Israel, A. C. (2009). *Abnormal child and adolescent psychology* (7th ed.). Upper Saddle River, NJ: Pearson Education.

Index